OPERA ANNUAL

Edinburgh Castle floodlit for the Festival

OPERA ANNUAL

No. 5

EDITED BY

HAROLD ROSENTHAL

DOUBLEDAY & COMPANY, INC.
GARDEN CITY   NEW YORK
1958

© JOHN CALDER (PUBLISHERS) LTD. 1958

LIBRARY OF CONGRESS CATALOG CARD NUMBER 58-12113

PRINTED IN GREAT BRITAIN BY
TAYLOR GARNETT EVANS & CO. LTD
WATFORD, HERTFORDSHIRE

CONTENTS

CONTENTS (continued)

ILLUSTRATIONS

ILLUSTRATIONS (continued)

INTRODUCTION

'O PERA ANNUAL' has now reached its fifth year of publication; and this year I have decided to modify the pattern that we have followed in our four previous issues. Instead of devoting the first section of the Annual to digests on the seasons in Great Britain, the United States, Germany, Italy, etc. I have relegated these to the latter end of the Annual and in a much reduced form. The record of the year's work in these different countries can be seen in the appendices and the many photographs reproduced; detailed criticism of important events has appeared throughout the year in the musical press, especially in the magazine *Opera*.

Following the suggestions made by many readers and critics, I have this year included several essays on specific works and composers. Thus Raymond Ericson writes on the new Samuel Barber opera, *Vanessa*; Edward Greenfield on Leoncavallo's little-known *La Bohème* which was recently revived in Italy; John W. Klein examines from a twentieth-century standpoint the works of Meyerbeer, which are surely due for revival; and Charles Reid looks at the additions to the opera repertory of this century, comparing and contrasting the more recent with those works that have established themselves firmly in the repertory. In addition we have an interesting account, by Robert Breuer, of the background to the Richard Strauss-Stefan Zweig correspondence recently published; an essay on the eternal question of Opera in English by an American University lecturer in that subject who examines some of the more recent 'American' translations of libretti; a study of the great teacher Manuel Garcia, the brother of Malibran and Viardot, who lived to be more than a hundred; and a short contribution from Margherita Wallmann, who produced *Aïda* and *The Carmelites* in London this year, on the place of ballet in opera.

In addition to these general essays, we have, as in the past, a main theme for the Annual; this year it is Festivals and Festival Opera. Accordingly we invited the Directors of the Edinburgh and Aix-en-Provence Festivals, Robert Ponsonby and Gabriel Dussurget, to contribute to our pages articles about their own particular festivals; then our old friend Joseph Wechsberg, who can hardly call himself a Wagnerian, writes about the post-war Bayreuth, while in complete contrast we publish a posthumous essay from the late Charles Webber, ex–Carl Rosa conductor who worked at Bayreuth before the first world war. Erich Leinsdorf, well-known American conductor of opera, recalls his work at Salzburg with Toscanini, and sketches a vivid pen-picture of the great Maestro; Lotte Lehmann has allowed us to reprint a few personal memories from her autobiography of her singing in *Fidelio* at Salzburg and elsewhere; Roy Henderson who was a 'foundation' member of Glyndebourne in 1934, recalls the beginnings of that magnificent venture; and Ernest Bradbury, critic of the *Yorkshire Post*, tells us about such operatic connections as the Leeds Festival had in the past in view of the coming production there of a Handel opera by the Covent Garden Company during the centenary year of both the Festival and the Covent Garden Opera House.

Last year's coloured prints of old singers seem to have been very popular, and this year I am devoting all eight of the coloured pages to pictures of great singers of the past, with some brief biographical notes about them.

I hope therefore that everybody will find something to please them in this year's Annual, and that they will approve of the new arrangement and pattern of the book. But please let us know what you feel, as we have to start planning next year's issue very soon.

H.D.R.

FESTIVAL OPERA

ROBERT PONSONBY

W HAT is there about opera?

Why is it that the vast majority of musicians and musical enthusiasts go to the opera, whatever their first musical interest may be? What has opera got that it should number among its devotees not only musicians who are primarily opera-lovers but also Professors of Music, plain amateur pianists, chamber-music players, enthusiasts for Gregorian plainchant and Troubadour music, Cathedral organists, madrigal-singers, players upon the lute and viol—even scholars of Byzantine musical notation? It is a very odd thing, for opera is the most vulnerable of all musical forms. Consider how vulnerable: singers crack, wobble, sometimes collapse, even occasionally swallow their false moustaches; choruses get at sixes-and-sevens, bump into scenery, are late in their exits and entries, periodically come undressed; technical equipment—lighting in particular—inexplicably acquires its own demon personality and indulges in uncontrollable eccentricities; even the conductor and his orchestra are by no means infallible.

Despite all this we all of us keep on going to the opera—and loving it, whatever we may say. What is there about it?

First—and there can be no doubt about this—opera combines in one form two of the strongest of all objective appeals to human emotion. These two appeals—music and drama—when combined in 'music-drama' each serve to heighten the other so that, for instance, the opera *Alceste* can be more moving than the play, while Mozart's *Don Giovanni* can be more moving than Strauss's *Don Juan*. In opera, there is a double appeal both to the musical ear and to the dramatic sensibility.

It follows that a finely co-ordinated performance of a music-drama which has sublime music and a libretto in the fullest sense dramatic can be an overwhelming experience. Such performances are few and far between owing to the elaborate and delicate machinery upon which opera has to rely—but sufficiently flawless performances do occur for the average opera-goer to apprehend the glorious potential of opera and to continue, therefore, to seek for it.

There are many other reasons for opera's extraordinary appeal—individual performances, the collector's instinct, a passion for the work of a particular composer, snobbism, fashion, even the hope of an operatic 'incident'—but it is, above all, the search for an overwhelming performance which draws us, like iron-filings to a magnet, back to the opera-house again and again. So it is that we all gravitate to the places where we are most likely to find such performances—places where the greatest artists are assembled, where the highest standards are expected and where the blinding spotlight of critical opinion is focused most sharply. In other words— to Festivals, which offer opera as the chief item on their bills of fare because of its unique appeal and its unique potential.

There are Festivals without opera, but they seem to me to lack, almost indefinably, the crowning glamour and *festiveness* without which a Festival is one in name only. To take the Edinburgh Festival, about which alone I am qualified to write: there have been many fine concerts and many fine dramatic performances, but more often than not, it has been the Opera—or an opera, or an individual performance— which has hall-marked the year in question. In eleven Festivals we have been visited eight times by Glyndebourne, twice by the Hamburg State Opera, once by La Piccola Scala: each Company has without doubt risen to the *Festival* occasion. As a result there have been remarkable achievements. To list a number of these is, even on paper, impressive: Grandi's Lady Macbeth, Stabile's Don Alfonso, *Ballo* with Welitsch and Silveri, Jurinac's Cherubino, Sir Thomas's *Ariadne* (in the early version), Busch's *Idomeneo* with Jurinac, Lewis and Simoneau; Grümmer's Eva and Agathe, Mödl's Octavian and della Casa's Sophie, Jurinac's Fiordiligi, Giulini's and Corena's *Falstaff*, Callas's Amina, di Stefano's Nemorino; not to mention the consistent distinction of Ebert's and Rennert's productions (in particular the former's *The Rake's Progress* and the latter's *Mathis der Maler*), Strehler's exquisite *Il Matrimonio Segreto*, the designs of Leslie Hurry, Osbert Lancaster, Oliver Messel, John Piper, Helmuth Jürgens, Luciano Damiani and others.

The mere recital of names such as these seems to me to convey an excitement not to be found in drama, ballet or pure music. We have been fortunate in our opera at Edinburgh but I am sure that other Festivals have the same story to tell and that Salzburg, Berlin, Venice, Holland, Aix—to name only a few—would never be prepared to do without their opera seasons. And it is significant, surely, that even the smallest Festivals in this country, Festivals such as Aldeburgh, Ingestre, Hovingham and Hintlesham, have decided that opera is the one essential ingredient. I am entirely certain that they are right. Despite the many maladies which constantly afflict operatic performances, despite the delicate balance which must be achieved between the claims of music, drama and design, despite the fallibility of operatic performers, despite unmusical librettists and composers with no understanding of the stage—despite all this, there is always latent in opera the possibility of a glorious fusion of all the elements which will result in an intensity of corporate achievement unsurpassable in any other artistic form. If this is so, and because the object of every Festival is the presentation of the best possible performance (in whatever artistic sphere), then opera must be the very core and heart of any Festival worthy of the name. (From this generalisation I would exclude only those Festivals which are 'specialists' in one subject—drama, for instance, or choral music.)

So far as the Edinburgh Festival is concerned, opera at the highest possible international standard is, I am certain, a vital ingredient and my hopes for the future are therefore directed toward the full maintenance of this standard. That it can be maintained I have no doubt, though it must be recognised that opera will always be the most costly of any Festival's undertakings—and that it is likely to become more, and not less, costly. There is no 'solution' to the high cost of opera, though there are a number of palliatives. The chief of these is, naturally, increased revenue from ticket sales—not only through high prices, but also through increased attendances. This second factor argues the need, which is pressing for other reasons also, for a larger theatre than is at present available. The King's Theatre, admirable as it is for the purpose for which it was built, is not an opera-house, nor is its capacity economical for opera. The Festival therefore needs a theatre, built with an eye to the technical requirements of opera (but suitable, obviously, for drama and ballet also), seating at least 2,000 people, an increase of 500 over the capacity of the King's Theatre. Such a theatre would have every artistic advantage, besides relieving the Festival's balance-sheet substantially.

Ultimately, however, the only thing that matters is the quality of the performances, and this I shall do everything possible to maintain.

THE 'MIRACLE' OF BAYREUTH

JOSEPH WECHSBERG

Bayreuth is terrific. I write this although I have little use for Wagner and less for festivals; there are far too many bad festivals these summers, dedicated to commercialism and primadonnaism, organised by promoters with little knowledge of music but considerable aptitude for extracting cash out of the pockets of tourists. Most permanent opera houses are run by artistically minded people; most festivals are run by Chamber of Commerce types who care more about profits than about quality. A dead, defenceless composer whose image appears on ash-trays and candy-boxes, is the star attraction. Big-name artists are hired and exploited. A beautiful idea deteriorates into Big Business. It's a successful racket though; the number of festivals increases every year. Obviously, there are smart hotel owners, travel agents and drumbeaters everywhere, and also snobs and innocents who are willing to 'do' Mozart or Wagner in forty-eight hours, as they've done the Louvre or the vineyards of France.

Bayreuth alone is different though it is by no means perfect. Certain hotels double their rates on important nights; and then there is something of the noisy carnival mood about town that doesn't go well with good music and good theatre. The Festspielhaus is an ugly, styleless red-brick building. Perfection is not always the keynote of the festival productions. Wieland and Wolfgang Wagner have the problems of opera managers everywhere—rising costs, higher wages, problematic subsidies, and a growing scarcity of voices healthy and powerful enough to withstand Richard Wagner's vocal demands. Everything takes on exaggerated proportions in Bayreuth, home of mad geniuses, heroes and giants: the beauty and the boredom, the emotion and the pathos, the acoustics (best on earth) and the discomfort (worst seats in the world), the length of the performances that start at four on a hot summer afternoon when people look as foolish in their evening clothes as a long-underwear chap would look in Albert Hall, and the endless intermissions filled with *Wurstbrote*, beer and goggling bystanders. It still is the same as thirty years ago when Romain Rolland wrote, 'The French flirt, the Germans drink beer, and the English read the

14

libretto,' except that there are now Americans who do all these things at the same time. This is a festival for people with physical stamina, large bank accounts and the capacity for sustained climaxes.

Despite everything, Bayreuth is wonderful. It has to be heard and seen to be believed. Bayreuth is today the most exciting experience in the contemporary musical theatre. The air is hot and humid but the artistic climate is healthy and invigorating. There are neither stars nor star intrigues; the first thing the Wagner brothers do is to make their stars forget that they are primadonnas and *Kammersänger* elsewhere. There is a happy tension about the Green Hill and a complete absence of routine. Everybody seems to be operating a little above himself which makes all the difference between a mediocre performance and an outstanding one. Bayreuth's intensity and enthusiasm are contagious, gripping everyone from trumpeter to tenor. It's the only place on earth where orchestra musicians don't grumble when the final rehearsals of *Meistersinger*, *Tristan* and *Parsifal* start out on three successive nights at seven and last until two in the morning, as they did last year.

'It could only happen here,' a dead-tired violist told me. 'It's what they call the miracle of Bayreuth. Perhaps the reason is that Bayreuth lasts only two months. You couldn't keep up this pace any longer than that.'

Maybe there is another reason, though, which was given to me by a prominent, hard-bitten singer with a widely known aversion to rehearsals. 'Elsewhere I'm fed up with a rehearsal before it starts. Here I enjoy it right down to the end. It's Wieland, of course. He listens to your ideas and may accept them if they are sound. Working with him you never have the feeling that you're improvising. I learn more in eight weeks here than during the rest of the year everywhere else. It's the most inspiring place in the world.'

The Wagner brothers have not only achieved the ideal of Grandfather Richard's 'total theatre', a blending of all components, music, staging, lights, voices, sound and action, into a magnificent entity; they've also been able to inject genuine enthusiasm into hard, painstaking labour. There's really a big, happy family on Bayreuth's Green Hill.

The family is indeed a big one. With soloists, orchestra, chorus, local schoolboys and supers, *Generalmusikdirektoren*, stagehands, technicians, lighting engineers, carpenters, there are almost a thousand people in all. Yet the administrative organisation is compact and unbureaucratic: Wieland and Wolfgang—anyone can get in to see them—Herr Klebe, Herr Eichner, half a dozen bright, devoted young women, that's all. It's a model how not only festivals, but artistic operations should be run.

*   *   *

My problem in Bayreuth (and it gets worse every year) is that so much of Grandfather's work is uninspired, pompous and simply boring. I sit unhappily through the slow-motion music and low-gear action of the first act of *Walküre* waiting for the love duet, and then I sit unhappily through the rest of the performance waiting for Wotan's Farewell. As I get older, the waiting periods seem to get longer. Many of us have gone through their adolescent stage of uninhibited Wagnerianism, and later through the post-adolescent stage of uninhibited anti-Wagnerianism. I didn't even laugh when I read that Grandfather had said—mind you, he wasn't joking, just making another extravagant statement—that during a good *Tristan* performance the audience should go nuts. During last year's *Tristan*, Grandfather would have been satisfied with me: there were moments—well, long half-hours, to be more exact—when I thought I was going nuts, though, I'm sorry to say, not the way Grandfather from Wahnfried had meant it. For one who loves the beauty of music— the heavenly inspiration of Mozart, the granite architecture of Bach, and, certainly, the immortal beauty of *Meistersinger*, of much of *Parsifal* and some of *Tristan* and the *Ring*—it's an ordeal to have to listen to Isolde's outbursts in the first act and Tristan's hallucinations in the last one, even when done by Nilsson and Windgassen. The romantic nonsense and silly mysticism of the early Wagner works, and the dreary alliterations and sentimental pathos of the later ones neither excite nor depress me; they just bore me. There remain some unforgettable moments and nightmarish hours when I feel sorry for the singers ruining their voices.

Evidently, I am a minority dissenter; the demand for tickets in Bayreuth always exceeds the supply. But I am not at all sure that the festival fans who drive up to the Green Hill—at last year's opening 1,204 automobiles were counted—are real enthusiasts. Neo-Bayreuth is fashionable, and it's considered smart to go there; insiders in the Festspielhaus estimate that less than one-fourth of the audience are hard-core enthusiasts who don't mind to walk there and would cheerfully cut Wieland's throat for cutting out a single note. Most enthusiasts are adolescents, some in their twenties and others in their sixties, soaking happily in the sound of horns and the steam bath of leitmotivs. The young ones are the genuine brand who discuss excitedly the revolutionary concepts of Wieland and Wolfgang. The old ones come back because Bayreuth reminds them of something that no longer exists (thank God). You see them pay their respects to Frau Winifred, the widow of Siegfried and mother of Wieland and Wolfgang. Frau Winifred loved to be photographed with those prominent Wagnerians, Hitler, Goering and Schirach. The old adolescents are really pathetic because they totally misunderstand the Bayreuth renaissance. In the brothers' concept, there is no room for nationalistic *Deutschtümelei*, papier-mâché castles and fat Rhinemaidens, of which the old ones were so fond.

AIX-EN-PROVENCE FESTIVAL

The Theatre in the Courtyard of the Archbishop's Palace, designed by Cassandre.

Lido

Jean Madeira as *Carmen*, Nicola Filacuridi as *Don José* in 'Carmen', 1957.

Bayreuth Festival

THE BAYREUTH FESTIVAL

The closing scene of 'Die Meistersinger' in Wieland Wagner's
1957 production at Bayreuth. Otto Wiener as
Hans Sachs

THE BAYREUTH FESTIVAL

A view of
the famous
covered orchestra
pit at the
Bayreuth Festspielhaus.

Bayreuth Festival

Act 3 of 'Tristan und Isolde' in Wolfgang Wagner's production, 1957.
Wolfgang Windgassen as *Tristan*, Gustav Neidlinger as *Kurwenal*.

Bayreuth Festival

The Piccola Scala at Edinburgh, 1957.
A scene from 'Il Matrimonio Segreto' with Graziella Sciutti, Gabriella Carturan,
Franco Calabrese, Carlo Badioli, Eugenia Ratti, Luigi Alva.

THE EDINBURGH FESTIVAL

Rosanna Carteri as *Adina*, Giuseppe di Stefano as *Nemorino* in 'L'Elisir d'Amore'.

The pretty, slim Rhinemaidens still chase each other through what Grandfather called 'greenish twilight', but they now wear one-piece golden bathing suits.

*   *   *

I remember my first afternoon in Bayreuth, in 1955. It was mid-July and I happened to pass through there, on my way to the Czech border, but when I saw the young men and women who seemed all excited about the *Rheingold* rehearsal with Hotter that was to begin in ten minutes, I got myself a pass and went into the ugly auditorium. About five hundred people—mostly young ones—had gathered in the middle of the long rows of straw-woven seats. As I sat down behind a young couple, the girl asked her companion where Wieland Wagner was going to sit. The young man showed her a makeshift platform in the rear, with a long table, a microphone and some telephones. 'He sits up there but his spirit is everywhere,' the young man said and the girl nodded raptly. Then the lights dimmed and went out, and I could hear a man talking quietly, probably into one of the telephones.

Then there was silence, and out of the darkness came a sustained E flat—so low that I couldn't distinguish exactly when the silence ended and the sound began. Nor could I be sure where the sound came from; it might have come from the sides of the auditorium, or the rear, or the ceiling. It was just there. Slowly the orchestra began to play the melodic passages, barely audible at first and gradually increasing in volume until the auditorium was filled with music—the music of the waters of the Rhine. When the curtains parted, the whole stage seemed filled with water— blue-green waves, ebbing and flowing in precise synchronisation with the music. The Rhinemaidens appeared, the music rose, and fell back to pianissimo, and Woglinde started her 'Weia! Waga!'

It took me a moment to realise that there were no props and no stage set; the whole scene, rock and all, was created by means of projected film and light. The music, the singing, the waters, and the lights blended perfectly. Although the brass dominated, it did not sound brassy, as it often does in the large orchestra Wagner calls for. The strings, particularly the first violins, were somewhat subdued, but that was a very minor flaw. I was under a spell. By the time Hotter (who sang in full voice at that rehearsal, God bless him) was leading his gods into his new Valhalla, which that year was a blue Impressionist castle and last year became a solid, square-stone *Burg*, I was convinced that Wieland Wagner is the greatest contemporary operatic producer—the only one who is creative, not merely reproductive—and that the grandsons have given a new lease on life to Grandfather's work which has been showing dangerous symptoms of senescence.

*   *   *

The four *Ring* productions are still the most important of the festival, and in many respects they are stunning productions. They change every year; Wieland still isn't satisfied, striving for more clarity and simplicity. He has thoroughly de-Germanized the Teutonic heroes and demoted Valhalla's gods. Wotan appears to be now a sort of Chicago gangleader, surrounded by a mob of scheming henchmen, who goes from perfidy to betrayal. He delightedly trades his own daughter for his new palace, and would just as happily trade his nagging wife for the ring, and he is sarcastic about the Rhinemaidens pleading to get them back the gold. Wieland has his arguments ready, in case some diehards should raise hell; and Wieland is a tough man to argue with because he knows the work and the intentions of Richard Wagner better than anyone else around. To him (and to Grandfather, he maintains) Wotan and Siegfried are the two anti-poles of the *Ring*, and the eternal split personalities of the German nation which produced Goethe and Goebbels. Wotan is driven into perdition by his lust for power, a dirty one-eye type who functions only with the help of Brünnhilde and is finished when he exiles her at the end of *Walküre*. To make matters worse, Siegfried, the hero, gradually changes from a fool to a crook who doesn't hesitate to commit perjury in *Götterdämmerung*. *Ja, ja*, and it's all in Grandfather's book.

There are other shocking moments. The Nibelungs in *Rheingold* are no longer dwarf-like monsters but tormented concentration-camp inmates. In the wonderful second act of *Götterdämmerung*, which Wieland turns into Shakespearean drama of action and suspense, Hagen manipulates his stupid mob as Himmler manipulated his S.S. men. The only great figure to emerge from this unappetising cast of super-people is Brünnhilde, who atones for Wotan's perfidy and becomes a Goethe-like figure, *Das Ewig-Weibliche*. It's a courageous conception; too bad that not many Germans can see themselves in Wieland's mirror.

The greatest Bayreuth production was, and still is, Wieland's *Parsifal*, left almost unchanged since it was first produced in 1951. It is a deeply stirring, nondenominational religious service. As musical theatre it is sheer perfection. What Wieland achieves with an empty stage, a cyclorama, and a few lights is magic, and a lesson to stage designers and producers everywhere. The mystic mood of the opening forest scene; the great transformation scene; Amfortas's torments in front of the Grail; Klingsor caught in his net; the ravishing poetry of the Flower Maiden scene; the Good Friday mystery—perfect miracles painted in light, the lights synchronised with sound. There is stark drama in the mass scenes. When I think of the cumbersome, monotonous *Parsifal* productions I've seen elsewhere, I am struck by the superbly simple yet deeply impressive solutions of Wieland Wagner. The astonishing precision of the chorus scenes; the bewildering revolt of the knights against Amfortas, a study in stylised drama; and of course, the superb singing-and-acting of all soloists; all that combines to achieve perfection.

Of course, Bayreuth has weaknesses. The inner circle of the soloists is small— Mödl, Nilsson, Varnay, Milinkovic, Rysanek, Greindl, Hotter, London, van Mill, Neidlinger, Schmitt-Walter, Vinay, Windgassen—and when some will have to bow out, owing to time and the demands of Wagnerian parts, it will be hard to find others who are not *Ersatz*. And who is going to take over when Knappertsbusch is no longer around? Many may be called but none seems chosen yet. Still, this is the greatest, and perhaps the only, true festival. In fact, I think Grandfather would like what Wieland and Wolfgang have done.

MEMORIES OF BAYREUTH—1914

CHARLES WEBBER

In 1914 I was conducting in Chemnitz; we were preparing Siegfried Wagner's opera *Herzog Wildfang*. Of the three or four performances of the work I conducted one. Siegfried Wagner was present and he thanked us all, singers, conductors and coaches, for our strenuous and conscientious work. He did this with so much kindness and charm that I took courage and asked him if he would let me help with the musical preparation of the *Festspiele*. He smiled and said he would be pleased if I came.

When I arrived I was taken to one of the eighteenth century mansions and had two rooms assigned to me for my own use. There were quite a number of such small mansions which I was told were erected at the time when Frederick the Great's sister was the Markgraefin of Ansbach-Bayreuth. I can only recall outstanding events and moments during my stay in Bayreuth which have impressed themselves deeply on my memory. We were about 8–10 assistant conductors besides the chorusmaster.[1] The latter had worked for many years in Bayreuth but in spite of his great reputation his name has slipped my memory. We worked hard with the singers, correcting false notes which had passed unnoticed and faulty time and rhythm. Occasionally I would make suggestions concerning nuances in tone colour, tentatively at first, then, when the singer responded, with greater freedom and authority. When the orchestral rehearsals started those of us who had no work to do with the singers would go and watch Muck or Balling directing the orchestra. The preparatory rehearsal with the orchestra would be held in a hall of a restaurant near the theatre. I recall at a *Parsifal* orchestral rehearsal Muck was so irritable that he interrupted his work and told us that the German oboes got on his nerves. The French woodwind in the Boston Symphony Orchestra, which he had been conducting, had spoilt him for the German woodwind, especially the oboe. We tried to pacify him and took him for a stroll in the woods on the *Festspielhügel*. It was a lovely June day and coming out of the hall we feasted our eyes on the beauty of the valley below. The lovely view helped to calm Muck's nerves and in a short time he went back to the hall

[1] *Hugo Rüdel—Ed.*

24

to resume the rehearsal, taking us with him, in a better humour. In the full rehearsals in the theatre we assistant conductors had a lot to do behind the stage as, for instance, to ring the bells in *Parsifal* which were always a tricky problem. They were never quite in tune. I had to play the grand piano which was meant to lend weight and body to the bells; it certainly did that but it couldn't make them sound more in tune. It would not be of sufficient interest to the reader if I mentioned all the things we had to attend to on the stage. I might say, though, that I was relieved to hear that one of the conductors who had for several years fulfilled a very difficult task to perfection was again going to give the signal for the curtain to rise in *Rheingold*. You remember that in the Prelude of *Rheingold* not only the key remains unchanged but also the E flat major chord over which it is built up until Woglinde sings the first phrase. The sign for the curtain to rise must be given in good time for her to see the conductor who gives her the cue. Unless the man on the stage who has the perilous task of giving the sign for the curtain has a full orchestral score at hand, or knows the scoring or at least the entrances of the various instruments by heart, he can easily lose himself and give the sign at the wrong time, either too early or too late, as it is impossible for him to count the bars, neither can he see nor feel the conductor's beat.

I remember the final stage rehearsal of the *Walküre* on account of a great experience. The mighty genius of Wagner revealed itself to me as never before. It happened in the second act. Brünnhilde overwhelmed by a wave of pity calls out to Siegmund that she will stand by him in his fight with Hunding. She hurries off, carried along as it were by the wild ecstasy of the tempestuous music and it was then that the revelation came to me. You must remember that in Bayreuth the conductor and orchestra are not visible to the public—they are under cover. The distance between the cover and the first row of the stalls is about five or six yards. The auditorium has a gentle upward grade. Therefore even those in the first row have a clear view of the stage. Let me repeat, the orchestra and the conductor are invisible. Where does the music come from? Is it played by human beings? Where *does* it come from? It comes from the *scene*. The scene, the characters, the rocks, the black rushing clouds, the sinister darkness, the lightning and thunder *are* the music. This miraculous illusion was my great experience. The *Festspielhaus* in Bayreuth is the only place known to me where this tremendous illusion is possible.

Let me say a few words about the receptions in *Wahnfried*, Richard Wagner's house. I think *Wahnfried* means an abode; peaceful and restful far away from the mad turmoil of the world. I was asked to two or three of these receptions. As far as I remember they were held before the actual performances had started. On the invitation card one was asked to be punctual. Believe me I was in the front garden before the appointed time. Many of the guests were there already, waiting for the front door to be opened. Among them I recognised Gerhart Hauptmann, the famous playwright, who may be remembered as the author of *The Weavers* and *The Sunken Bell*. Then I saw Humperdinck, to whom we owe the lovely opera *Hänsel und Gretel* and the almost as lovely *Königskinder*. And then a king, the King of Bulgaria! Soon the door opened and the guests, of whom there must have been about a hundred, streamed in. They were received by the Countess of Gravina, Bülow's and Cosima's daughter, a charming, gracious lady. The guests moved on round the oval-shaped hall until they came to a recess where Eva, Wagner's daughter, stepped out to welcome the guests and speak with the celebrities. Humperdinck, a little man with kind, humorous eyes and a beard, was just in front of me. Eva was very pleased to see and speak to her brother Siegfried's great teacher in composition. She only shook hands with me, albeit very nicely. I was not a celebrity.

The guests dispersed and I found myself alone. I walked along a carpeted corridor and suddenly I found myself on the threshold of a fairly large room. The door was open. I knew it at once and a feeling of awe came over me when I stepped in. It was the sanctum sanctorum. Here the great man had worked. I stood reverently there alone. Then I heard some movement behind me; I turned and saw Houston Stewart Chamberlain, Eva Wagner's husband. I had seen photographs of him and recognised him at once. His features had something of an ecclesiastic and professional. He was apparently searching for a book on the bookshelves. He gave me a friendly look and showed me some books of Celtic legends, among them *Mabinogion*, which he thought might be of interest to me. He found the book he wanted and was leaving the room when he said he thought I should not miss the concert. 'Certainly not,' I said, 'Sapelnikoff is playing is he not?' He nodded and left the room. I was following him when Sapelnikoff himself entered. I knew him quite well personally from days in Leipzig where we had occasionally lunched together. We shook hands and he sank into a comfortable chair. I said, 'You want to be alone with yourself in this room and rest before you play. You'll be starting in about five minutes I think. I shall not disturb you. I must find the music room and be there in time to hear you play in Wahnfried! What are you playing?' 'Liszt and Chopin,' he answered. 'I shall love it,' I said.

War broke out and put an end to the festival. *Parsifal* was the last performance. *Parsifal*! War! Imagine the contrast. I heard that already, during the performance, a number of the musicians in the orchestra had to leave; they were called up. I was allowed to stay in Bayreuth. I did a little work with two American singers. Occasionally I went for short walks with Mildenburg, who was the unforgettable Kundry, and her husband the playwright Hermann Bahr, and also with Siegfried and his sisters and his Aberdeen terriers who used to make us laugh. Soon I had to leave for Lubeck where I was engaged as conductor. My engagement did not last long. The morning after I had conducted *Mignon* I read a notice in the newspaper. The headline was 'French opera conducted by an Englishman; a few days later I was interned in Ruhleben. Farewell Bayreuth!—I remember the Countess of Gravina saying to me on the day of the outbreak of the war as we stood before the Festspiel-haus, 'This is the end, the *Götterdämmerung* of Bayreuth.'

TOSCANINI AT SALZBURG

ERICH LEINSDORF

IN the fall of 1934, I attended every rehearsal which Maestro Toscanini held with the Vienna Philharmonic Orchestra. A performance of the 'Ninth' Beethoven, preceded by Kodaly's *Psalmus Hungaricus*, promised to be the climax of that particular series. To make the occasion a completely international one, a chorus and three soloists from Budapest had been invited to participate, and the program was to be repeated in Budapest after having been presented in Vienna. During intermission of one of the rehearsals for this program, I ran into the Manager of the Vienna Philharmonic Orchestra who seemed completely frantic and harassed, explaining to me upon my inquiry that he was unable to locate anyone who could or would play the piano the following morning for the rehearsal which Toscanini had scheduled for the solo quartet of the 'Ninth' and the tenor soloist in the *Psalmus*. I eagerly offered my services, having prepared the Kodaly work a few years earlier with a choir in Vienna and being, of course, familiar with the 'Ninth'.

I practised rather intensively that afternoon and arrived in the green room of the Musikvereins Saal a quarter before ten in the morning. I thought that I would be early to try the piano, but I was by no means the first. Richard Mayr, the famous and beloved Viennese basso, the only non-Hungarian of the solo quartet, was already there. He was quite nervous and wanted to know from me what to expect from the famous and much feared Maestro. It was his first encounter with Toscanini and I could not advise him as it was also my first time with Toscanini. Mayr said in effect (trying to conceal his obvious apprehension behind a façade of bluster) that he had sung the 'Ninth' for a quarter of a century; that he knew it one way; that he was too old to change and if the Maestro did not approve of the way he was doing it, he was just going to walk out and suggest that somebody else take over. The other soloists arrived; Toscanini came in accompanied by the Manager of the Philharmonic. I sat down at the piano and Mayr began the famous recitative, sang it straight through in the way in which he had done it for the past quarter century and at the end of it, Toscanini patted him on the arm, said 'bene' and that was the sum total of his comments or criticisms. It was invariably the case when Toscanini met an outstanding artist, that he would recognise instantly the calibre that was before him and instead of the fireworks which some members of the ever-present coterie expected (maybe hoped for?) peace and serenity prevailed.

There was one notable incident, tactfully omitted from many recollections, which I witnessed at close range. During the 1936 Salzburg Festival, Toscanini found it necessary to ask one of the principals, who had been engaged with his specific consent for one of 'his' operas, to withdraw from the cast. I was with the Maestro after several piano rehearsals when he paced up and down the rehearsal room talking more or less to himself, trying to solve a situation, which meant that he would either have to bend his own conception of a great work or that he would have to hurt— and very deeply—an artist for whom he had great esteem and personal affection. He finally wrote a personal letter in which he explained that there was such a divergence of interpretations between the singer and himself that no useful collaboration could be accomplished. The artist who replaced the one who withdrew was definitely inferior, but completely pliable to the wishes of Toscanini.

It has often been remarked that in his later years, the Maestro selected singers more according to their pliability than to any other vocal or musical qualifications. The friction with the famous singer who was asked to withdraw illustrated for me, at least, that at a certain point in an artist's career, the ability to change and to adjust ceases and when two artists meet, both of whom have reached that particular point, the world is treated either to the proverbial fireworks or there has to be a parting of the ways.

All seriousness and iron discipline ceased once a show had been launched. The run-throughs prior to repeat performances remain most pleasantly in my memory.

Once we had a complete *Meistersinger* ensemble rehearsal because Lotte Lehmann had dwelt over a phrase in the second act somewhat too long and I remember that the whole rehearsal consisted of nothing but story-telling by the Maestro and by members of the cast and that after this *Kaffeeklatsch* had gone on a while, Toscanini said with a broad smile and mock indignation toward Lotte (for whom he had boundless admiration), 'Now here we are—a whole rehearsal just because you made me wait for the end of a phrase in the last performance.' These story-telling rehearsals were a very conscious practice of Toscanini's. We would meet ostensibly for a run-through prior to a repeat performance and the actual work would be only a few minutes of repeating a phrase here or a phrase there, while the rest of the time would be devoted to swapping stories (especially with the Italian cast of *Falstaff* with whom the Maestro had many common memories). He explained to me one day after such a conversational rehearsal that it was most important to see each other a day prior to the

29

performance just to have everyone's mind alerted to the fact that another performance of the work was coming up and it might be advisable to think again of one's
role and to practice again a passage here and a passage there.

In *Zauberflöte* which Toscanini conducted in 1937, he was desirous of creating a
sonority for the 'magic flute' passages distinctly different from that of an ordinary
instrument and he finally decided to have the passages in question played backstage
and not, as is customary, in the pit. To make the sound bigger, better audible and
more 'magic' four flautists performed them in unison, one of them using an alto
instrument in G. I had to conduct these four gentlemen and Toscanini seemed very
taken with the strange effect of that unusual combination.

In *Fidelio* and *Zauberflöte*, Toscanini would always consult a libretto in his typical
attitude of peering intently at the printed page from a distance of just a few inches;
he wanted to be certain to know the dialogue cues so that he could alert the orchestra
on time and start the next music number at the right moment. It was never clear
in these rehearsals nor in *Meistersinger* how much German he really understood.
An occasional remark to a singer pointing up an important word to be emphasised,
made one believe that he was very much aware of the meaning of the language, yet
he never spoke or read a phrase in German.

During these three summers, I played every piano rehearsal which Toscanini held
for his operas and, I am sure that I assisted at every orchestra rehearsal and every
performance. There are many false notions and misconceptions about Toscanini's
work in circulation and I want to correct them. The first is the idea that Toscanini
rehearsed more than anyone else. This is not so. He made the utmost use of his
rehearsal time, but he never over-rehearsed anything. When he was satisfied with a
singer's rendition of a role at the first run-through at the piano, he would never go
over that particular part again. One such case was Hermann Wiedemann's Beckmesser. The artist came to a solo rehearsal with Toscanini at which I played the
piano. We went through the entire role, Toscanini conducting ever so lightly just
to be sure that *his* tempi were being taken and, understanding immediately that he
had before him a singer of experience who had completely mastered the role, he
declared himself fully satisfied because, as he explained to me later 'even if I should
do a certain phrase in a different way, I find that it is better for the total effect, if I do
not correct a good artist who has his own conception, just to impose my own,
so long as his idea is in good taste and generally acceptable.' He used to make
elaborate fun of conductors who repeated passages just to use up time left at their
disposal. The second and third years of *Fidelio* and *Falstaff* he would rehearse very
little with orchestra—I should say less than other conductors rehearsed for operas
which had not been given for eleven months.

The second misconception to correct is the one that Toscanini was so terribly concerned with presenting everything 'exactly as it is written'. He was never interested in precision for its own sake. I noticed with amazement when I first played rehearsals for him how he would pay no attention to certain incorrect note values in the rendition of singers. I never heard him make a puny correction, but what he said was always prompted by interpretation and expressive motivation. Characterising his art as being so great because he produced that 'which was written by the composer' is a gross understatement which is bound to lead to an erroneous idea of Toscanini.

He studied all his life to get closer to the meaning of music, to the intentions of the great composers. He was not an uncritical slave and he always looked for the meaning behind the notes. When he found things which did not seem right, he changed, he added. His scores were full of annotations, and the librarian would be asked up to the last minute before a performance to mark another accent for the first oboe here and another special staccato dot for the bassoon there. He transposed freely when he felt that a singer's performance would be enhanced by a transposition. One year, he even tried, in the big 'Abscheulicher', to make a new harmonic sequence in order to keep the recitative in the original key, while transposing the aria proper. He suggested transposing the second aria of the Queen of Night. He changed a harmony in the first movement of the Beethoven 'Ninth' because he was convinced that there had been an error by a copyist or printer. I do not believe that Toscanini was always right, but I do believe that he was always interested in getting the utmost intensity and the fullest meaning out of any work he tackled.

This is an entirely different concept than that which has been so widely publicised of 'the strict precisionist who played everything as the composer wrote it'. I suggest that Toscanini's greatness lay in his ability to read in a score that which the composer meant, but which no conventional symbols of notation are able to convey to the average reader. His intuition to understand that which lies under and between the written notes and to bring those invisible indications to full sound—that was his greatness.

'FIDELIO' MEMORIES*

LOTTE LEHMANN

I HAVE known unforgettable experiences with each conductor with whom I have sung *Fidelio*. Schalk, who first induced me to sing this beautiful role, imbued the opera with all the nobility of his being. Singing it with him I felt liberated from this earth. I am grateful that it was he who, through many intensive rehearsals, first revealed Beethoven to me. The Beethoven Centenary, in which I sang Leonore for the first time, in a new production of *Fidelio*, was a great event for the people of Vienna. There was scarcely a person who didn't take a vital interest in the celebration. Music was the very breath of life to the Austrians. They grew up with it and were so intimate with the treasures of their musical heritage that every one seemed to regard Beethoven and Mozart as his own personal property. Those days of the Centenary festivities when even the baker's boys, delivering their rolls, whistled Beethoven airs through the streets, painted Vienna in all its loveliest hues.

*　　　*　　　*

Bruno Walter gave his whole soul to this noblest of all operas. It was as if the whole gamut of human emotion from the depths of tragedy to the heights of joy pulsed from his heart.

And Toscanini? He made *Fidelio* flame through his own fire. There was thunder and lightning in his conducting—his glowing temperament, like a flow of lava, tore everything with it in its surging flood.

*　　　*　　　*

Fidelio in Salzburg, Vienna, Paris, London, Stockholm, Hamburg, Berlin—was always the same tremendous experience. I could never become 'accustomed' to

* Reproduced from *My Many Lives* by Lotte Lehmann (by arrangement with the Publishers, Boosey and Hawkes

singing Leonore—for me she was always new, always deeply exciting and utterly moving.

*　　　*　　　*

Oh these hours of happy sublimation! This pure ecstasy of artistic creation, of artistic bondage with the other personalities in *Fidelio*, with the conductor! The Vienna opera—the Salzburg Festival Playhouse—London's Covent Garden—the Paris Grand Opéra—in them there lies for me the whole wonder of years which have vanished, of beauty which has passed away. . . .

Schalk, Walter, Toscanini shine like a constellation of three stars in my memory. And ever again I say: 'Thank you' to them in my heart.

GLYNDEBOURNE—1934

ROY HENDERSON

It was while on a railway journey in company with some fellow artists that I heard of the project of Opera on the Sussex Downs. All of us discussed it with the feeling that this was another mad scheme, far more crazy than any of the well meaning attempts to form an opera company which had from time to time foundered on financial rocks. Here was a man evidently determined to give opera four miles from the small country town of Lewes, a mile from the nearest bus stop, presumably in the open air. My only experience of open air singing had been at a private party on a Thames island, with the newly appointed musical director of a recording company in the audience. We were rather excited to see that he appeared most interested; dreams of a five-year contract loomed large in our minds. Alas, he was only fascinated by the number of flies and midges that each singer inhaled. Opera on the Downs during a warm evening, with a fine local hatch of Olive Duns, and bats attracted by the lighting, might at least be entertaining.

Later I heard that a theatre was in the process of being built. Sheer madness! Had no one warned this Mr. John Christie that opera in the best of conditions would ruin him if it were undertaken seriously? Where could he find an audience? Of course he could probably afford a week of semi-professional performances, with the local choral societies providing the chorus; the nearest amateur operatic society supplying the producer and most of the principals, and a promising youngster from one of the Colleges as conductor. The orchestra could be two pianos, or some local amateur string players with rather down-trodden professional stiffening at the most. It would be fun: but fancy building a theatre just for that.

Early in 1934 I was asked if I would like to meet Mr. Christie and Hans Oppenheim, with a view to taking part in a fortnight's opera at Glyndebourne, during the off-season for concerts. We met, talked it over, and Oppenheim wanted to hear me sing. I well remember the walk we had to a studio. John Christie led the way charging through the London traffic, while Oppenheim and I stood gasping on the kerb. I collected sufficient breath, sang, and was asked if I would undertake the part of the Count in *Le Nozze di Figaro*. So far my career had been confined to the concert platform with very few exceptions, but I decided to accept the offer as it would only be a sort of village performance anyway.

I was soon disillusioned. When rehearsals started very little was right. Phrase after phrase was repeated over and over again. Our rhythm was not firm enough; our time was not exact; metronomes were employed to show how careless we were. Fritz Busch, they said, was a terror for rhythm. He would make us sit up, and Carl Ebert—when he came (sardonic laughter)—the rest was left to our increasingly apprehensive imaginations.

Gradually things began to take shape. We got to know one another and to work together in ensemble. The first singer I met was Audrey Mildmay who I learnt afterwards was the real inspiration behind her husband, John Christie. It was the beginning of a close friendship and an association on the stage which will remain one of my proudest and happiest memories.

Foreign artists were due to appear and we all wondered what they would be like. Aulikki Rautawaara, the Finnish soprano who was to play the part of the Countess, was as attractive as her name but at that time could speak no English. I still possess the little pocket German dictionary with which she presented me, and which, with the further aid of carefully chosen sentences from lieder, enabled us to understand each other very well. The following year her English surprised us all.

Willi Domgraf-Fassbänder was singing and acting at his very best. His amazing vitality and enthusiasm were quite infectious, and there was never a dull moment when he was on the stage.

Luise Helletsgrüber was the remaining foreigner in a cast that contained eight British artists. How gracefully she moved on the stage. She taught me a lesson I am constantly quoting to youngsters. I looked into the theatre one day and saw it was empty but for Helletsgrüber, who was on the stage. In the last act she had to run across the stage, up a long flight of steps and arrive in a certain position on a particular beat of music. Actors have no conception of the difficulty of exact, split-second timing required of an opera singer, at any rate at Glyndebourne. I watched her start on this foot, then on that, a foot in front, and a foot behind her original starting point until she got it right. She then practised the run at least forty times more. Needless to say it was perfectly timed and looked quite spontaneous at the performance.

It was this meticulous rehearsal that made the deepest impression on me. I had seen nothing like it before. My own experience of Covent Garden rehearsal in the late 'twenties (I am glad to say it bears no resemblance at the present time) was ludicrous. As Donner, a lesser god in *Das Rheingold*, in the second cycle of *Ring* performances, I met the producer twice, first when he said how do you do, and instructed the stage manager to show me how to swing the thunder god's hammer. I was further told to keep near Froh who had played the part before and knew where to go. Our one rehearsal was to be without Wotan, who had appeared at Covent Garden the previous year and presumably knew the dimensions of the stage. He was a magnificent singer and when he appeared on the night he gave a dignified and static performance, as befits the mightiest of gods, but often caused embarrassment in his choice of lodgement, as when he stationed himself firmly on the trap which was about to open for Erda to make an appearance from the bowels of the earth. Frantic gesticulations and a chorus from the wings, which I can only describe as resembling a group of Welshmen arguing in their native language the validity of a try near the corner flag, enticed him away just in time for her to sing 'Weiche Wotan' as she disentangled herself from his cloak. On another occasion he stretched out his arms just in front of me and held them there, completely obliterating both conductor and audience as I was about to sing a few bars that I felt were rather important. This wouldn't do at all, so I strode heavily across the stage, as I felt the lesser god of thunder ought to do, and from a hitherto uncharted region addressed the Giants who were busy piling up the gold. It was amusing to see their indecision before they found in which direction to make their customary rude answer.

After that I met the producer the second time and was soundly reprimanded for leaving my position alongside Froh, who in any case had completely ignored me since he had spent the evening with his arm round the waist of a comely Freia. The following year I asked for a rehearsal but was told I did not need one as I had played the part a year ago.

How different it was at Glyndebourne. With infinite patience and understanding Professor Ebert took us through our parts, often acting the role for us, instilling into us a sense of movement and drama which matched the music. He was tireless, working into the small hours of the morning at stage lighting and the hundred and one things that go to make a successful production. He treated us as colleagues and encouraged us to make suggestions about our own personal problems. Many times in the course of six seasons I had what I felt was a bright idea. He would always listen patiently and either tell me the reason why it wouldn't do, or say 'let us try it', usually after dinner in rehearsal periods or round about 11 p.m. when the season had begun. If he liked the idea he was delighted and would incorporate it in production.

I was especially interested in the way he made characters out of the members of the splendidly trained chorus, quite a number of whom have since made big names for themselves in opera and on the concert platform. I can think of no finer training for any young singer than to spend a couple of seasons in the Glyndebourne chorus

A scene from Act 2 of Verdi's 'Falstaff'.

THE
LYNDEBOURNE FESTIVAL

ofessor Carl Ebert rehearsing a scene
om 'Idomeneo', 1957.

A scene from Rossini's
'Le Comte Ory'.

THE MUNICH FESTIVAL

Paul Hindemith and Rudolf Hartmann at a rehearsal of Hindemith's 'Die Harmonie der Welt'.

A scene from Hindemith's 'Die Harmonie der Welt' at Munich, 1957. Josef Metternich as *Kepler*.

Franz Novak

THE SALZBURG FESTIVAL

Two scenes from Herbert von Karajan's production of 'Fidelio' at the Felsen-reitschule. *Above* the Prisoners' Chorus; *below*, the finale.

A scene from Act 2 of 'Le Nozze di Figaro' with Elisabeth Schwarzkopf as
The Countess, Irmgard Seefried as *Susanna*, and Christa Ludwig as *Cherubino*.

THE SALZBURG FESTIVAL

A scene from Liebermann's 'The School for Wives' with Christa Ludwig,
Kurt Böhme, Nicolai Gedda (Anneliese Rothenberger and Walter
Berry on balcony).

if he or she is lucky enough to be selected for it. Today the competition for places is very keen, and involves continuous auditions for many weeks.

As the production unfolded itself in that first season we were all caught up by the enthusiasm and activity of the producer. Norman Allin, who had been in opera for over twenty-five years at that time, told me he had experienced nothing like it before.

I mentioned Professor Ebert's infinite patience: perhaps it is not quite the right adjective. Once a year, and very occasionally twice, he became thoroughly exasperated by incompetence or inattention. There would be a warning rumble, then something would occur that truly rent the heavens. A torrent of words in German (and what a wonderful language it is on these occasions), would reverberate through the theatre as he paced up and down the gangway. The theatre would be tactfully cleared and sometimes there would be a short interval. Rehearsal would start again as though nothing had happened, except that we were very much on the alert, and the Professor's hair looked neater than when we had last seen it.

On the musical side we had Hans Oppenheim, Alberto Erede, who has since become a famous conductor, and Jani Strasser, who is still there to give Glyndebourne the benefit of his long experience. Meticulous to a degree, these three saw to it that we were thoroughly prepared for the exciting moment of the first rehearsal with the conductor. Fritz Busch was pleased with his team; under him the music sprang to life; he got the best out of us. It was noteworthy that several of the press critics said they had not heard the British artists, with whom they were well acquainted, sing so well before.

At the end of the first rehearsal the artists were invited to listen to the orchestra playing the overture to *Le Nozze di Figaro*, which they had rehearsed for the best part of three hours. I had sung with the L.S.O. on many occasions and I knew their playing well, but this was quite thrilling. Each player knew exactly what to do in every phrase and note, and obviously wanted to impress the singers. One of the 'cellists, who was prone to considerable head movements, looked to me as though he would break his neck anywhere in the last forty-five bars. Busch knew exactly what he wanted and insisted on it. His splendid sense of humour was a great asset, and respect grew to the affection in which he was held by all who came under his inspired leadership.

I can remember how on one occasion, when things were going rather badly in rehearsal, we were all rather tired and tension was high on the stage, Fritz Busch saved the situation. Temperament had got the better of a lady artist who said a polyphemic mouthful terminating with a sentence which could have been rightly punctuated by several exclamations and one large question mark. There was a dramatic pause while sufficient breath was being stored for a suitable reply, when the opening bars of Mendelssohn's 'Spring Song' wafted through the highly charged atmosphere from the conductor's rostrum, to general laughter in which the infuriated parties themselves joined.

Those of us who had only little operatic experience began to appreciate what was happening behind the scenes. The management under Alfred Nightingale must have had many difficulties during the first season. Hamish Wilson designed the scenery which was made from start to finish, besides properties and much else, by the ubiquitous 'Jock', who to this day is the mainstay behind the stage. With the help of men who had never seen the back of a theatre before he organised a team of stage hands second to none.

For myself, I have never enjoyed anything like the Glyndebourne seasons and these rehearsals. The superb music under the most expert guidance, the congenial company, the wonderful gardens and surroundings left little to be desired, especially when I found some trout fishing nearby for my leisure hours. No wonder we felt on top form in this most delightful theatre.

How wise John Christie was in his choice of the two main pillars on which the future of Glyndebourne was to rest, Busch and Ebert. They knew each other's value and worked together in perfect harmony. It is my firm belief that Glyndebourne could not have succeeded without their standard of performance. John Christie himself never interfered with their work. He watched everything and yet was strong enough to leave the job to his experts. At the performances he was always the best member of the audience from the actor's point of view and we used to listen for his hearty laugh ringing out above those of the rest. He showed an immense interest in everything that was going on and when each season was over he was full of plans for the next. Every year brought new improvements, some of them vast structural additions, during the building of which any Glyndebourne guest was liable to be whisked away to climb perilous-looking ladders and bits of scaffolding, while the scheme and its purpose were unfolded.

His sayings could fill many books. What a field day he had when the electricity failed during a performance of *Die Zauberflöte* and he made over a dozen short speeches which left the audience in the best of spirits. His sense of humour is distinctly boyish.

He is the first to say that he owed it all to his wife. Audrey Mildmay was an asset, not only for the roles she played so charmingly, for the part she played as Glyndebourne's most gracious hostess, but also for the inspiration with which she enthused her husband and the wise counsel she gave him. No one who was not in the inner circle of discussion during those early years can imagine the complicated problems and decisions which had to be made. Her advice contributed in no small way to the success of Glyndebourne.

The first night came. I was a little nervous of course, but felt a confidence after I had sung my first phrase that can be acquired only through painstaking rehearsal. We all knew exactly what to do and constant repetition made every movement second nature.

The six men soloists were together in one room, as the dressing-rooms were not built until the following autumn; the ladies dressed somewhere in the dark recesses behind the stage. None of us realised that within a few hours we would have helped to make history, together with all those numerous workers behind the scenes who get no applause. The overture was finished, brilliantly played, and the curtain went up most fittingly on Audrey Mildmay and Fassbänder, the first artists to be seen on the Glyndebourne stage.

After *Così fan tutte* had been performed on the following night, with Souez, Helletsgrüber, Eisinger, Nash, Fassbänder and Bettoni in the cast, Glyndebourne had set a new standard of operatic performance which the Press said outshone the performance of Salzburg. The theatre, empty at first, soon filled, and in subsequent years had to be enlarged over and over again, for seasons of opera five times as long as the 1934 season.

The lessons of Glyndebourne were many. I learnt to respect great music. Ever afterwards I felt I was one of the lucky ones to be entrusted with a part in the performance of a great masterpiece, which I could disfigure or in some small way bring to life. It was my duty to do as well as I could. I learnt the value of careful preparation and benefited from close association with great artists, from whom I found inspiration and example which all artists who wish to improve must obtain.

It is not easy to assess the value of Glyndebourne to the musical life of Britain. Busch and Ebert set a pace which made all the others run faster. One big change was the end of the star system. In the old days at Covent Garden the front of the stage was reserved for the more important artists and lesser characters were expected to keep at a distance up stage. I knew nothing of this, but well remember the angry gesticulations of a rather odious Walther as I approached the footlights to address him as Kothner, the master of ceremonies. The other lesser masters, all British, let forth a volume of muttered abuse, encouraging me to take no notice but go on, which of course I did. I was not engaged at Covent Garden the following season. In Glyndebourne it was team work, where nobody, however distinguished, was allowed any special favours and the name of Childs, John Christie's butler, who played a first-class deaf mute in *Entführung*, was written in just as big letters as Kipnis and Stabile. I am certain it was the happiest opera company in the world.

At Glyndebourne we felt we were not working for a company or an association or an impresario, who naturally had to make his living, but for one man whom we all loved and respected. John Christie had such faith in his ideal, we could not let him down.

It would be impossible to measure the enjoyment John Christie has given to music lovers from all over the world, or the prestige he has gained for this country. He is that rare combination, an idealist and a man of action. He has had help from public funds on one occasion only, during the Festival of Britain, but whatever the difficulties he has wended his way through them in that direct way of his, with his eye fixed on his objective, as he charged through the London traffic on the day I first met him.

THE AIX-EN-PROVENCE FESTIVAL

GABRIEL DUSURGET

(TRANSLATED BY LIONEL DUNLOP)

'OPERA ANNUAL' has greatly honoured and pleased me in asking me to write about the Aix-en-Provence Festival. All who know me appreciate how dear this subject is to me. The Aix Festival is, indeed, my pre-occupation, my sole care and, I should add, my great joy.

This festival was born by the purest chance. It came about first as a result of a visit to the town, and then from an interview with Monsieur Bigonnet. It was while travelling in Provence and at Aix itself that during my sojourn in this ravishing city I could not but be struck by the harmony of Aix with Mozart's music. This harmony aroused my desire for performances and, hence, for a festival.

To realise this, I called upon M. Bigonnet. I described to him my plans and, after some reflection, he told me of his. We were soon in agreement and so, thanks to this daring, understanding man, something of a poet and above all courageous, the Aix-en-Provence Festival was created in 1948. The first festival was dedicated to Mozart. His music fitted this setting so well that at the end of the first season M. Jean-Louis Vandoyer of the Académie Française wrote: 'A predestined union. Mozart's charms and those of Aix are the same charms'—'Going from streets to squares, from squares to courtyards and from courtyards to gardens, the artists who raised this succession of mansions and fountains have composed a setting whose well-spaced order is laid out as a concert for the eyes. How many times whilst walking about this marvellous town have we heard the perfect melody which this concert in stone embodied.'

I am not going to retrace here the growth of these performances. Rather I wish to describe how the preference for and boldness in staging our operas with young singers came about.

In 1949 we had decided to put on *Don Giovanni*. Our casting was complete except that we lacked someone for the principal role, that of Don Giovanni. Being unable to find someone to suit us among the acclaimed and celebrated singers of Don

Giovanni, we had resort to the young. And so it was that, attending auditions at Milan, we happened to be present at the arrival of the young Capecchi, then twenty-three years old, who gave a very brilliant audition. After much hesitation we decided to entrust to him the principal role of Don Giovanni. He had ten months to study the score; he was a good musician, actor and hard worker, and so our boldness was rewarded and Capecchi proved a very fine Don Giovanni. His career has, too, continued, most brilliantly; he was singing a year later at the Metropolitan Opera, and he has been at the Scala for eight years.

Encouraged by this success and, too, having acquired a taste for novelty, I was looking a year later for a Susanna for *Le Nozze di Figaro*, when at the Théâtre des Champs Elysées, after a rehearsal by the Société des Concerts du Conservatoire a timid young girl introduced herself and asked me to hear her. She sang Susanna with such charm that I immediately engaged Graziella Sciutti to sing the role at Aix. She had had no experience of the stage and in Italy was considered solely a concert singer. She was then only twenty and had just left the Rome Conservatoire; but she had won an Italian radio prize. She has since shown herself one of the finest singing-actresses of our generation.

Emboldened by the success of these experiments and also gaining self-confidence, there followed our engagement of Leopold Simoneau and Rafael Ariè (after his Geneva prize). The following year two singers, who have since become very famous, made their débuts on the Aix-en-Provence stage. They were Teresa Stich-Randall and Nan Merriman.

Henceforth, to find young singers, I go to all the Swiss, Spanish, Italian and French singing competitions. I listen very carefully to all the candidates. I do not concern myself with the prizes they may be winning but only with those qualities which I believe I have found in them. It is as a result of these patient auditions—and re-auditions—that Antonio Campo, our present Don Giovanni, and Teresa Berganza have graduated, after Aix, to the great stages of the world. We now know of the amazing success in the role of Dorabella last year of Teresa Berganza whom the Scala has just engaged and for whom we are this year putting on at Aix *Il Barbiere di Siviglia* in the original version.

Nor should it be forgotten that the Cour de l'Archevèché has seen the début too of Maria Morales, Pilar Lorengar and certain young French singers about whom less is heard, but who have no less talent: Vivette Barthelemy (she is singing at the time of writing at the Scala), Jeanne Berbié (at the Scala), Irène Sicot.

I am ending this list of successes by mentioning the young French tenor Michel Sénéchal, who made such a brilliant and remarkable début in the role of Platée in Rameau's opera of that name.

The 1958 Aix-en-Provence Festival will include *Il Barbiere di Siviglia*, *Don Giovanni* and *Die Zauberflöte*. In this last opera there is again an unknown young singer, a German called Fritz Wunderlich.

You asked me how I find these young singers. I look for them, of course, and I find them by listening to them. As you see, it is quite simple. It is a question of not allowing oneself to be too easily deceived, for a serious error would be disastrous both for the festival and for the singer. Aix-en-Provence is beginning to prove a great bait, and so we are often approached by all the youthful artists who are dedicated to the lyric art. Since, on the other hand, those who have some talent know that they have the chance of an engagement, a very large number of these 'young hopefuls' ask to be heard; and, since it is always the one who is not heard who is good, I always take the trouble to listen to those who ask me.

All this does not prevent us, of course, from frequently calling upon the services of such famous singers of the top rank as Suzanne Danco, Janine Micheau, Consuelo Rubio, Leonie Rysanek, Rolando Panerai, Franco Calabrese, Marcello Cortis, Boris Christoff, Jacques Jansen, Gérard Souzay, etc.

THE LEEDS CENTENARY MUSICAL FESTIVAL

ERNEST BRADBURY

1958 is the centenary year of three British musical institutions, two of them permanent, the third periodic. The Hallé Orchestra celebrated its hundredth birthday in January; Covent Garden held similar festivities in May, and in October the Leeds Musical Festival is claiming its centenary and is honouring the event by including opera in its programmes for the first time. As a fact opera is but one of several new paths (jazz is another) to be explored by Leeds for this special occasion, in keeping with modern trends when festivals try to provide something for everybody. Opera might not be included in another, non-centenary year, for the basis of the Leeds Festival is not opera but choralism, on which its fame has rested exclusively for a hundred years.

So is history made, and thus do musical patterns establish themselves. Not for England the pattern whereby national opera should develop from the petty princedoms and private courts of the aristocracy, as in Germany. Instead, and especially in the North, we had the grim march of industrial expansion, the rapidly increasing populations in the townships, the spread of the sight-singing movement, the foregathering—on winter nights in church or chapel or public hall—of artisans of every class willing and anxious to make music with the voice, concerned that their standard should not be lower than that of their nearest neighbours and withal mightily assured that such activity was pleasing in the sight of heaven. In all this, no doubt, nature herself had a hand. The Colne and Holme valleys of the West Riding, say some, produce the richest-voiced basses in the land. Certainly there is evidence that the Northern choirs soon regarded themselves as leaders in the field; and when, for the opening of Leeds Town Hall by Queen Victoria in 1858, extra activities of a festive nature were considered desirable, what more natural than that Leeds should copy the choral festivals established elsewhere and stage a similar event of its own?

A scheme drawn up by the city fathers met with unanimous approval; but alas! enthusiasm is not the same as experience. The committee of Leeds gentlemen, says

Baur

THE ZÜRICH FESTIVAL

The third scene from Schöenberg's 'Moses und Aron' which had its world
première at the 1957 Zürich Festival

'Carmen' at Trieste

SUMMER OPERA

'Norma' at the Verona Arena

FESTIVALS IN ITALY

'Turandot' and 'Otello', both at the Arena Flegrea, Naples.

Troncone

LOTTE LEHMANN
IN LONDON

Two moments during Lotte
Lehmann's Master Classes at
the Wigmore Hall, London,
last autumn. Mme. Lehmann
rehearsing a scene from 'Der
Rosenkavalier', and with
Ivor Newton, taking a call
at the end of the class.

Anthony Pant

Anthony Panting

the record, 'seem to have been puzzled by the super-sensitiveness of the artists in arranging terms. As business folk, the committee thought they were purchasing a marketable commodity in the ordinary manner—the buyer giving as little and the seller obtaining as much as possible, without sentiment on either side. It was not for them to understand why money negotiation is distasteful to a public vocalist,[1] or why he or she must be approached, as Agag drew near to Samuel, "delicately".' There were difficulties of several kinds, including sectarian rivalry, the pretensions of local soloists who thought they had some divine right to a place in the scheme, and the outcry from singers in Leeds when it was decided that only eighty of them were good enough for the Festival Chorus and that the remainder would be drawn from other parts of the West Riding. Beside these disturbances (though the records are lean) the great ones from London seem to have behaved with exemplary decorum. Alboni, only pupil of Rossini, who had figured in the opening night of the Royal Italian Opera House, as Covent Garden was called in 1847, was content to appear at four concerts for an inclusive fee of £250. Mr. Sims Reeves accepted £210 for the whole festival.

From the first there had been talk of engaging Michael Costa as Festival Conductor; but in the end Yorkshire partisanship prevailed and the position was offered to Sterndale Bennett, who wrote his Pastoral *The May Queen* for the occasion. The Festival was held from 8 to 11 September and included Rossini's *Stabat Mater* alongside Mendelssohn's *Elijah*, Beethoven's *Mount of Olives* and the *Messiah* and *Israel in Egypt* of Handel. The miscellaneous programmes, with an average of twenty-four items in each, were made up of operatic arias and duets, instrumental solos and symphonies. *The Times* found that 'such vigorous, powerful, and full-toned voices as these Yorkshire choristers possess, it rejoices the heart of the jaded Londoner to hear. The trebles and basses, especially, are unrivalled anywhere'. And *The Morning Post* thought that 'the Yorkshire choir displayed some of the freshest and finest voices in Europe, and sang with a precision and pulmonic vigour quite unsurpassable'. Yet in spite of this success, and a festival profit of £2,000 handed over to the General Infirmary at Leeds, an attempt to renew the Festival in 1861 proved abortive, and it was not until 1874 that the second Festival was held, after which—the years of the two world wars excepted—it continued triennially until 1953, over which period accumulated profits of some £24,000 were distributed among medical charities in Leeds.

The second and third (1877) Festivals were conducted by that great figure Sir Michael Costa who, among other things, claimed Rossini as his godfather. For the first (but not the last) time the Leeds Committee now faced an inflexible and

---

[1] The species seems to have overcome this little weakness in the intervening years!

imperious artistic temperament. In the opening negotiations for both festivals Costa insisted on being waited on in London. In vain did the Committee plead with him for a simple answer as to whether or not he would accept the conductorship. Countless details had first to be settled. Against the Committee, he wishes to repeat the overture to *William Tell*. ('Excus-a me, gentlemen, it is the finest thing you can do for the audience. When the storm comes in I will lift the people off their seats.') Against the Committee, he refuses to do Bach's *Magnificat*—written for a *small* choir. In spite of the Committee, and because of the near-breakdown of Henry Smart's *Bride of Dunkerron* in 1874 (for which some members held Costa responsible) he vows never again to conduct a work by a living composer. The following characteristic letter to the Festival's Hon. Secretary, dated from Winchfield, Hants, 16 January 1877, gives the stamp of the man. (Only three days earlier, from London, he has asked that the Festival shall 'take place as late as possible, since at too early a period (*sic*) would interfere with my baths in Germany'.)

Dear Mr. Atkinson,

I have received here this morning your letter, and am sorry to see my good advices are not followed! The old saying never fails, the more are the cooks the more the broth is spoilt. Let everybody, if you please, be at their post, and nothing else. The Choral Symphony, except the *andante*, is an awful work, and a perfect infliction on principals and chorus. It failed at the Philharmonic, at Bradford, Exeter Hall, Birmingham, and at the Crystal Palace. The Handel selection is very good. Bach's selection and the Raff symphony can be done.

And now let us avoid wasting useless time in going over again upon matters which ought to be settled once for all.

Please let me have the final decision of the programme, and I shall give you mine.

Yours very sincerely,
M. Costa.

For the 1877 Festival, too, another great operatic character had been proposed; but the declining health, throughout the summer, of Therese Tietjens, caused the Committee much anxiety. She died in August. Meanwhile the great soprano Albani had been engaged, through her husband Ernest Gye, for a fee of 550 guineas, 50 guineas to be returned as a donation to the Leeds Medical Charities Fund. When this Festival was over the cheque for 500 guineas was sent with an accompanying note explaining that the promised donation had been deducted. Gye, however, returned the cheque and demanded the full fee of 550 guineas which, after a little consideration, was sent; whereupon Gye immediately returned a cheque for 50 guineas as arranged, all honour satisfied!

It is perhaps not surprising that Costa was not engaged a third time, and the next seven Festivals were conducted by Sullivan, who appears to have thought more of his *Golden Legend* (produced at the 1886 Festival) than of all the operas that now keep his name alive. Dvorak was also present at the 1886 Festival, conducting the première of his oratorio *St. Ludmila*. Later conductors were Stanford (till 1910), Elgar, Nikisch, Sir Hugh Allen, Albert Coates, Beecham, Sargent, Barbirolli, Maurice Miles, and Josef Krips, and among other notable works first given at Leeds might be mentioned Humperdinck's *Moorish Rhapsody*, Stanford's *Stabat Mater*, Vaughan Williams's *Toward the Unknown Region* and *A Sea Symphony*, Elgar's *Falstaff*, Walton's *Belshazzar's Feast*, Lennox Berkeley's *Jonah* and, in 1958, Fricker's *A Vision of Judgement*. All these composers turned also to the field of opera, though Elgar's *The Spanish Lady* was only partly sketched, while Fricker, of course, still has opportunity before him.

As for Handel's *Samson*, to be produced for the Centenary Festival, that work comes near enough to the Handelian traditions that have formed the choral backbone of the Leeds Festival since its inception, and its stage version may even make Yorkshire choralists think of opera in a new light. For the rest we shall have further opportunity to consider the production, in a bi-centenary context, when it is restored to Covent Garden in the 1958-9 season.

MEYERBEER AND HIS 'EXTINCT VOLCANOES'

JOHN W. KLEIN

'Those extinct volcanoes !' In such disparaging terms did an eminent critic recently refer to Meyerbeer's operas. It would of course be futile to deny that the works whose success was once so universal are now practically forgotten. Saint-Saëns in his old age voiced his amazement. 'Who could have predicted,' he exclaimed, 'that the day would come when it would be necessary to rush to the defence of the composer of *Les Huguenots*, of the man who at one time dominated every stage in Europe by a leadership that was so extraordinary that it looked as though it could never end ?'

And yet, occasionally, one of Meyerbeer's works is revived or broadcast; and, despite the hankering after effect and the excessive ornamentation that disfigure them, once again we become aware of the composer's remarkable gifts: his vivid sense of orchestral colour which so deeply impressed Elgar, his superb handling of crowds; above all, the highly developed instinct for the stage which enabled this most criticised of operatic composers to establish himself firmly for the better part of a century.

To a great extent, Meyerbeer was, however, the product of his meretricious environment: the showy, fundamentally unmusical Paris of Louis Philippe and Napoleon III, the Paris that broke even the indomitable heart of Berlioz. What, quite frankly, appals one is the low level of the theatre of this period. The chief playwrights imagined that drama consisted entirely of far-fetched intrigues; everything depended on variety and complexity of incident; the more startling and fantastically improbable the situation the better. (Even Victor Hugo was no exception to this rule.) Any genuinely human problem was contemptuously ruled out. Eugène Scribe, the most popular playwright and librettist of the period, appears childish and almost unreadable today, though many of his most blatant characteristics would still undoubtedly appeal very strongly to Hollywood.

Yet what we fail to understand is why the most eminent musicians clamoured for his shoddy wares; he was even 'too busy and too important' to receive Wagner when he first came to Paris. Nevertheless, his talent nowadays strikes one as negligible, though he was certainly not, like Verdi's browbeaten librettists, a mere servant but an autocrat avid of power.

His influence on Meyerbeer was undoubtedly deplorable; and it is significant that, when the composer decided to interpolate an absolutely indispensable love duet in *Les Huguenots*, Scribe stubbornly refused to provide the necessary 'verses', for he imagined that his ramshackle work was already perfect! Meyerbeer was consequently compelled to have recourse to an obliging friend, Emile Deschamps; and thus, incidentally, he saved his work from oblivion.

Not that Meyerbeer himself was blameless for the sad fate which has overtaken his once celebrated operas. His inordinate passion for coloratura still repels one. If, however, we remain objective, we are compelled to admit that we encounter, at no less unsuitable moments, very similar vocal acrobatics in Rossini, Bellini, Donizetti and Gounod; and even in such consummate musical dramatists as Mozart and Verdi. But Meyerbeer, encouraged no doubt by singers of exceptional virtuosity, carried this senseless and superfluous ornamentation to unexampled extremes, thus undermining the very foundations of the drama. (The second act of *Les Huguenots* is a deplorable example of this.) It is amazing that Meyerbeer should not have realised how fatal this weakness might eventually prove. For in 1849, at the time of *Le Prophète*, his prestige was already such that he could have afforded to dispense with his numerous concessions to the poor taste of both his vocalists and his audience. He could have led the vanguard instead of endeavouring to outdo Donizetti who— despite his superior melodic gifts—never possessed Meyerbeer's powerful sense of drama. We can accordingly sympathise with Wagner's violent reactions at a performance of *Le Prophète*: 'When the famous mother of the prophet gives vent to her grief in the well-known series of ridiculous roulades, I was filled with rage and despair at the thought that I should be called upon to listen to such a thing!' And Berlioz, after emphatically declaring that he was unable to renounce his musical principles even for Meyerbeer's sake, could not refrain from growling: 'Dear and revered master, you know how much I love and admire you, but I dare affirm that if at such a moment you had been close to me, and your powerful hand which has written so many great, magnificent and sublime pages had been within my reach, I should have bitten it to the blood.' Meyerbeer, however, might have retorted ironically: 'Ah, but didn't both of you meet with utter disaster in Paris?'

Modern criticism, taking its cue from Wagner, has played havoc with Meyerbeer's reputation: constantly we are reminded of his opponents' disparaging remarks to the effect that his operas are like variety programmes, piling sensation upon sensation. And yet how, we exclaim incredulously, could an art all hollow sham and empty display endure so long and penetrate to the most remote corners of the earth? At first sight, it seems a mystery that no amount of reasoning can solve.

Nevertheless, it is significant that, Wagner excepted, none of the great musical dramatists ever despised Meyerbeer. Verdi may have deprecated his mania for publicity; but he found him an unusually stimulating influence: curiously enough, he ranked him as a musical dramatist far above Mozart, 'a mere quartettist'. Mussorgsky also praised his exceptional skill in writing for the stage: 'he was a man who knew what he was about'. Moreover, he learnt much from Meyerbeer, particularly from his remarkable sense of movement in the handling of excitable multitudes. Finally, the youthful Bizet was full of enthusiasm for the fourth act of *Les Huguenots*, which redeems all the frivolities and absurdities of the first three.

Now the composer of *Carmen* possessed an unerring instinct for what was effective or moving on the stage; immediately he discerned Meyerbeer's significance for opera, his imaginative widening of its scope. He did not, however, realise that these great gifts were offset by equally great defects. It would, indeed, be difficult to revive most of Meyerbeer's operas. *L'Africaine* is, on the whole, little more than a jumble of incongruous styles. *Le Prophète*, despite the extraordinary brilliancy and dramatic power of the Cathedral scene, falls to pieces in the last act. The same criticism has, incidentally, been levelled (though with considerably less justification) against *Les Huguenots*, the last act being usually omitted. But that final scene, with its beautiful church choruses and its uncanny suggestion of the approaching massacre, is vital to the drama; and the producer who eliminates it is scarcely less culpable than he who omits the Revolutionary Scene in *Boris Godunov*. For Meyerbeer's masterpiece is far from being an 'extinct volcano'; and if it were subjected to a fairly drastic revision (such as *Simone Boccanegra* and *Don Carlos* have successfully undergone) it might still score a genuine success, formidably difficult though it is.

1836, the year of the première of *Les Huguenots*, remains, after all, a memorable date. For it witnessed the production of the first great historical opera. (I know scholars will indignantly refer to Spontini's *Fernando Cortès*; but in this case we are, indeed, confronted with an obsolete work.)

In *Les Huguenots* a uniquely dramatic historical theme was, at last, boldly tackled. Apparently Scribe was astounded at his own daring, for he frittered away his magnificent subject (the massacre of the Huguenots on St. Bartholomew's Eve) on a particularly far-fetched story, obtusely endeavouring to subordinate monumental history to childish intrigue. It is, nevertheless, to Meyerbeer's credit that he skilfully avoided a complete debâcle. For in the impressive fourth act he created what is, chronologically, the third great scene in opera, at any rate, as far as sheer drama is concerned. First, surely, Don Giovanni's supreme encounter with the Commendatore; secondly, no less compelling, the dungeon scene in *Fidelio*; but, thirdly, the 'Benediction of the Daggers' in *Les Huguenots*, a scene seething with fanatical fury, and followed by what is perhaps the most stirring example, before *Tristan und Isolde*, of the love duet in danger, but with a more vivid sense of the peril threatening the doomed pair. Camille Bellaigue, a particularly discerning critic, nearly half a century after Meyerbeer's death termed this duet 'the most chaste and idealistic duet in all opera'—and yet he revered the *Otello* of Verdi, and that great composer valued his judgment. It has been objected that the duet possesses little unity, that there is a lack of balance in the design of even its loveliest melody; nevertheless, how ethereally does the music suggest the sudden and ecstatic revelation of mutual love! Admittedly, both Gluck and Weber are greater and purer musicians than Meyerbeer; but did they ever succeed in creating an effect as powerful or as poignant? Verdi and Bizet greatly admired the whole of this noble act, perhaps partly because they were not disguised symphonists such as Wagner and Schumann, but vital and innate musical dramatists. Echoes of the duet linger in works that represent their creators perhaps at their most subtle: in Verdi's *Aïda* and Bizet's *L'Arlésienne*. Without this scene Meyerbeer's great prestige would have been wholly inconceivable, for it is in striking contrast to the established view that his music is merely the emptiest of façades.

But even Wagner owed something to *Les Huguenots*. Kurwenal is partly based on Marcel, the sturdy and outspoken Huguenot soldier, an entirely original creation. I should be surprised if Mussorgsky did not recall Marcel's truculent 'Piff-paff' (quite revolutionary for its time) when he was writing Varlaam's boisterous song: 'Beneath the walls of Kazaan.' Meyerbeer has frequently been accused of creating merely stage puppets; but Marcel is scarcely one of them and can claim, moreover, a lengthy line of impressive descendants.

The customary attitude of most critics is that Meyerbeer may possibly have been endowed with certain gifts, but that his successors surpassed him so immeasurably that his works have forfeited all interest. As criticism this is, however, unconvincing: equally plausibly one might argue that Verdi surpassed Bellini and Donizetti to such an extent that the works of the lesser composers are nowadays no longer worth performing. For, no less than the Italians, Meyerbeer still deserves an occasional revival; though to undertake such a difficult task perfunctorily, as was done at Covent Garden in 1927, would naturally be courting disaster.

It has been too frequently suggested that Meyerbeer's phenomenal success was chiefly due to his immense wealth. No doubt this was a contributory factor, just as Bernard Shaw would have found his career considerably more arduous if he had not—as he himself frankly admitted—at a critical moment married a green-eyed millionairess. But Meyerbeer was no futile plutocrat squandering his wealth for want of anything better to do; he did succeed in creating something new and significant: a kind of colourful, spectacular opera which prepared men's minds for Verdi's *Aïda*, not to mention Wagner's operas. There are many passages in *Tannhäuser*, no less than in *Rienzi*, that are curiously Meyerbeerian. It is consequently unjust to denounce the master's whole output as one vast inflated sham.

Admittedly, he appealed too often to the spirit of his age whereas he should have guided it; obviously the fact that his music was so astoundingly popular (with philosophers and novelists such as Herbert Spencer and Balzac down to the man in the street) dazzled and even led him astray. For let us be just: his operas were as successful when performed in some tawdry little theatre at Vera Cruz as when produced with the utmost pomp and splendour at the Opéra in Paris.

The widespread notion that nobody had a chance against him with his vast fortune, his innumerable rehearsals and his vociferous bodyguard of bribed critics is, in fact, preposterous. (This idea was sedulously fostered by Wagner, who himself owed so much to the financial support of a wealthy and eccentric monarch.) The critics conveniently overlook the fact that during the long period of his hegemony he wrote exceptionally little. There was a gap of no fewer than thirteen years between *Les Huguenots* and *Le Prophète*. (An uncharacteristic as well as unsuccessful little Singspiel: *Ein Feldlager in Schlesien* may be safely ignored.) There were, surely, plenty of opportunities for other composers, including the indolent Rossini, whom people were ceaselessly pestering to create a new masterpiece which unfortunately never materialised.

One final critical injustice: Meyerbeer is consistently represented as so calculating and Machiavellian that he never helped a man unless he had some ulterior motive. That he was avid of praise was notorious; and yet how many careerists (or idealists, for that matter) would have gone to endless trouble to ensure the production of two of the works of an obscure, but obviously extremely gifted and dangerous rival! (Wagner's *Rienzi* and *Der fliegende Holländer*.) How many opportunists would have attended almost every performance of an unsuccessful opera by an ageing and consistently unpopular musician: Berlioz's *Les Troyens*; particularly when that composer had ceased to be the formidable critic of *Le Journal des Débats* and could no longer either harm or help him. The upright Verdi, who was repelled by Meyerbeer's thirst for publicity, was, nevertheless, deeply shocked at what he termed Berlioz's ingratitude. He was aware that Meyerbeer had a rare flair for recognising talent and encouraging it to the best of his ability. The unjustifiably belittled composer can scarcely be blamed for occasionally expecting some acknowledgment on the part of his numerous protégés; and it is natural enough that Wagner's duplicity should have filled him with

Act 3 of 'The Trojans' with Blanche Thebom as *Dido*, which was revived during the Centenary season.

THE COVENT GARDEN SEASON, 1957-8

Act 1, scene 2 of Margherita Wallmann's production of 'Aida' which opened the 1957-8 season. Sets by Salvatore Fiume.

Birgit Nilsson as *Brünn-hilde*. An action photograph taken during 'Götterdämmerung' in which the new Swedish Brünnhilde scored a great success.

David Sim

THE COVENT GARDEN SEASON, 1957–8

Daily Mail

Gerda Lammers as *Elektra*, Georgine von Milinkovic as *Klytemnestra* in the revival of 'Elektra'

A moment in the 'auto-da-fè' scene in Verdi's 'Don Carlos' in Luchino Visconti's production. Boris Christoff as *King Philip*, Jon Vickers as *Carlos*, Gré Brouwenstijn as *Elisabeth de Valois*.

THE COVENT GARDEN SEASON, 1957-8

The closing moments in Poulenc's 'The Carmelites', which was produced by Margherita Wallmann, with sets by Georges Wakhevitch.

THE SADLER'S WELLS SEASON, 1957–8

Victoria Elliott as *Judith* and David Ward as *Bluebeard* in Bartok's 'Duke Bluebeard's Castle'.

Denis De Marney

A scene from Act 3 of Lehár's 'The Merry Widow' with Thomas Round as *Danilo*.

Denis De Marney

distaste. Yet, generously, he refrained from publishing his rival's obsequious letters teeming with fulsome protestations of undying gratitude.

On the whole, Meyerbeer emerges from this welter of intrigue as an amiable figure, unusually generous and patient (until ill health rendered him increasingly and sometimes understandably irascible). As a composer he remains significant, for surely he was one of the seminal influences of opera. The modern attitude of scorning him is unwarrantable, as both Elgar and Bernard van Dieren felt very strongly. However opportunistic he may have been, one can not imagine his saying like his cynical rival Auber: 'I only work when I am bored; and when I work, then I am still more bored!' For in every fresh development of music he was passionately interested. It was he who abolished the elaborate academic overture that was becoming redundant, replacing it by the short and dramatic prelude, later on so characteristic of the works of Verdi, Bizet and even Mussorgsky. But, above all, he helped to keep opera alive when it was dogged by ill fortune; when Rossini was idling, Bellini dead, Donizetti insane, Verdi feeling his way only tentatively towards mastery, and Wagner far too abstruse and complicated for the general public. This dangerous gap Meyerbeer alone seemed capable of filling, somewhat in the sense that Puccini still does today. Not only did he save the Opéra from closing down; he also gave his art a new lease of life by wrenching it away from the graceful trivialities of Rossini, and forcing it to tackle great themes, however conventionalised. (Even *Le Prophète* has almost as striking a subject as *Les Huguenots*.) Thus Meyerbeer successfully transformed opera into a large-scale musical form and, not altogether unconsciously, built for the future. Even so stern a judge as Hans von Bülow termed *Les Huguenots* 'one of the greatest experiences of my life.'

Nevertheless, something fundamental was lacking in Meyerbeer; however convinced he might be of the importance of his work, he always remained curiously unsure of himself. Unlike Verdi, he could not mould recalcitrant librettists such as Scribe to his will; too frequently he was the slave, not the master of his singers: that is why at the most vital moments of the drama we are irritated by those meaningless cadenzas which he, like Gounod (with whom he had much in common) was too amiable or too subservient to refuse; or which he may foolishly have imagined would enhance the brilliance of the spectacle. Throughout his life he remained too hesitant, introspective, morbidly anxious. 'Never shall we know how much suffering his operas caused him,' wrote a contemporary, 'how he was worn out with toil, suspicion, terror and even despair.' His strange letter to Berlioz (twelve years his junior and immeasurably less successful) before the première of *Le Prophète* signed 'your trembling Meyerbeer' is the most startling proof of this harassed frame of mind. In some respects he strikes one as the Hamlet of opera, an extremely gifted man with a sensitive, ascetic nature, entrusted with a task beyond his strength.

For Wagner did his rival a cruel injustice when he asserted that the latter regarded his art merely as a trade. In reality, it became, after the death of his children, his very life, a torturing obsession. Ceaselessly, with unremitting zeal he revised his work, with at times an agonising realisation of its inadequacy wholly at variance with his proverbial notoriety as a conscienceless popularity-hunter. In his strange way he was disinterested, for he revealed a fine disdain for money that other *grands seigneurs* such as Lord Byron have not always displayed. A word of praise, a glimpse of understanding would bolster up his vacillating self-esteem; and it was perhaps the greatest consolation of his life that the aged Goethe, who had been so scornful of Schubert and Weber, had proclaimed him the only contemporary composer capable of setting his own mighty 'Faust' to music. And, moreover, had not even the hostile Wagner referred to the love duet of *Les Huguenots* as 'one of the most perfect of music's works' and that at a time when, disclaiming all flattery, he had resolved to voice only the most unpalatable truths?

MANUEL GARCIA, CENTENARIAN

VIKTOR FUCHS

To reach his hundredth birthday is an extremely rare privilege for any human being, especially so when the centenarian still enjoys physical and mental freshness. However, if the centenarian is an outstanding personality it is a sensation which will long be remembered.

Just over fifty years ago Manuel Garcia II, who won fame as a voice teacher, an author of books on singing, but above all as the inventor of the laryngoscope, celebrated his hundredth birthday in a unique manner. On the morning of St. Patrick's Day in 1905, Garcia, a resident of London since 1850, drove to Buckingham Palace to receive the insignia of a Commander of the Royal Victoria Order from King Edward VII. Afterward the astonishingly vigorous maestro attended a reception at the Royal Medical and Surgical Society where, seated upon a crimson throne, he received the eulogies of numerous distinguished speakers. The Ambassador of his homeland, Spain, conveyed the felicitations of his King and presented him with a high decoration and the German Emperor sent him the great Gold Medal of Science. A number of medical societies all over the world bestowed honorary degrees and medals to the man whose invention marked the start of an important medical achievement—Laryngology. After a short rest in the afternoon, Garcia drove to the Hotel Cecil where another less official but splendid reception was arranged.

To evaluate the amazing life of Manuel Garcia II, one should know first the story of his family and above all that of his father, Manuel Garcia del Popolo Vicente, who already at the age of seventeen made his successful début as a singer and composer in Madrid. During the following years Garcia, known as 'Garcia the elder', became one of the most successful operatic tenors of his time, singing also in Paris, London, and Italy. In Naples in 1812 he became court singer of the King Murat of Sicily. At the world première of Rossini's *Il Barbiere di Siviglia* in 1816, he created the role of Count Almaviva which part he also sang successfully in Paris and London. Nine years later, in 1825, Garcia brought the very first Italian opera company to New York, where he opened his season with Rossini's masterpiece *The Barber of*

Seville. He himself sang Almaviva, his seventeen-year-old daughter Maria Felicita (Malibran) appeared as Rosina, his wife sang Berta and his son Manuel II, the subject of this article, sang Figaro. Subsequently the Garcia opera company performed several operas, including three by his friend Rossini: *Tancredi, Semiramide* and *Otello*; in the latter the father sang the title role, Maria was Desdemona and the son appeared as Iago. The success of Garcia and his singers was imposing but the most enthusiastic reception came from Lorenzo da Ponte, the librettist of Mozart's *Nozze di Figaro, Don Giovanni,* and *Così fan tutte*, who was then Professor at Columbia University. After an extremely adventurous life, da Ponte had landed in New York just twenty years before Garcia's appearance with his company and was living there as Professor of Italian language and literature at Columbia University.

At that time, already seventy-six years old, he had outlived the seven-years-younger Mozart by forty-seven years. The story of the meeting between Garcia and da Ponte is most characteristic. When da Ponte visited the singer he introduced himself as the author of *Don Giovanni* ('My *Don Giovanni*,' as he modestly said) and Garcia, embracing the old man danced around the room like a child, singing 'Fin ch'han del vino'—the famous drinking song from Mozart's masterpiece.

It was probably the influence of da Ponte which decided Garcia to include also *Don Giovanni* in his company's repertory. However, there was no tenor available for Don Ottavio (Garcia himself, following the Italian habit, sang the baritone role of the Don) and da Ponte not only found the right singer for Don Ottavio, but with the help of his friends and pupils, he even took care of paying for his services.

The elder Garcia later went with his company to Mexico where he won laurels and a tremendous amount of gold; however, on the return journey he and his group were robbed by brigands. Garcia who had known such romantic scenes in opera now, in real life, lost in a few moments the earnings he had garnered for the last three years. Poor, but not at all in despair, he set up in Paris as a voice teacher and dedicated himself to the composition of operas and ballets. Altogether he wrote eighteen operas in Spanish, twenty-one in Italian, and eight in French. Garcia was extremely musical and so was his whole family. During his stay in New York he gave a number of concerts during which he would strike a single chord, and then with his wife, his son and daughter, he would render a difficult operatic quartet, unaccompanied. At the end he would strike the chord again to show that they had not deviated from the pitch even a hair's breadth. But the most marvellous evidence of his musical memory took place after his arrival with his company in Mexico. During the journey nearly all of the musical material of the group was lost, and so Garcia wrote out from memory the whole score of *Don Giovanni*, Rossini's *Otello* and *The Barber of Seville*.

68

In order fully to understand the exceptional life and influence of this musical genius, not only the father's career but also that of his two daughters must be at least briefly reviewed.

Maria Felicita inherited her father's genius as an opera singer; according to many critics she even surpassed him as an artist. In fact, her career was one of the most sensational in the history of opera. While still in New York she made a most unfortunate marriage to a supposedly rich French merchant many years her senior. A short time after the marriage he was sentenced to jail for debts, and the poor girl not only had to pay off these debts, but for years she could not get a divorce from this unworthy man whose name—Malibran—she made immortal. Although her career lasted all-in-all only eleven years (she died when only twenty-eight), her name will always be remembered: the memory of her unprecedented career is honoured by the fact that one of the most beautiful opera houses in Venice still bears her name.

Pauline, the younger daughter, who studied first with her father and later with her brother, became one of the greatest singers of her day. Although her voice was not as beautiful as the voice of her sister, she overcame the natural obstacles with her unusual art. She made her début in London in 1839 as Rosina. Years later she created in Paris the part of Fidès in Meyerbeer's *Le Prophète*; she also was the first contralto who sang Gluck's *Orfeo*. She was an excellent pianist—her teacher was Franz Liszt—and like her sister, she also was gifted as a composer. At the time when Richard Wagner was trying to interest German opera singers in his *Tristan und Isolde*, Pauline Viardot-Garcia, as she was known, sang at sight the part of Isolde (in the second act) with Wagner singing Tristan. Pauline was also very successful as a voice teacher, Marianne Brandt, Aglaia Orgeni and many other of her students bringing her honour. She died in 1910 in her eighty-ninth year.

One cannot imagine a greater dissimilarity between two outstanding personalities than the character and life of the two Garcias, the father and the son. Manuel the Elder was a highly romantic genius while his son was a highly gifted and most serious theorist. The latter was the great teacher of teachers, who finally in his endeavour not only to hear and to develop, but also to *see* that mysterious instrument—the human voice—invented in 1850 the laryngoscope. A contemporary of the elder Garcia, the singer Garat, wrote that the tenor Garcia took his audience by storm whenever he appeared on the stage. With his Andalusian furor, he overpowered all in the audience as well as on stage. Three days after his arrival in Paris he was famous not only as a singer but also as a composer. From Spain he had brought a lot of successful music. All Madrid sang his song of the smuggler: 'Yo que soy contrabandista'. Romantic brigands were a great vogue in opera at this time, though probably the elder Garcia had lost his taste for brigands in Mexico. . . .

Manuel, the son, neither inherited the romantic temperament of his father, nor the beauty of his father's voice; however, like his father, who at thirty-seven as a tenor of highest esteem went to take voice lessons from the famous tenor and voice teacher Ansani, Garcia the younger strove during his whole life for perfection of voice technique.... Already in 1829 Garcia II had given up his singing career and dedicated his life—and what an amazing long life it was—not only to teaching but to exploring the essence of the most subtle and individual of all musical instruments—the human voice. Like his father before him he taught his sisters Maria Felicita (Malibran) and Pauline. Both sisters were by nature contraltos, but with their great art of singing, which was not only inborn but developed by studying with their father and brother, they were able to sing the soprano parts in *Norma* and *Sonnambula*, with the greatest ease. The unique greatness of Manuel II was that he, like his father, was a thorough master of the traditional art of *bel canto*. As a young man he was even introduced by his father to Ansani and had a few lessons from this great master, who himself probably got some precious hints from the legendary maestro Porpora (1686–1766). In other words, the younger Garcia grew up in the world of the old empiric Italian masters who liked to hand down their great art of singing from mouth to mouth. Some of them would even cover their windows with curtains when they started to initiate their students in the mysteries of *bel canto*. It was Garcia, the son, who was the first to open the window and unveil the mysteries which he knew as well as anyone of his predecessors. However, it was certainly not his fault that during his long life the art of 'beautiful singing' became more and more rare. It would lead us too far astray from our subject if the many reasons for this obvious decay were to be further discussed in the framework of this essay. One could call him the first theorist in voice culture, but he was a theorist in the service of the art.

In Paris where he had lived and worked in 1829 he submitted, in 1840, the essence of his research, to the Academy of Science. Seven years later he edited his main work: *L'art du chant*. It was the first attempt to analyse the great art which he had learned from the many great artists he had heard, and of course from the famous members of his family. But he was aware that the wisdom and the skill of the teacher is always limited: he can develop the instrument, he is able to teach the student how to use it, but he never can succeed in breathing a soul into a human being who does not *feel*. Goethe says in *Faust*: 'Doch wardet ihr nie Herz zu Herzen schaffen,Wenn es auch nicht von Herzen geht.' !¹ It is characteristic that many of his numerous students became successful voice teachers, singers like Mathilde Marchesi and Julius Stockhausen. His greatest success was, however, the fabulous

¹ 'But that which issues from the heart alone, will bend the hearts of others to your own'—translated by Anna Swanwick.

Jenny Lind, the 'Swedish Nightingale', who at eighteen years of age was already famous and who came to him when twenty-one in order to put the final touch to her singing. But her audition before the maestro was a catastrophe; Garcia was forced to tell the successful young singer: 'Mademoiselle, I am sorry to tell you that there is no voice left.' He gave the desperate singer the advice to be silent for six weeks and then to come again. Luckily, Jenny Lind followed his advice strictly and after the six-week period they could start again. Ten months later she returned to the Royal Opera, Stockholm, and undertook the same part which she had sung before she left for Paris, Norma. Her success was tremendous. The Swedish King bestowed a high order on Garcia and the University made him an honorary doctor. Jenny Lind became afterward the greatest singer of her time. . . .

The revolution of 1848 drove Garcia from Paris, and he settled down in London where he remained for the rest of his life. There in 1855 he invented the Laryngoscope.

Manuel's father was primarily a singer who also taught and composed. Garcia the son had started as an opera singer but he abandoned this profession in order to dedicate his life and efforts entirely to teaching. Admittedly, he never was a great success as a singer; his voice was by comparison with the outstanding voices of his father and his sister Maria Felicita without brilliance. In our time we would call him a 'utility singer'. In New York in his twentieth year he was Figaro opposite his father's famous Almaviva and his sister's superb Rosina, but he was also Leporello in *Don Giovanni*, Iago in Rossini's *Otello* (written for tenor), and sometimes he even took over his father's tenor part. It seems not improbable that his tremendous musical ability and the dominating wish of his father had strained his vocal power. He was forced to sing too often widely divergent parts—a fact which certainly was harmful for the improvement of his young voice. Here may be the great mistake. A girl, especially if she is born in a southern country, may sing as early as seventeen, parts like Rosina and Zerlina, provided that she is exceptionally developed and gifted, and above all if she is wisely trained. Garcia, the elder, who sang in opera when he was only seventeen, was probably not aware that he himself was a very rare exception, and besides he was probably only singing lyric tenor parts during the first years of his career. It is an idle question whether the younger Garcia would have developed a more beautiful voice and could have become a singer of importance if he had not been misused in his young years. But posterity is fortunate in any case, for his failing success as opera singer saved for the musical world one of the greatest and most important authorities in voice theory.

Although the father's life ended when he was fifty-eight, his son when already over ninety was still teaching and could advise a student who came for an audition: 'You

71

had better wait a whole year and then we will start.' In fact, he accepted the young man as a student. It was this same student, M. Sterling-Mackinlay, who reported the story in his excellent book *Garcia the Centenarian and his time*.[1] He had studied with Garcia for four years. Manuel Garcia the elder wrote an unmeasurable amount of music for the common grave of forgotten musical creations, while the son wrote books—the last one in 1895 (*Hints of Singing*)—which today are still standard works for voice teachers and singers as well. Manuel the younger obviously had seen Napoleon when his father took him as a boy to the Opéra in Paris where he appeared in an opera of Paër, the favourite composer of the Emperor. Napoleon was ousted, the Bourbons returned, the Civic kingdom came, and only the revolution of 1848 expelled the maestro from Paris. . . .

What an expanse of time and history was covered by the life of the younger Garcia! He was already singing in New York at the time when Beethoven and Schubert were still alive, and in the same year that he celebrated his hundredth birthday, Richard Strauss's *Salome* had its première at Dresden. Garcia was a boy when Wagner and Verdi were born, and he already was an accredited voice teacher when Brahms was born. He was a contemporary of the majority of all the great composers of the nineteenth century and outlived them all. At the day of the birth of Queen Victoria he was already fourteen years old, and when she died in her eighty-third year, Manuel Garcia still was active as a voice teacher. When he was a boy, Jefferson was President of the United States. In 1905 when he celebrated his hundredth birthday, Theodore Roosevelt succeeded as mediator in the Russian-Japanese War.

But this miraculous man was able even to celebrate his 101st birthday by picking up a guitar and singing a Spanish song. He attended with great interest a concert of the Philharmonic orchestra several weeks later, and in June, 1906 he attended a performance of a play of one of his friends. On Sunday, 1 July, 1906 Garcia, who was born in Madrid on 17 March, 1805, died in his sleep.

What an amazing life and what a great personality! His name will not be forgotten as long as we have a cultured world.

---

[1] *Garcia the Centenarian and his time*, by M. Sterling-Mackinlay; publishers, William Blackwood & Sons, Edinburgh and London, 1908.

Marietta Piccolomini as *Violetta*

Pauline Viardot as *Azucena*

Marietta Alboni as *Arsace* in 'Semiramide'

Anna Zerr as *Queen of Night*

THE OTHER 'BOHÈME'

EDWARD GREENFIELD

THOSE who know Caruso's magnificent record—H.M.V. DB 122—of two highly attractive arias from Leoncavallo's *La Bohème* must often have wondered what the rest of the opera was like, and whether it might deserve—at least in the composer's centenary year—a token revival.

The story has often been told of how two *Bohèmes* came to be written at the same time by two composers who had until then been friends. Meeting Leoncavallo one day in a Milan café in the early nineties of last century Puccini boasted of his new idea for a libretto. It was to be based, he said, on Murger's novel *Scènes de la vie de Bohème*. Leoncavallo was incensed. He pointed out that it was he, some time before, who had originally suggested the idea to Puccini, but Puccini had rejected it. When it had not been wanted, so Leoncavallo claimed, he had decided to use it himself. It was his preserve, he said, and not Puccini's. 'Then there will be two *Bohèmes*.' was Puccini's laconic comment. And two *Bohèmes* there were. On the following morning in the *Secolo* came the news that Maestro Leoncavallo was writing an opera on Murger's novel and in the afternoon (so the story goes) the *Corriere della Sera* published the news that Maestro Puccini was writing one too.

So far as I am aware this story has not been dated exactly, though anyone with access to the files of the Milan papers in the 'nineties might be able to help there. At least it seems clear that it took place before June 1893. In a letter dated 5 June of that year Giulio Ricordi, Puccini's publisher, urges his recalcitrant composer to work on the libretto saying 'An inadvertent word which slips out may serve as a guide to your rival in *Bohème* and give him ideas for his libretto'. The first performance of Puccini's opera did not take place until 1 February, 1896 (exactly three years to the day after the première of his previous opera *Manon Lescaut*) and Leoncavallo's 'lyric comedy' as he called it not until well over a year after that on 6 May, 1897. Such long delay by both composers is strange when each knew he had a rival. It is strange unless when the incident first took place their determination to use the idea was not so strong as each made out. Certainly Puccini even as late as August 1894 had not entirely renounced the idea for an opera to be called *La Lupa* (The She-Wolf) based on a Sicilian play by Varga about a suitably devouring female.

The three years Puccini spent on his *Bohème* were generally well occupied, with the composer typically driving his librettists Giacosa and Illica—the latter also at work then for Giordano on *Andrea Chénier*—to produce exactly what he wanted before he wrote the music. With Leoncavallo there is on the face of it less reason for detecting time well spent. Leoncavallo wrote his own libretto, and as so often when composers are their own librettists he failed to be as critical of what he produced as Puccini was with the work of his collaborators.

To us, knowing Puccini's libretto, the whole balance of Leoncavallo's seems decidedly off-centre. The tenor part is given to Marcello, and for the first three acts the Mimi-Rodolfo relationship is so far in the background it could scarcely be dignified with the description sub-plot. Only with Act 4 when the scene (on Christmas Eve 1838) reaches Rodolfo's attic does their love become of central importance, and it comes almost as a surprise when Mimi's death, as in Puccini's opera, provides the opera's final climax—Mimi dying, weakly whispering the words 'Natale! Natale!' (reasonable enough in French translation as 'Noël! Noël!' but 'Christmas! Christmas!' might be the last straw). The allocation of the female parts adds if anything to the off-centre feeling, for though Musetta's is the principal role it is given to a mezzo, and Mimi's is the only high soprano part. Eufemia, Schaunard's partner, is also a mezzo.

The characterisation is not so well realised as in the Puccini opera. Though Puccini's Mimi is not very close to the character in the novel, she is at least a living character, and would have contrasted less effectively with Puccini's Musetta had she followed the Murger prototype. Leoncavallo does not manage his contrasts very well. While his principal tenor and mezzo pair, Marcello and Musetta, slip easily enough into fairly conventional hero and heroine roles, Mimi and Rodolfo do not really add any character-part interest, so that we are presented rather with reflections of the principal pair, and (as with Puccini) Mimi's infidelity is not conveyed with any great conviction. For the first two acts indeed Leoncavallo relies very little—far too little—on conflict of character. The beginning of Act 2, when Musetta is being evicted from her apartment and Marcello in his aria '*Io non ho che una povera stanzetta*' tenderly offers her a home with him, provides some feeling of genuine emotion (this was one of the arias Caruso recorded) but generally in those two acts such incident as occurs, most of it heavily high-spirited, conveys little of the emotions underneath, and not really as much of character as one would expect. The last two acts are predominantly emotional, but this division of the work, two acts boisterous followed by two acts sentimental, has nothing of the nicety of balance which so marks the Puccini opera.

Act I is set on Christmas Eve 1837 in a room on the first floor of the Café Momus. A billiard-room can be seen through the doorway. The opening motif representing the Café Momus has a suspicious likeness to the theme of Puccini's at the beginning of Act 2, which also represents the Café. Leoncavallo's Momus theme is in a fairly brisk 2/4—admittedly marked 'Andante Mosso' but directed to be taken at crotchet equals 144, in fact much faster than Andante—and the point which links it irrevocably with the Puccini motif is that much of it is in parallel triads.

This leads at once to a long harangue by Gaudens, the proprietor of the café, to which Schaunard, the only other character present, listens patiently. Gaudens complains of the noise made by the Bohemians, that models pose for Marcello (they will no longer pose in the nude, promises Schaunard) and of gambling habits. Schaunard is given a short aria 'tempo di gavotta' in which he answers the complaints *elegantissimo* promising with tongue in cheek that the Bohemians will not cause trouble in future. The parallel with the gavottes in *Manon Lescaut* (1893) and *Andrea Chénier* (1896) is clear.

The Bohemians enter. Leoncavallo's habit of imitation here takes the form of direct quotation from another composer. Marcello's greeting to Musetta is specifically given the stage direction 'Marcello in a romantic pose gazes at Musetta and parodying the recitative of Raoul de Nangis in *Les Huguenots* sings softly'. The parody amounts to a quotation of the phrase 'O qual soave vision' from the recitative before Raoul's aria 'Bianca al par' in the Meyerbeer opera, when he tells of the fair one, once only seen and sought ever since. It has certainly been bad luck on Leoncavallo that *Les Huguenots* should itself have lost its popularity. The parody is taken up again later in the act when Gaudens threatens to turn the Bohemians out for not paying their bill. They have a mock knightly battle with some of the kitchen boys (cf. Act 4 of Puccini's opera). It is only after Mimi has sung a pleasant little song about Musetta with a rising scale opening that strongly recalls Puccini's bonnet motif in his Act 2, that the first distinctively Bohemian theme appears in 3/8. The Bohemians as they sit down to their meal are interrupted by the equivalent of Puccini's Alcindoro, called here, Barbemuche. He comes in and sits down uninvited. Musetta describes him in a short lyrical passage as a platonic lover of hers.

In the meantime the 3/8 passage has developed and the most notable of its motifs comes rather surprisingly.

Here of course the imitation is of Leoncavallo's own work—a diminished seventh version of the opening of *Pagliacci*. Musetta in return for the song about her sings a charmingly French-sounding salon song about Mimi ('Mimì Pinson, la biondinetta') in which the others join much as the ensemble joins in Musetta's Waltz Song in Puccini's opera, though here the passage is not so extended. A shortish trio in 6/8 'O Musette, o gioconda sorridente!' for Marcello, Musetta and a slightly drunk

Colline follows, charming enough, but like so much of this music with harmonies so conventional that they make Puccini's seem dazzlingly advanced.

The Bohemians find they cannot pay their bill, looking at it horrified. Gaudens appears—to the opening theme of the opera—and the battle-scene follows. At this point Barbemuche calls on them to stop. He offers to pay the bill himself. At first the Bohemians refuse. Then after a heart-on-sleeve revelation from Barbemuche that he always wished to lead 'la vie de Bohème' it is agreed that acceptance of this offer will depend on the result of a game of billiards between Schaunard and Barbemuche. The whole ensemble sings a mock-pompous chorale-like passage as they enter the billiard-room for the contest (further parody) leaving Marcello and Musetta behind. Their duet begins with a waltz-like passage which calls to mind Lensky's aria from Act 2 of Tchaikovsky's *Eugen Onegin* in its progression if not its rhythm. This leads finally to a reprise of the 6/8 trio theme. The other Bohemians return, triumphant at Schaunard's victory. Almost immediately after with joyful—and rather unexpected—cries of 'Natale! Natale' the curtain falls.

The second act shows the courtyard of the house where Musetta lives. It is evening and Musetta's furniture is piled up in the middle of the courtyard. She is being evicted, as is explained by the porter, Durand. Musetta and Marcello enter, and when they realise what is happening Marcello sings his aria 'Io non ho che una povera stanzetta' that I have already mentioned. With the arrival of the other Bohemians the horse-play becomes fast and furious, with plenty of gallumphing 6/8 sections as Musetta's furniture is carried about the stage. (One of the more staid inhabitants of the house is tripped up by a carpet to everyone's uncontrolled mirth). What Leoncavallo obviously regarded as the big climax of the Act (it is the only item from the opera listed separately in the frontispiece) is the Bohemian Hymn which follows, sung by the full chorus of Bohemians which has by this time arrived. This chorus turns out to be like nothing so much as Mendelssohn's 'War March of the Priests', only squarer and weaker.

In the confusion Mimi's lover, the Viscount Paul arrives and he and Mimi sing a lyrical if rather inconsequent duet. He persuades her to come with him and enjoy the life of luxury. The duet stops indeterminately when the other Bohemians call on Musetta to sing the waltz of love. She is finally persuaded and her song proves to be an attractive French-style waltz with hints of *Faust* and *Les Filles de Cadiz*. Musetta's piano is still in the courtyard, and Schaunard after making much play of a hammer in the piano which hits two strings at once, sings an amusing parody of a florid Rossini aria, 'imitating the Rossinian style' as Leoncavallo is careful to explain in the score. In the confusion which follows Mimi and her viscount slip away. The noise and confusion grows more and more. A final vivacissimo is shattered by Rodolfo's revelation that Mimi has gone. 'Vengeance!' cry the Bohemians, 'Boemi! All 'assalto!', and the curtain falls to a very loud reprise (tutta forza) of the Bohemian Hymn.

The opening of Act 3 shows Leoncavallo trying on a nice new Wagnerian suit. If that man, Puccini, can imitate Wagner, one almost hears him saying, so can I. Puccini's cribbing from *Tristan* in *Manon Lescaut* is at least reasonably well integrated with the rest of the musical texture. Leoncavallo's manages at the same time to stick out for the palpable imitation it is while remaining inept musically.

The scene is set in Marcello's attic. Musetta has decided to leave her lover. She writes a letter of explanation to an aria in A minor 'Marcello mio, non stare ad aspettarmi'. Hardly has she finished and sent it off than Mimi enters. She, it seems, has tired of her viscount so that at the very moment when her friend is impelled to leave her Bohemian so Mimi must try and return to hers. Cox and Box is hardly in it, and the situation is exploited to an even greater outburst of tremolos, chromatic scale passages and dramatic arpeggios than Leoncavallo lavishes on this score at other points. The agitato subsides and Mimi's Grand Tune enters.

If indeed Leoncavallo had not heard Puccini's opera before he wrote this, it is the most curious of coincidences, for the hints of 'Che gelida manina', the middle section of Musetta's Waltz Song and 'O Mimì, tu più non torni' in Act 4 (all themselves related) are staggeringly obvious. And if Leoncavallo lifted the idea deliberately can he really have thought no one would notice? Perhaps after all Leoncavallo was as naïf as some of his music.

The tune has a good showing and is expanded into a duet for the two ladies, ending up in a lush D flat major. Another Grand Tune enters, and the outburst continues, only to be assuaged when Marcello enters, the letter in his hand. Mimi hides. There is another agonised duet with arpeggio accompaniments ranging from rustles of spring to revolutionary studies. Marcello finally turns on Musetta herself for being so inflexible, and the duet ends shatteringly with an optional top C on the words 'Ah! sei vil!'

The main situation coped with, it is time to deal with Mimi and Rodolfo. Mimi's approaches are rejected ('Everything between us is finished') and Rodolfo slams the door in her face. She falls down sobbing convulsively, but recovers sufficiently to leave conveniently before Musetta's and Marcello's final parting. Before going Musetta breaks off a dead flower from those by the window and presses it to her bosom. Accidentally she drops her bonnet and Marcello is left pressing that to his bosom while singing the aria 'Testa adorata' (the other that Caruso had on his record). Owners of that record incidentally have for years been squabbling whether in the opening recitative he sings 'Mimì!' (which would be quite wrong but an understandable mistake) instead of 'Musetta!' as he should.

The last act takes us to Rodolfo's attic. It is Christmas Eve once again, and a storm is raging outside—cue for tremolos, chromatic scales and diminished sevenths in arpeggio. Rodolfo's first aria is neatly conceived. It is a setting of Murger's own 'Ballade de Désespoir' with its simple form of question and answer. The aria is interrupted by Marcello, followed shortly by Schaunard bringing fried potatoes and red herrings, and he pronounces an ironical 'Requiescat in pace' over the fish. There is a forced attempt in a reference to the 3/8 Bohemian passage from Act 1, but in dejection Marcello and Rodolfo talk of their frustrated loves. Marcello has been waiting for Musetta for a week, ever since a letter came from her saying she would return if only she could be sure of at least some bread every day.

Mimi arrives to the surprise of the others. She tells of being in hospital for a month. 'What irony! They say I am cured.' After a little resistance Rodolfo is reconciled. 'I have taken nearly an hour to climb the stairs,' Mimi says, 'but the desire to see you again before dying. . . .'

It is at such a point that the full contrast with Puccini is felt. There is here neither the contrast of Mimi's arrival as in the Puccini nor the terrible shock to Rodolfo when in the end he does find her dead. In her own words at the very start of the scene Mimi's condition is all too explicitly stated. The only dramatic coup of which Leoncavallo avails himself here is that Musetta when she enters does not notice Mimi. She gaily sings once more her song about Mimi from Act 1 only to realise suddenly that Mimi is there. In pity Musetta gives her bracelet and ring to be sold so that medicine can be bought.

The last few pages are left entirely to Mimi's dying monologue. She remembers

Edmark

A scene from the Oxford University Opera Group's production of Verdi's 'Ernani' at the Town Hall, Oxford.

OPERA AT OXFORD AND ON BRITISH TELEVISION

Barratts

Helga Pilarczyck as *Salome* in the successful Television performance of the Strauss opera, produced by Rudolf Cartier.

A scene from Act 2, with Eleanor Steber as *Vanessa* and
Rosalind Elias as *Erika*.

THE SEASON AT THE METROPOLITAN, NEW YORK, 1957-8

The world première of Samuel Barber's first opera, 'Vanessa'.

Samuel Barber
the composer.

Act 3, scene 1 with Giorgio Tozzi
as the *Doctor* and George Cehanovsky as the *Major Domo*.

Two scenes from Peter Brook's production of 'Eugene Onegin' which opened the season. Act 1, scene 1 with Martha Lipton as *arina*, Rosalind Elias as *Olga*, Belen Amparan as *Filip-yevna*.

Louis Melançon

The final scene of Act 3, with Lucine Amara as *Tatiana*, and George London as *Onegin*.

Two scenes from the new production of 'Don Giovanni'. The Supper scene with Cesare Siepi as the *Don*.

Theodor Uppman as *Masetto*, Fernando Corena as *Leporello*, Robert Peters as *Zerlina*, Siepi as *Don Giovanni* in the finale to Act I.

the night at the Café Momus only a year back. There is a hint of the 3/8 theme and a faint whisper of the joyful Christmas music which ended Act 1. She murmurs 'Natale! Natale!' in echo of that occasion, and the orchestra simply repeats fortissimo the brief coda which in quieter form ended Act 3.

As must be obvious even from this outline the dramatic construction has little of the neatness of Puccini's. Coming after Puccini's work as it did it had little chance against so strong a rival. But if given better ideas the libretto might have just passed muster, the chances of the opera achieving success on its musical merits would have been slim. I have tried to indicate some of the obvious derivations in the score. What I have only hinted at is the comparative absence of what one might describe as a musical driving force of the kind which has put *Pagliacci* into the permanent operatic repertory everywhere. Playing through the score one quickly becomes open-mouthed at the bare-faced padding on almost every page—arpeggios, scales both diatonic and chromatic sweeping up and down, feeble sequences and feeble modulations. Puccini's love of modulating at the interval of a third is well known, but Leoncavallo's favourite modulation is into a key a semi-tone or tone higher, so that when the sequence happens to be an arpeggio or scale figure the result is like the most primitive of singing exercises.

The pianistic inspiration behind much of this music seems fairly clear. It would be very surprising if most of it had not been composed at the piano, and much of the score when played on the piano sounds like very feeble first-period Beethoven, with harmony if anything less advanced than that. Indeed there is a longish section in Act 2 where I would stake gladly on Beethoven's 'Pathétique' sonata being the model. With the solitary exception of the Wagner imitation I have already mentioned the influences rarely seem to relate to models in any way advanced. Even when Verdi is the model it is the early Verdi of *Rigoletto* and *Traviata*. Even the express parodies are of composers writing half a century earlier.

The dramatic tricks in the music are also handled clumsily. To convey a jolly atmosphere Leoncavallo has remembered the device of making singers laugh in staccato rhythms, which can certainly be highly effective. Nevertheless if it is successful at its first appearance it is decidedly less so at its fifth and when in the first two acts we find that Leoncavallo has used it no fewer than eleven times, it is not surprising that the gaiety begins to sound forced. Then like Puccini with his soh-doh flip that forms the binding motif of his Act 3 Leoncavallo also has a soh-doh motif, but unlike the highly memorable Puccini motif it is the simple straight-rhythmed falling effect which is almost inevitably a cliché. Another motif is a simple scale of four demi-semi-quavers running up or down to the tonic—an equally unoriginal effect.

There is little here to remind us of the vitality of *Pagliacci*. One suspects that Leoncavallo once having committed himself to writing a *Bohème* out of rivalry for his former friend would not abandon it at any price however little it inspired him. That Leoncavallo could be pig-headed is also suggested by his unforgiving bitterness against Puccini, tempered (according to Del Fiorentino) at the last but still contrasting with the more fluctuating feelings that existed over the years between Puccini and his other former friend, Mascagni.

Nevertheless there are positive qualities in Leoncavallo's *Bohème*. The attraction of the two tenor arias on the Caruso record is not simply the result of Caruso's singing. There is genuine lyricism in the true Italian tradition, nowhere near as individual as Puccini's but still very appealing. And Leoncavallo unlike his rival did make some attempt at a genuine French feeling in some of the music. It often led to cliché, but as with Musetta's song about Mimi the result could be charming. Certainly there are, say, half a dozen numbers that it would be agreeable to hear from time to time—besides the two tenor arias, the duet sequence in Act 3 (Puccini imitation and all) the Rossini parody, Musetta's 'Faust' waltz song and perhaps Rodolfo's 'Ballade de Désespoir'. At the very least they have the great merit of being capable of showing off Italian voices well.

THE PLACE OF BALLET IN OPERA

MARGHERITA WALLMANN

In determining the place which ballet occupies in opera, I should like to make a clear distinction between some five different ways of how the relationship can be made.

Firstly, there is ballet as divertissement: that is to say, as a part independent of the dramatic action, which can be included or omitted without the argument of the opera being affected. In *Aïda*, for instance, the famous ballet in the triumph scene in Act 2 enriches the impression of magnificence which is important to the action but not of it. The ballet here stands in the middle of the Victory March, dividing the heroic first part from the more ritual character of the second, which prepares the climax for the entrance of Radames. But the omission of this ballet would in no way make the plot less convincing. We find the same situation in *La Traviata*. Here the first dance of the Gypsies could be performed by the chorus, or in some other way, while the second Spanish dance could be completely dropped without any harm being done to the opera.

I could name many more examples where ballet in opera is just incidental dancing and neither linked up with the characters nor with the progress of the libretto. It appears for purely decorative reasons, often also because custom or fashion obliged the composer to put a ballet into his opera in order to please the taste of the audience of a certain epoch. It is for this reason that we have today forgotten many once-familiar ballet-divertissements, as for example the dances in *Otello*; they are no more performed and are quite forgotten. This could, obviously, only happen because the ballet was here insignificant by comparison with the real value of the opera, as well as being divisible from the action. Sometimes, indeed, the composer sensed the uselessness of the ballet in this place, and composed for these sequences music far below the level of his genius. There are many such cases.

Yet often we find ballet to be an integral part of the opera. I can think of many situations in opera where the action can only be held back or pushed forward or completed with the help of ballet. There is, of course, *Un Ballo in Maschera*. Though

91

we are only listening to some simple dance patterns in the finale of the opera, the ballet contrasts its gaiety dramatically with the tragic fulfilment of the plot. And in hiding the conspirators between the masked dancing groups the ballet becomes an important fact which cannot be obliterated. At the beginning of *Tannhäuser* (in the shorter as well as the longer Paris version) Wagner established an overpowering need for ballet to convey to the audience the enchanted atmosphere which would hold Tannhäuser under Venus's spell. The music of the Venusberg ballet is an inseparable part of the whole and the opera would be unthinkable without it and without the realisation of this music through a ballet imagined by the composer himself, not an associate choreographer. I could call to mind countless other examples of this type of integral ballet—Humperdinck's *Hänsel und Gretel* is one and there are many more. But these particular two operas present a great contrast in style and thought, though in both, ballet has become an artistic collaborator inseparable from story and music alike.

There are also instances where ballet acts as a decisive leading element of the opera, equal in importance to the prima donna or the principal tenor. This is the case in *Orfeo*. Through pantomime and dance the ballet determines the happenings. The dancers, becoming shadows of the underworld or blessed spirits of the Elysian fields, decide the destiny of the protagonists. The dramatic events are the results of ballet action that leaves Orpheus and Eurydice either together or apart. Without the intervention of ballet, that is, the singers would be unable to act their parts. In a sense the ballet can here be compared to the ocean and the singers to the waves; for just as the wave does not exist without the ocean, so the solo singer would be obliged to sing his part rather as if on a concert platform instead of on a stage. I should even go so far as to say that in this case the real protagonist has become the ballet, not in an individual sense but as an expression of mass movement. Another example is in The Dance round the Golden Calf in Schönberg's *Moses und Aron*. This ballet is the climax of the whole opera, and without it everything that happens before or after it would be utterly pointless. The ensuing action is determined by the ballet.

Ballet may also be an illustration to opera. It appeared in this manner in a famous Russian production of *Le Coq d'Or*; the chorus and the singers were seated throughout the duration of the opera without ever taking part in any action on the stage, while the ballet danced and mimed the corresponding events in perfect identification with the singing. Here ballet as a new art form had conquered opera. I should like to call attention to the fact that the opera was not originally intended to be given in this way by the composer; it was an experiment on the part of the producer. There have been many imitations. I myself produced *Jeanne d'Arc au Bûcher* in

America in a similar manner, though it was informed by different principles owing to the fact that this is really a scenic oratorio and not an opera in the traditional sense. Recently the Paris Opéra has staged a version of *Le Martyre du Saint Sébastien* in which the ballet had the rare task of governing the action not only according to the singing but also to the spoken chorus. In such a manner ballet may become dominant on the opera stage.

I should like also to mention briefly some cases in which ballet, though of minor importance to the whole opera, is nevertheless absolutely irreplaceable. There is *Prince Igor*, for instance, and *La Vida Breve*. The music written by these operas' composers for their ballet scenes has been inspired by folk elements; strangely, this music has become the most famous part of the whole opera and this is due not least to the fact that the ballets were created in perfect harmony with the specific character of the works. Further, these ballets have proved themselves able to stand on their own, to travel all over the world, to make the name of the opera known where it has never been performed. They have established themselves in the world repertoire of ballet as independent entities and have almost made one forget their provenance. One can truly say that in these cases ballet has outgrown its parent opera, and though based on opera, has established respect for the place ballet should occupy in opera. This shows that in many similar cases opera may need ballet. Though it may be of very short duration—perhaps only a few minutes as compared to the hour or two of singing—ballet may stand out in the performance (especially in these two instances of *Prince Igor* and *La Vida Breve*) as a sparkling and typical example of the entire atmosphere which the composer wanted to be heard and seen and felt by the audience.

But ballet should not be introduced into opera where it has no real mission to fulfil. It should not be inserted just to animate the action, for often this places a false interpretation on the plot. Ballet and opera are two different worlds, two completely different languages, and the choreographer who wants to produce an opera should first of all forget that he is a choreographer, in order to view opera with new eyes and a new creative spirit.

OPERA IN ENGLISH - IN AMERICA

ROBERT H. NEWALL

As a teacher of the English language by profession and as a fervent operatic devotee by avocation, I have been consumingly interested in the rather glibly dubbed 'opera-in-English' problem. Although the problem admits of no single solution since so many personal tastes are involved (sometimes belligerently so), the Metropolitan Opera of New York has made enviable strides in sanely coping with this thorny troublemaker. Undeniably mistakes—some lamentable—have been made, but under the régime of Rudolph Bing, the General Manager, the question of the language in which a given opera will be sung has been frequently decided with heartening perspicacity and with reference to the demands of the work itself.

As a result of some rather arbitrary decisions on the choice of language in opera houses here and abroad, some unnecessarily ludicrous developments and overtones have occurred. In Europe, for example, where the general practice of singing an opera, regardless of its origin, in the language of the country in which it is performed smacks of nineteenth-century nationalism. I have heard Wagner's *Die Walküre* intoned in French, the graceful phrases of which are inanely incongruous to the blatant barbarism of the gods and demi-gods. The elegant French is not only ill-suited to the opera because of the crude strength of the Wagnerian figures, but also because the costumes and the décors bespeak the battlefield rather than the boudoir or the salon. The guttural quality of the German is felicitously suited to the speech of the earthy or heroic characters who populate the Wagnerian music dramas. To use a French translation is to sandpaper away the essential power of his work and, in a sense, to emasculate it. The 'bite' is effectually eliminated. Though the Parisians usually do *Die Walküre* in French, they sensibly retained the original German when they revived *Tristan und Isolde* in 1955, by which time, one is not unmindful, the German tongue was less of an anathema in France than it had been at any time since the Occupation. But even before the war, the Opéra and the Opéra-Comique cleaved quite rigidly to the use of French even for German operas.

But probably the most absurd outgrowth of this linguistic imbroglio occurred in London when, some years ago, I attended a performance of *Il Trovatore* at Covent Garden. The company had rehearsed the opera in Italian and had no choice but to sing it in that language even though the indisposed Leonora was replaced by a Sadler's Wells soprano who evidently knew the role only in English. (Sadler's Wells, as an organisation, adheres chiefly to English as the medium through which the operatic texts are conveyed.) In any case, the simultaneous use of two languages on one stage in one opera borders slightly on the preposterous. This experience recalled faintly the days when Ezio Pinza used to sing Boris in Italian whereas the rest of the cast and the chorus used Russian!

As a student of language my own conviction is that opera is preferably heard in the language in which its libretto was written and for which the music was expressly composed. This position—so far as I am concerned—becomes more unassailable almost every time I hear an opera sung in a tongue foreign to its composition, for more often than not the results of tampering with the words, which are normally wedded happily to the music, are painful and perturbing. On too many occasions when opera is presented in English, my enjoyment of the music has been severely compromised of straining to catch individual words which, by and large, are unintelligible. One seldom has the pleasure of both words and music. Lacking the opulent vowels of Italian, the facility of French and the crispness of German, English is hardly the ideal form of communication unless the music has been expressly adapted to it. Even then understandability is not guaranteed. But if singers polish their enunciation of English and cultivate a flawless accent, they can contribute an aesthetic experience which will do much to prove that English, despite certain deficiencies in sound, can be a delicate and entirely beautiful means of communication.

So far as the Metropolitan goes, it has, indisputably, made errors; at the same time it has admirably solved some of the knotty problems connected with furnishing certain of its productions with new English texts of taste and style. On the debit side, the irony of casting Leonard Warren, the American baritone, as the High Priest in Gluck's *Alceste* in an early revival in French and Paul Schoeffler, the Austrian, in a later production in English of that opera comes instantly to mind. Though the German accent of the latter sometimes shrouded the meaning, it is to Mr. Schoeffler's credit that he enunciated carefully. Curiously and damningly enough, it not infrequently is the native American and English artists who articulate in a most slovenly fashion, whereas their European colleagues—Kirsten Flagstad is a notable example—have enviably refined accents which allow us to catch their words without listening so acutely that we lose the effect of the music. The moral of all this is that if opera in English were readily understood—as its proponents argue—much of the criticism against adopting such an innovation (now attacked as reactionary in many circles) would radically diminish. But the complexities of opera are already legion and should not be augmented by another totally unnecessary complication.

Several seasons ago Mr. Bing made an interesting and, as it turned out, a most enlightening experiment which was to determine whether the opera-going public would prefer to have the operas of the standard repertory equipped with English texts. The work under scrutiny was *La Bohème*, an opera whose poignant, almost bitter-sweet plot is so straightforward that, even for the neophyte, translation is presumptuous. The will of the public—and, generally, the critics—was to retain the Italian version. Though the signal fact remains that *La Bohème* is a comprehensible entity almost without a text, it must be confessed that the translation used for the experiment was inadequate. But I decidedly question that *any* translation in English could lay hold of the mellifluousness of the Italian without being drab or, what is worse, vulgar.

Indeed, because of its enduring popularity *La Bohème* has not wanted for translations. In 1950 the Charles O. Wagner company used one which was hopelessly coarse and which unfortunately defeated the intentions of the composer. Again, I witnessed another feeble endeavour to use English at Covent Garden. Though the lovers strived gallantly to be passionate, the translation defeated them and kept the opera earthbound. When *La Bohème* is sung as Jussi Bjoerling and Bidu Sayao, as Rodolfo and Mimì, sang it at the Metropolitan in the late 'thirties and early 'forties, it would strike its mark even in Coptic!

At any rate the prospect of *La Bohème* in English was prudently dropped at the New York house, but experimentation there has steadily gone on. And, typically enough, the operas which best lend themselves to revamping in English are comedies or those works with substantial spoken dialogue (*Singspiel*). In Europe the linguistic problem is not nearly so pressing as it is in this country because a European audience (save in Great Britain) can usually cope with one or two or possibly more alien tongues. At the least many know enough to make sense of spoken dialogue even if it is thrust into another language. But in the United States only a very, very few are comfortable with a second language much less a third or fourth. Therefore the spoken parts of an opera like *Die Zauberflöte* would be entirely incomprehensible to most listeners. So long as there is music, words are almost nugatory. Lacking the music, which often gives clues to character and situation interpretation, the words suddenly assume significance. Thus it was that *Die Zauberflöte* became one of the earliest and assuredly one of the most successful operas to be translated into English. Though the words are sometimes mutilated in the singing, the spoken dialogue at

Bosio and Mario in 'Martha'

Aïno Ackté as *Ophélie* in 'Hamlet'

Felia Litvinne as *Alceste*

Tamberlik and Miolan-Carvalho in 'Faust'

least gives a hint as to what is going on. Though I aver once more that I prefer—infinitely—the opera in the original because of the essential marriage of words and music, I do believe that it is far more practical for the Metropolitan to use the English text than the German simply because the work is then more urgently communicated to the audience.

Two other operas—or, more exactly, operettas—to be translated with phenomenal success at the Metropolitan are Strauss's *Die Fledermaus* and Offenbach's *La Périchole*, both of which have long stretches of spoken material which would grow tedious to an uncomprehending audience. Yet, to the eternal glory of the Viennese meteor, I once saw a sprightly version in Stockholm which had been translated into Swedish (not a word of which do I understand) and which bored me not one whit. But I make a habit of reading an unfamiliar libretto before hearing an opera, a practice which would solve many difficulties if opera-goers could be convinced of its efficacy. Too many, indeed, take the easy—and lazy—way by appearing at the opera house without having done an ounce of research just as they would do were they to go to the movies. By examining the complexities of a given plot, a person would then not merely grasp the essentials of an opera but would, as well, gain insights into its dramaturgy, its subtleties and its histrionic difficulties.

In a sense, *Die Fledermaus*, though surely not the first opera to be given an English text, was a *cause célèbre* inasmuch as gargantuan efforts were made to apply palatable lyrics to the mercurial music instead of the usual banalities. Making no attempt to cleave slavishly to the German, Howard Dietz minted an idiomatic 'translation' which wholly eschewed sentimentality. Consider the following lyric in which Rosalind, discovered with Alfred, protests:

Original: Mein Herr, was dächten Sie von mir,
Säss ich mit einem Fremden hier,
Das wär doch sonderbar!
Mit solchen Zweifeln treten da
Sie wahrlich meiner Ehr' zu nah';
Beleid'gen mich fürwahr.

Dietz: If this affair were clandestine
Then I would not have let you in
To find us here alone.
Nor would I sit my lover down
In my dear husband's dressing gown—
No. He would have to wear his own.

Or Adele's saucy rebuff to Eisenstein at Orlofsky's ball:

> Original: Mein Herr Marquis,
> Ein Mann wie Sie
> Sollt' besser das verstehn,
> Darum rate ich,
> Ja genauer sich
> Die Leute anzusehn!

> Dietz: Look me over once,
> Look me over twice,
> Examine the line of my spine.
> Make a resumé
> Of my vertebrae
> Appraising their rare design.

These examples will suffice, at least, to point up the brittle, but undeniably lilting quality of the translation Dietz has supplied. It is certainly no overstatement to say that not a little of the enormous popularity of the revamped *Die Fledermaus* at the Metropolitan stems from this 'translation', which, though it may lack some of the mellowness of the German, is not an unworthy mate for the bubbling score. Wisely Dietz avoided exactitude on one hand and cavalier dismissal of the librettist's ideas on the other, these being the Scylla and Charybdis of translators. Few can steer between the extremes and produce the sort of thing the original librettist would have done had he written in the language into which the opera is translated. To conjure up the spirit of the original is probably just as apposite a goal for operatic translators as it was for Dryden when he addressed himself to Virgil's *Aeneid*.

But let me affirm once more that Dietz's new lyrics, admirable as they are, are not invariably adequate. One must always observe taste. In working with a libretto this is doubly important inasmuch as the words, lacking taste, may compromise the music. In the first act of *Die Fledermaus*, for example, Rosalinda, in mock seriousness, bewails the fact that her husband must spend a fortnight in jail:

> The graying sea—the leaden sky—
> The autumn leaves that fall—
> Will be symbols of my sadness
> When you're beyond the wall.

This is, in point, a little too free in addition to its rather crass reference to 'the wall'. I also submit that the lyricist is straining for effect (or for rhymes) as he does as well in Orlofsky's aria *Chacun à son gout*:

> With someone feeling an inner demand
> To eat upon the floor,
> I've never taken a difficult stand—
> I let him have the floor.

This is twisting the Muse's arm pretty savagely, and in the company of lyrics of some distinction, such a pedestrian rendering as this shows up badly. Yet Dietz' version of Falke's 'Brüderlein, Brüderlein und Schwesterlein' air seems indisputably right:

> Happy Days!
> Here's to all the Happy Days!
> Drown your sorrow and pain
> And love will remain.
> Happy Days!
> We'll recall the Happy Days—
> We'll recall all their song and laughter,
> But the time is now
> Once again we vow
> To be friends forever after.

In this passage inheres the nostalgia of Old Vienna. Though the lines are hardly inventive (Dietz does his slickest work with the more witty parts of the libretto), they *are* satisfying and they come to grips with the music remarkably well. Here, especially, has *Die Fledermaus* weathered its sea change. In working with his elements liberally and dexterously, Dietz has fashioned lyrics that are not only generally well adapted to the music but lyrics which have demonstrated the falsity of the hitherto seemingly incontrovertible fact that opera could not be successfully forced into an English mould.

The latest rebuff that those who have opposed opera in English have suffered is the immensely popular Offenbach concoction, *La Périchole*, unveiled during the 1956-7 Metropolitan season. So handsomely mounted and so stylishly acted and sung was this volatile piece that it probably could have rivalled *My Fair Lady* had the Metropolitan chosen to give it a Broadway run. Again one cannot underestimate the influence of the lyrics of Maurice Valency, a man who seized upon the poetry of the original French and, preserving its essence, threw over it the mantle of idiomatic English. This is no easy job. Mr. Valency's lyrics, which, like those of Howard Dietz, scrupulously shy away from stiltedness, craftily mirror the intentions of the original and yet undergird the music most unobtrusively. Take this tart passage, sung by La Périchole after she has accepted the Viceroy's invitation to live in the palace:

> I've dined so well I feel divine!
> Oh, what an extraordinary wine!
> My head is in a lovely whirl,
> I am a very happy girl!
> I might be a little tight, a little tight,
> But oh! But oh, not a soul must know,
> Not a soul must know!
>
> A little vague my words may seem—
> Yes, I am floating in a rosy dream.
> I feel a smile upon my face
> Which I'm unable to erase!
> I might be a little tight, etc.

Here is the near-delirium of a young girl who, a short time before on the edge of starvation, has eaten—and drunk—far too liberally. Further, the words unquestionably suit the iridescent music. Still another pertinent illustration is the droll little song in which the Viceroy, in the disguise of a jailor laden with keys, comes to thwart the plans of La Périchole and Paquillo to escape, a tune whose emphasis on the single word 'jingling' gives an easy pretext for a chorus in which the three join:

> A jolly jailor, I—
> I hope my whiskers don't confuse.
> I grow them not to terrify
> But principally to amuse.
> And, ting, ting, ting, ting,
> I am forever jingling.

The lyrics superbly underscore the farcical situations of the operetta as well as play upon some of its rather indelicate, but quite inoffensive themes.

So far as the problem I posed at the beginning of my essay is concerned, how, then, can these somewhat disparate remarks be distilled into a sane appraisal of opera in

English? As I have already declared, my own preference—prejudice is perhaps more nearly the word today in this country—is still geared to hearing opera in the original tongue (with certain exceptions). But this is, after all, a special (some might say 'snobbish') approach to an art form which, like its sisters, has become increasingly subject to the pressures of democratisation. This argument has it that opera must be made as intelligible as possible to the common person if it is to survive. But, if I may digress a moment, one can powerfully argue that no matter how many changes are effected in opera to bring it into the realm of the average person, it will still remain a luxury to be relished by the few comprehending souls who have always demonstrated an infectious enthusiasm for it. This same argument, indeed, has fostered 'popular' editions of the classics in the foolish hope that by this method more people could be weaned from trivial to significant music. But there seems to be an utter lack of realisation that what these people are listening to—these mutilated 'classics'—are no longer supreme works of art. The magic has been milked out and they are little removed from the level of popular music. Arnold Bennett once observed that only the passionate few were responsible for the preservation of great literature. This principle is no less true of music in general and opera in particular. Great art, itself mercilessly autocratic, resists democratic blandishments with stubbornness.

NOW THAT MELODY IS DEAD....[1]

CHARLES REID

(*a*) Give your impressions of new or newish operas you have heard in your time.

(*b*) On the basis of these impressions, state whither, in your opinion, opera is tending.

Ignoring the remaining letters of the alphabet, I cull the foregoing from an examination paper devised by the Editor.

Let me deal summarily with (*b*) right away. In my opinion opera is heading straight for the clouds and specialist stratosphere. In its more viable days (Mozart—Weber—Meyerbeer—Verdi—Gounod), opera was addressed to the Plain Man. He had to be fairly well off as well as plain, it is true. The combination is not unknown. By plainness in this context, I mean the ability to know a good tune and a telling dramatic situation when you hear or see either.

Of these two criteria, the first has gone by the board. The Plain Man is as fond of tunes as ever, but he no longer gets them in the contemporary opera house. When it comes to tune-making the operagoer naturally invokes Mozart–Verdi standards. He has every right to do so. By these standards he has been given increasingly thin gruel these forty years. In the matter of tune—still more in the matter of rounded melody that is capable of bearing *da capo* strains—even Puccini and Strauss make a poor showing alongside *Giovanni, Così, Entführung, Boccanegra, La Forza, Don Carlos, Aida.*

All this, let me remind the harried reader (himself a specialist, no doubt) is written from the Plain Man's point of view. If not served by melody the Plain Man does not give a fig for the second criterion, that of the telling dramatic situation. Increasingly, therefore, he is turning his back on modern opera—and on not-so-very modern opera as well. In London the rarity of *Wozzeck, Katya Kabanova* and *Turn of the Screw* performances, as well as the smallness of the audience (as a rule) when they *are* performed, is a depressing but undodgeable truth, the sort of truth with which the wise man quickly makes terms, since he will have to go on living with it indefinitely.

[1] The fact is undeniable—but this title does not commit anybody but me.—C.R.

In our own time 'melody opera'—which is as external and objective in its appeal as the Parthenon—has given place to 'analytical opera', the type of opera which, relying on phrase, motif, timbre and, above all, harmony, probes the souls not only of the people on the stage but of those who are out in front, listening and watching. This is a distinctive and vast achievement. But it means retraction, a shedding of numbers. I should say that for every fifty citizens who relish and whistle 'Voi che sapete' or 'Patria mia', only one is capable of savouring, or even attending to, a typical page of Alban Berg.

I do not say that analytical opera will be with us for ever. Schönberg's *Moses und Aron* is a monumental reversion to opera of the external, objective type. But Schönberg lives in a stratosphere of his own. To *Moses und Aron* I will return later.

Meantime, a glance at one or two other new or newish works.

Raking about among the fustier of my recent memories, I come upon Tomasi's *Sampiero Corso*. This work, much in the operatic news two or three years ago, shows what happens when general-utility musical talents are applied to a neo-Verdian theme. Doublets, hose, casques and general military commotion on the stage. A lone rebel leader who reluctantly strangles his faithless wife. Bloodletting with stilettos. Funereal rites and prancings in a remote mountain pass. And so on. A theme which would have had certain possibilities in the 1850s (not that these were realised by Tomasi's librettist) wears a false, even comic look a century later. All I can remember of Tomasi's music is that it was resourceful and well-meaning—and that I haven't the slightest wish to hear it again.

Another case of dramatic anachronism is the much-performed *School for Wives* of Rolf Liebermann. I am more than willing to put up with Molière originals, mainly because of the dazzling economy and shrewdness of Molière's style. But, especially after Rossini, the crusty, stick-thumping guardian who schemes to marry his fourteen-year-old ward is a theme tepider than yesterday's tea. As conscious as I of the thwarted operagoer's appetite for tunes, Mr. Liebermann turns out a lot of little ones and one big fellow. The little ones he patterns pleasantly in a tart, quasi-Hindemithian manner. For the big fellow, 'Amo, amas', which is sung by the crusty old guardian in person, he clears the stage and suspends the action so we may be quite clear that something important is happening. But 'Amo, amas' turns out to be of no importance at all: singable, true, but exasperatingly glib and 'catchy'. Noting this and other switches of style, I regretfully concluded long before the curtain fell that Mr. Liebermann is enormously clever. Too clever by half, in fact.

Our great Simplicist, Carl Orff, on the other hand, makes a point and virtue of not being half clever enough. I have seen only one of his pieces, *Catulli Carmina*, in the theatre. Against my will and better judgment I found myself being carried away at first by Orff's elementary choral iterations and the Stravinskian top-dressings of his percussion squad. Better judgment prevailed in the end. The yearning, cynicism and despair of pagan poetry are here stated, restated and rubbed in with rudimentary plainchant techniques. Catullus and Lesbia and the rest recline for necking to choral and solo tunelets which smack of the cloister. Lust and its pains are confused associatively with vespers and mattins. Personally I find this a repulsive mixture.

The musical content of *Catulli Carmina*, like that of all Orff's music I ever heard, is, of set purpose, negligible. The intention is, of course, unexceptionable. Orff tells us, in effect, 'Music in our time has become introspective and technically so elaborate that only a handful of specialists can relish or even understand it. To hell with music for the few. Long live music for all!'

Other composers think to achieve the same end by judicious re-manipulation of traditional devices. Hence *The Rake's Progress*. Stravinsky's alleged dependence in this score on *Così fan tutte* has been ludicrously overstated. As has happened invariably since his *Pulcinella* pastiche, he does not ape, mimic or steal from the classics; he *transubstantiates* them, making the essence of their music the essence of his. Even so, after the warblings have died down and the orchestral filigrees faded away, all that I am left with from *The Rake* is Anne's lullaby in the bedlam scene. Music's most ruthless formalist has always been good at childlike tenderness of this sort. One has only to think back to the *Firebird*, *Symphony of Psalms* and *Apollon* finales. But one has to wait a long time for the Lullaby, and it doesn't last for long. Much as I hold with traditionalism, I cannot but feel that *The Rake* is an operatic cul-de-sac. A point comes at which Stravinsky seems to be rejoicing in form and conciseness for their own sakes. I come away feeling parched.

Our other outstanding traditionalist is Gian Carlo Menotti, tradition in his case being sketchily summarised by one name, that of Puccini. Far more important than the merits of the work (which are considerable) was the mixed and embittered reception accorded to *The Consul* in London when it first came here in 1950. This puzzled me at the time and has puzzled me ever since. The Britten faction were especially 'anti'. One of its leaders used to go round collecting adverse opinions of *The Consul* and making them up into shattering posies. He would pop his head round one's door at ten in the morning and announce with raised forefinger and a beam of triumph, 'I've found someone else who doesn't like it!'

For my own part I still listen with intent ears to Magda's show-stopping number, 'To this we've come.' The mesmerised dance of the poor, oppressed tiny people in the same scene still wrings my withers. I still wait, knowing it will mean as much as ever it did, for the Secretary's arioso, 'Oh, those faces' and the 'cello obbligato that goes with it. I still admire the aptness and daring of the Secretary's colloquial lines—'It's getting late. I must hurry or I'll miss the pictures. . . . It's cold in here. I must complain to the janitor.' Magda's monologue, like the corresponding focal number of *The Saint of Bleecker Street*, 'Ah Michele', which Don Marco sings, is much more than a Puccini re-hash. Although not innovatory, the harmony of both numbers bears the Menotti fingerprint. Certainly, the man has a musical quality of his own. But, all too clearly, he is not, in the box office or vogue sense, the Puccini of our times. His success, although exceptional as operatic success goes nowadays, has not reached plugging or tea-shop eminence or anything like it. The tunes are there, but they are not compulsive enough. Nor does the 'contemporary' character of his librettos popularise them to the degree that might have been expected.

Over now to the analytical or introspective school.

It may be argued that this school is every bit as old as *Tristan*. Others may trace its roots to *Pelléas et Mélisande*. For me the true beginnings are in *Elektra*. Not *Elektra* wholesale, to be sure, but one particular scene: that between Elektra and her mother Klytemnestra.

Strauss's music hereabouts is the radiograph of a diseased soul. More than that, the wail of conflicting triads and the clash of seventh chords opens up new vistas in the listener himself. Apropos Klytemnestra we learn something about ourselves.

The same may be said of Klytemnestra's magistral successor, Lulu. Berg's score means a new chapter or lease of sensibility for any man who masters its idioms. When I speak of *mastering* the score, I mean that quite literally. Berg's harmonic range and spectrum are much too subtle to be savoured or even suspected in the acoustical rough-and-tumble of the theatre. It demands homework. I will content myself with one example. In the second scene, Lulu and her artist husband have a duettino in two strophes. In performance this invariably flits by without making the slightest impression on me. But I know perfectly well from long experience of the *Lulu* vocal score that it is one of the most deliciously invented pages in modern music. To enjoy it I have to go to my piano.

The same applies, on the musical plane, to half a dozen other Lulu episodes. Always I am left marvelling at Berg's resource and *vision* as a harmonist. His vocal line, on the other hand, strikes me as about as relevant as a bit of grit in the eye. I peg away at the proclamatory Lied der Lulu ('I never pretended to be other than a bad lot. Take me as I am or not at all. I haven't the slightest intention of reforming') without being able to convince myself that it is a lied at all. Lulu's vocal line is rambling, gawky and, when it breaks into demi-semi-quavers, incredibly tortuous. No doubt it all has something to do with Wedekind's philosophy —that of 'human renewal through the purgatory of untrammelled sexuality.' To which I reply: 'Stuff. There's much more to be said for the classical and Christian doctrine that untrammelled sexuality leads to human disintegration.' With one apoplectic fit, one throat-cutting, one fatal shooting and one immensely tempestuous orchestral interlude, *Lulu* makes quite a night at the theatre. But, as compared with *Wozzeck* —or, for that matter, with *Peter Grimes* and *The Turn of the Screw*—it remains a parcel of disparate elements, certain of which are experimental rather than rounded and realised.

Britten undoubtedly is the man who put the coping stone on analytical opera as an art essentially of our time. The simplicity of his means when compared with the subtlety and strength of his effects is often uncanny. Among the most haunting pages I know is the scene where little Miles sits pondering at night ('O I've been sitting, sitting and thinking'—*Turn of the Screw* v.s., page 146 on). His soul is cleft and in the balance. The crisis within him is symbolised with extreme beauty by swaying triplet figures on the harp. The harmonic essence is an alternation of major seconds and perfect fourths, with a shifting back and forth of tonality.

No composer has ever, as it seems to me, probed more deeply into the human soul than Britten does at this point. To those who say (rightly) that Britten couldn't write a Verdi or Gounod tune for toffee, one may properly reply that neither Verdi nor Gounod had the gift to write a *Turn of the Screw*.

Is *Moses und Aron* going to swing us back from introspection to the outward look?

Another question perhaps takes precedence. Can so head-breaking a work be expected to determine any general artistic tendency? Schönberg makes nothing easy for us. The very first line is theologically foxing. Accompanied by chords that are pure Tristan-and-quinine, Moses speaks of God as Inconceivable. How Moses contrives to believe (as he evidently does) in Something or Somebody he can't conceive is quite beyond me as, in many aspects, are the conflicts between him and Aron.

Certain of the stage directions in the Golden Calf orgy obviously ask for trouble. I simply do not believe in operatic tribesmen who gallop on to the stage, then smartly rein in their horses. Or in prancings around altars by wholly naked young women, a requirement which usually ends in wrinkled fleshings and fiasco. Nor am I wooed and won by Schönberg's extraordinary mixtures of vocal line, *sprechstimme* and outright talking.

But his straight choral writing knocks me over the head. It is as massive and 'external' as anything by Handel. The polyphony is so grandly shaped that I no longer crave for recognisable keys or try to imagine them when they're obviously not there. Listening to this as to most Schönberg is hard work. For that reason the *Moses und Aron* choruses can never, in my opinion, become public art in the full sense of that term. But certainly they are an incentive in that direction. Here is the germ, perhaps, of some future *Aïda*, some far-off *Messiah*.

THE STRAUSS-ZWEIG CORRESPONDENCE

ROBERT BREUER

THE long-awaited correspondence between Richard Strauss and the Austrian writer, novelist and dramatist Stefan Zweig, covering a span of somewhat more than four years (October 1931 to December 1935), will arouse the interest not only of readers especially familiar with the life and work of the two protagonists, but of all people eager to learn how free creative artists struggle under the drastic regulations of a totalitarian régime.

The book has been excellently edited by Willi Schuh, the eminent Swiss Strauss biographer. It deals with artistic, literary and musical problems arising from the spirited collaboration between Strauss and his new text-writer. It discusses not only the creation of the one and only completed work by Strauss and Zweig—the opera *The Silent Woman*—for which Zweig based his libretto on Ben Jonson's play, but also many interesting plans that Zweig brought to Strauss's attention, only to see them utilised in later years by "substitute" writers, because Zweig himself has long been silenced by the party in power in Germany. In their letters, Strauss as well as Zweig reveal both their friendship and respect for each other and their artistic and philosophical wisdom.

After the death of Hugo von Hofmannsthal in 1929, Strauss's dramatic output had come to a sudden stop. It was the noted German publisher Anton Kippenberg who introduced Stefan Zweig to Strauss, suggesting that Zweig present to Strauss a copy of a rare Mozart manuscript. This epistle, dated 5 October 1777, was printed privately for Zweig in fifty numbered copies. It bears the title: 'Ein Brief von Wolfgang Amadeus Mozart an sein Augsburger Bäsle, zum erstenmal ungekürzt veröffentlicht und wiedergegeben für Stefan Zweig in Salzburg 1931'.

In his first communication, Zweig confesses: 'I wished to be granted the pleasure of visiting with you one day, to lay before you a musical plan. But wherever I come as admirer I feel rather ill at ease. Were I sure you would not consider it an hour lost, I would gladly call upon you some day . . .' Strauss's reply, by return mail, expresses gratitude and delight. Putting 'a simple guest room' in his villa at Zweig's disposal, he writes: 'Perhaps I am allowed to confess what I would like from the author of "The Poor Man's Lamb", "Volpone", and of the excellent "Fouché"? I miss—amid all the feminine characters of my operas—one female type which I would love . . . to compose for the stage: the woman as swindler or the grande dame as spy.'

The idea of *Sir Morosus* (first chosen title for *The Silent Woman*) was offered to Strauss in the spring of 1932. With characteristic modesty, Zweig stated that he would try his hand at the subject. Should he be unsuccessful, he would gladly let any author chosen by the composer finish the book 'without any material claim whatsoever except the one of having had the pleasure to serve a great man'. As the work progressed, Strauss repeatedly had occasion to show his approval: 'Act I just received, "Bravi, bravi"!' 'Act III excellently done: thanks and congratulations! There is nothing to correct except that during the process of composing the need for some cuts may arise. . . . I am sketching already the first act—it works splendidly.'

A year later, in April 1933, Zweig expresses his satisfaction about the news that Strauss's work is progressing: 'I am very happy about it—politics don't last for ever, art remains, and that's why one must work towards enduring goals, leaving agitations for those who find exhaustion and happiness therein. History proves that artists have found greatest creative concentration in the most unruly times, and so I feel blissfully elated about each and every hour that transforms words into music for you, that lifts you soaring above our times, for the enchantment of future generations.'

Without previous notifications, Strauss, on 15 November 1933, has been made president of the Reichsmusikkammer, 'an office that gives me quite some extra work but which I had to accept in order to avert many a calamity'. The German minister of propaganda, Goebbels, questioned Strauss whether his new text-writer was the 'unwanted' author Arnold Zweig (not related to Stefan Zweig). Strauss established his collaborator's identity, 'and I asked Goebbels directly whether there was something political against you, whereupon he answered me with a "No". Therefore we will not encounter any difficulties with *Morosus*. . . .'

Although political developments became more unbearable from week to week, thoughts as to future operas grew in intensity. In a letter dated London, 17 June 1934, Zweig showed scepticism regarding an Achilles plot; 'I am sure you felt already in the *Egyptian Helen* that the classical figures with whom we are so deeply familiar do not exist any longer for the present-day non-humanistic form of education. All the splendour we find in those names has lost its lustre for this generation—and people are not even ashamed of their ignorance.'

From England, where Zweig thrived on the peoples' dispassionate character and sense of justice, he, for the first time, offers to submit some more subjects to Strauss 'even though you will choose someone else to work them out', a theme that recurs again and again during the remaining part of the correspondence. Of interest is Strauss's 'strictly discreet' message to his friend: 'I tell you that you were "shadowed" in London and that your excellent behaviour was classified as "correct and politically unobjectionable". Don't get worried about it, everything will go well with the *Silent Woman*!'

Returned to Austria, Zweig dispels Strauss's own worries: 'I never was plagued by fears regarding the *Silent Woman*. The most essential part is finished: the work. Everything else we will leave to the future. Well—up to this day one pays homage to Mozart's *Don Giovanni*, although its good, librettist, Da Ponte, was a genuine member of the clan of the brave Venetian Shylock, without doing damage to the work and its lasting fame in Germany. . . .'

In August 1934 after Zweig had sketched ideas for *Friedenstag* and *Capriccio*, Strauss wrote: 'It might be a good idea that we don't speak a single word about our future collaboration. In case someone asks me, I will answer: "I don't work on anything, I have no more librettos at my disposal". In a few years, when our works are finished, the world most probably will show a different face.'

When Zweig tried to interest Strauss in the Swiss poet Robert Faesi, Strauss rejected his drama *Opfergang*, remarking jokingly to his friend: 'With your permission, I'll stick to Stefan Zweig'. A few months later he lamented: 'If you now leave me in the lurch, I will have to lead the life of an unemployed, sick private man. Please believe me: even if you offer your generous help, the writer who would furnish me with a good libretto does not exist!'

Strauss continues to tell Zweig about his discussions with Goebbels and Göring. The composer informed them that he had not found a single librettist except his 'only Hofmannsthal'. 'Why worry about problems that will exist no longer in two or three years? Everything will remain a secret between us two until the time comes that we can tell the world. . . . I also wanted to suggest to Dr. Goebbels that he propose a contest for an operatic libretto! We could see the fruits. . . . And if the minister on top of all this had to read all entries—God help him!'

Zweig, somewhat uncertain about the possibility of a stage performance of the *Silent Woman* writes: 'We are living in unsettled times changing from one week to the next, and we have to get used to blotting out the word "security" from our vocabulary!' Again the author tried to interest Strauss in other writers, this time in Alexander Lernet-Holenia and Joseph Gregor, both of whom Strauss rejected, assuring Zweig of his unswerving faithfulness towards him. In the pre-Christmas season of 1934 he writes: 'I utilise this boring time to compose an Olympic Hymn for the proletarians—I, the dedicated enemy and despiser of sport. Indeed: laziness is the cause of all evil.' Somewhere else Strauss adds the following P.S. to a letter: 'Please give it up, once and for all, recommending another writer to me!'

Affairs came to a climax when the Gestapo opened and confiscated a letter which Strauss, on 17 June 1935, had directed to Zweig. It contained passages which necessitated an immediate visit of high party officials to the Strauss villa where the composer was given curt permission to "resign" from his office as president of the Reichsmusikkammer. The Saxonian Reichsstatthalter submitted a photostat of this letter which Strauss had addressed to 'the Jew Stefan Zweig' for the personal perusal of Adolf Hitler.

Willi Schuh, in providing additional material pertaining to this incident, publishes a memorandum jotted down by Strauss, on 10 July. It contains the following noteworthy comment: 'Since Bach's time, we compose all that is in the realm of our individual talent and are Aryans and Germans without paying special attention to it. One can hardly call this high treason, although in the case of Mozart and in my own, non-Aryans have written the texts.' In one of Strauss's little grey and blue school-notebooks another entry was found: 'I was accused of being a servile, selfish anti-semite, when, on the contrary, I declared again and again in front of influential persons that I condemned the anti-Jewish hate campaign of Streicher and Goebbels, holding it a disgrace to German honour. . . . I confess openly that I have benefited by so much furtherance, so much sacrificial friendship, generous help and also artistic stimulation of Jews, that ingratitude on my part would be almost a crime. Of course, I had several enemies in the Jewish press too; on the other hand, my relationship to Gustav Mahler can be called a cordial one. My worst and most malevolent adversaries were "Aryans", I name only Perfall, Oscar Merz [a Munich critic], Theodor Göring [a music writer], Felix Mottl, Franz Schalk, Weingartner, and the entire press connected with the [National Socialist] Party, *Völkischer Beobachter*, etc.'

Strauss states that while the *Silent Woman* was slated for its Dresden première 'the anti-semitic bomb exploded all around after the attack of a certain Will Vesper in "Freiheitskampf".' At that time, Strauss, who conducted his first *Parsifal* in Bayreuth, met with Goebbels. Strauss wrote: 'It may have been of some significance that I, in the house of Wagner, the great martyr, had to endure my own smaller martyrdom.' Anyway, Strauss and Goebbels decided to send Hitler the score of the opera. The minister observed casually that he was able 'to muzzle all newspapers', but he could not guarantee that 'no tear-gas bombs would be thrown at the première'. In conclusion, Goebbels stated that there should be no further difficulties about the first performance, if Hitler approved of the opera, aside from the fact that its libretto was written by 'an unpleasantly talented Jew'.

Strauss writes: 'And so it came to pass: the work alone has won, although Hitler and Goebbels did not attend the première. In the city hall, State Commissary Hinkel made a warm speech. But it is a saddening time when an artist of my calibre has to ask a little boy of a cabinet member for permission what to compose and to perform and what not to. Now, I, too, belong to the nation of the servants and the waiters—and I almost envy my persecuted Stefan Zweig, who refuses definitely to work with me, either openly or secretly, as he does not want to get "special treatment" by the Third Reich. . . . My lifework seems to have reached its end completely with the *Silent Woman*. On the other hand, I could have created much more and, as I believe, it would not have been entirely worthless. What a pity!'

The new opera, conducted by Karl Böhm, and with Maria Cebotari and Friedrich Plaschke in leading roles, was warmly acclaimed at its première. There was an incident, however, a couple of days before the first performance that again showed Strauss's strong feeling for Zweig. While playing cards with some Dresden friends, he was shown the printed bill. The programme read: 'From the English of Ben Jonson'. Stefan Zweig's name was omitted. 'Strauss got his famous red head'— Friedrich Von Schuch, the noted conductor's son, recalls—'and threatened to leave Dresden immediately unless Zweig's name as the author of the libretto were included at once'. His wish was granted, yet the opera 'disappeared' from the repertoire after three performances, undoubtedly upon 'higher order. . . .'

The correspondents became very cautious in not prolonging their exchange of letters, inasmuch as strictest censorship in Germany made it imperative for both not to run into further trouble. In his last letter addressed to Zweig, Strauss writes: 'I mail this letter in Tyrol, and I entreat you not to write me any more across the German border, because all mail is being opened. Just sign your letters Henry Mor —and I will sign mine Robert Storch. It would be advisable to use special messengers to exchange our mail. . . .' (Strauss had used the fictitious name of Robert Storch in his opera *Intermezzo* where he portrayed himself in the figure of Storch.)

Aside from a last note mailed in London, in which Zweig displays again his highest regards for Strauss, historic events made any further correspondence impossible. An artistic friendship that developed most felicitously despite unforeseen political handicaps was finally trampled to death by the ruthless dictatorial régime that silenced Strauss for many years and caused the tragic end of Zweig, who took his own life in exile.

'VANESSA'—THE NEW SAMUEL BARBER OPERA

RAYMOND ERICSON

IF operas were ever designed to be sure-fire successes, *Vanessa* would fall in this category. Receiving its world première at the Metropolitan on 15 January 1958, this first opera by Samuel Barber was given the red-carpet treatment. The Bing management shrewdly left nothing to chance in its plans to make this production popular. As if remembering the stigma of American opera at the box office, it hired personalities well known in the theatrical as well as the musical world. The opera's librettist, Gian Carlo Menotti, staged the work; Dimitri Mitropoulos was engaged to conduct; and Cecil Beaton was brought in to design the elegant sets and costumes. And in matters of casting great care was obviously taken to select the right singers for the right roles.

Naturally, with all the publicity that preceded the opening night, the première generated uncommon excitement. The celebrity-studded audience was a show in itself and was willing to express its approval with vociferous applause, as if afraid it might not recognise an historic occasion.

Fortunately, the excitement and the ballyhoo concerned an important occasion: the production of *Vanessa* was a milestone in the history of the Metropolitan. Not only is Barber an American composer of first rank whose each new work is greeted with interest, but also *Vanessa* is the first American opera that the company has produced since 1947 (the ill-fated one-act opera *The Warrior* by Bernard Rogers) and the first full-length opera by an American-born composer heard since 1934 (Howard Hanson's *Merry Mount*). To say the least, American opera has not prospered at the Metropolitan, if it has anywhere. Thankfully, the company cannot be criticised for not giving an auspicious start to an opera well deserving of the chance.

And what did the audience hear and see on the evening of 15 January? It heard an opera that is tailored to the present status of the Metropolitan's repertory, which means that *Vanessa* is not experimental in any way and is content to express what it has to say—musically and dramatically—with forms long since established. This does not mean that it is a bad opera. On the contrary it is successful in many ways.

Louis Melançon

A scene from Act 1 of the new production of 'Madama Butterfly' with Antonietta Stella as *Cio-Cio-San*, Alessio de Paolis as *Goro*, Mario Zanasi as *Sharpless*, Eugenio Fernandi as *Pinkerton*.

THE SEASON AT THE METROPOLITAN, NEW YORK, 1957-8

A scene from Act 3 of the revival of 'Otello' with Mario del Monaco as *Otello*, Leonard Warren as *Iago*, Nicola Moscona as *Lodovico*.

Louis Melançon

OPERA IN AMERICA

A. Nokimos's design for Lady Macbeth's costume in Verdi's 'Macbeth' at the New York City Center.

Robert Lackenbach

Leyla Gencer as *Violetta* at San Francisco.

OPERA IN SAN FRANCISCO

Eugene Tobin as *Calaf* in 'Turandot' at San Francisco.

A scene from 'Ariadne auf Naxos' at San Francisco with Rita Streich as *Zerbinetta*.

bert Lackenbach

A scene from Cilea's 'Adriana Lecouvreur' at the Chicago Lyric Opera, 1957.
Renata Tebaldi as *Adriana*, Tito Gobbi as *Michonnet*.

OPERA IN CHICAGO

The 'Letter Duet' from Act 3 of 'Le Nozze di Figaro'.
Eleanor Steber as *The Countess*, Anna Moffo as *Susanna*.

A scene from Kurt Weill's 'Die Bürgschaft' revived in
Carl Ebert's production at the Städtische Oper.

OPERA IN BERLIN

A scene from Boris Blacher's 'Abstrakte Oper, Nr. 1'
performed by the Studio of Städtische Oper.

A scene from the revival of Meyerbeer's 'Les Huguenots' at the Hamburg State Opera.

OPERA IN GERMANY

Rudolf Heinrich's design for the first scene of Britten's 'Albert Herring' at the Komische Oper, Berlin.

THE KOMISCHE OPER, BERLIN

A scene from Act 4 of Felsenstein's production of 'Les Contes d'Hoffmann' with Melitta Muszely as *Giulietta*, Hans Nocker as *Hoffmann*.

Jürgen Simon

Eva-Maria Baum as *Blöndchen*, Manfred Jungwirth as *Osmin*, in the new production of 'Die Entführung aus dem Serail'.

THE SEASON
AT FRANKFURT

Erika Schmidt as *Die Frau*,
Erich Witte as *Josef K.* in
Einem's 'Der Prozess'.

Cünter Engler

A scene from 'Eugene Onegin' at Frankfurt.
Claire Watson as *Tatiana*, Rosl Zapf as *Filippyevna*.

Gunter Englert

But it is to say that *Vanessa* is an opera that could have been written thirty years ago and that (perhaps luckily) it seems strangely apart from our times.

There is nothing remotely American about the work, and typical is its romantic setting 'in a northern country, the year about 1905'. The plot centers around Vanessa, 'a lady of great beauty'. When the curtain rises, she awaits a guest in her drawing-room, whose unusual features are the covered mirrors and the draped portrait over the fireplace. As a snowstorm rages outside, she is beside herself that he will not arrive safely, and, as we soon learn, because she has waited many years for the fateful moment of his return. Vanessa's niece, Erika, and Vanessa's mother, the Old Baroness, are also on the stage, the former giving orders to the Major-Domo for the supper, the latter maintaining silence, as she has not spoken to Vanessa for many years. When the guest's arrival is announced, Vanessa is left alone to greet him, but when she sees his face she realises that he is not the expected guest, and she rushes out of the room. Erika returns, tells him that he must go immediately, and discovers that he is Anatol, the son of Vanessa's lover, who is dead. The act closes with Erika and Anatol beginning to enjoy the meal that has not been prepared for them.

A month has passed when the second act begins. It is a Sunday morning, the scene is the same. While Anatol and Vanessa are out skating, Erika tells her grand-mother that Anatol seduced her the night he arrived. The Baroness asks if he will marry her. The answer is yes, but Erika has not accepted the offer. She is not sure Anatol loves her, and she knows that Vanessa has now fallen in love with him. After Vanessa and Anatol return, the family doctor arrives. While he and Anatol have coffee together, Vanessa conveys some of the happiness she feels. Later the Baroness warns Erika that she must act or Vanessa will marry him. Then Anatol repeats his offer to Erika, telling of the marvellous times they could have together. They are interrupted by Vanessa, who beckons them to church. Erika is left alone. Slowly she unveils the mirrors and then the portrait of Vanessa. As she says that she must refuse Anatol's offer, the curtain falls.

The third act is set in the castle's entrance hall, which has a large staircase in the rear. Through a large door on the left, we see a brilliant ball in progress. Vanessa is frantic because neither Erika nor the Baroness are present, and the Doctor, who has had a great deal to drink, goes to find out what has happened. Anatol appears, and he and Vanessa sing a brilliantly effective, though somewhat contrived, duet about the bitter nature that love can have. The Doctor returns, his mission unsuccessful. As he begins to make the announcement of Vanessa's engagement, Erika appears on the stairway. She hears the words and faints. Recovering, she murmurs that the child cannot be born, and she rushes outdoors unnoticed. The Baroness enters, full of fears of what might have happened. The curtain falls.

Of the final act's two scenes, the first takes place in Erika's bedroom later that evening. Erika has not been found, and Vanessa questions the Doctor as to why this had to happen. Suddenly they see men bringing her back. Erika is still alive. After the Doctor has assured them that she will recover, the stage is empty save for the Baroness, who has remained silent through the action, and Erika, who has been put to bed. To the Baroness's questions concerning the child, Erika replies that it will not be born. Now the Baroness will not speak to Erika.

Anatol and Vanessa have been married when the final scene, which is the same as Act I, takes place and are about to depart for Paris. Vanessa asks Erika about the fateful night, and the latter tells her that she did not attempt suicide because of Anatol. Now it is time for good-byes, and after the couple has departed, Erika orders the mirrors to be covered again. Now she has taken Vanessa's place, and the time has come for her to wait.

Whether or not one likes Menotti's libretto, it is skilfully constructed in terms of theatrical effect and in its adaptibility for being set to music. Set pieces—arias, duets, a quintet—abound, in addition to other devices that have proved in the history of opera to be dramatically and musically effective—a quasi-folk song and dance, a ballet, a hymn sung by off-stage voices. In short, many of the ingredients thought necessary for grand opera are here, if sometimes used too self-consciously.

The characters themselves are not particularly human or interesting, and their motivations are often sketchy. Vanessa is made to seem rather silly in that she has brooded twenty years for her lover and then without apparent explanation we find her (in the second act) in love with his son. Erika, like Vanessa, is without a sense of humour, and one often feels that Menotti is manipulating her emotions so there can be effective second- and fourth-act curtains. Why the Baroness speaks so seldom is mainly left to the imagination. The carefree opportunist Anatol, however, is logically drawn and believable. So is the Doctor, the only likeable character, and he brings humorous relief to an otherwise laughterless atmosphere. But still operatic characters live in a world of their own, and considering many famous operas, it is perhaps unfair to pick at their traits mercilessly.

Barber's music is essentially lyric and not dramatic. Like the libretto, the score, to our ears that have been hardened by the music of Schönberg and Stravinsky, seems old-fashioned. Unabashedly romantic, it occasionally brings to mind other composers—Puccini, Richard Strauss—but Barber's personal stamp can be found on every page of the music.

Many critics have thought that the Quintet that comes near the end of the last act is the most inspired section in the work. Its melody, though not the most noteworthy in the opera, falls pleasantly on the ear and is easy to remember. The mood reminds one that parting can be such sweet sorrow, and it is this bitter-sweet poignancy that pervades the atmosphere of the opera. Other memorable moments are Erika's 'Must the winter come so soon?' (Act I), the folksy 'Under the willow tree' (Act II), Anatol's aria 'Outside this house the world has changed' (Act II), and the Doctor's 'For every love there is a last farewell'. The orchestral Intermezzo between the two scenes of the last act contains beautiful pages, and it also describes the yearnings, the regretfulness, the bitterness of love and farewell,

The second and fourth acts are the strongest of the four. Dramatically, the first takes too long to get started, and, musically, its conclusion seems vague and unconvincing. The third act is fragmentary and emotionally indeterminate, and is more noteworthy for business-eye professionalism than inspiration. It is the other acts that provide the uplifting musical experiences and indicate that important operas should come from Barber's pen.

When reading the libretto, one has the impression that Erika and not Vanessa is the heroine. But when hearing the score this proves wrong, for Vanessa's music clearly dominates. Sena Jurinac was originally announced to sing the title role, but because she was indisposed, Eleanor Steber assumed and learned the part on short notice. It is difficult music that Barber has given her to sing, and Miss Steber did not seem always entirely sure of herself. In general, she acquitted herself well if without distinction. As Erika, Rosalind Elias achieved her greatest triumph at the Metropolitan to date, and hers was a striking characterisation, dramatically and vocally. Though she had relatively little to sing, Regina Resnik met the challenge of the Baroness's part with great success and created a vivid impression on the stage. Giorgio Tozzi is rapidly becoming one of the greatest assets of the company, and judging from his portrayal of the Doctor, it is easy to see why. Strange as it may seem (though perhaps not really so strange), the English of Nicolai Gedda (as Anatol), who was the only non-American among the principals, was by far the easiest to understand. His acting and singing were immaculate. Mr. Mitropoulos kept the music moving at a nervous pace.

The production itself was quite beautiful, though Mr. Beaton's sets seemed a little too lush for the atmosphere of the opera. Mr. Menotti's direction was excellent, except for the third act. Why Erika should faint on the stairs in easy view of the dancers without being seen was inexplicable. And the third act was also unnecessarily cluttered with too much stage movement.

Vanessa may not be the great American opera, as if any opera ever could be, but its music stands up amazingly well on repeated hearings. The Metropolitan has announced that it will be in its repertory next year, which is a hopeful sign that it may be able to establish itself firmly with the public. And, in conclusion, a good question to ponder is: What American opera can compare favourably with it?

THE AMERICAN SEASON 1957-1958
including a note on the
TANGLEWOOD FESTIVAL

RAYMOND ERICSON and FRANK MILBURN, Jr.

Nᴏɴᴇ of the ten operas in the five-week season presented by the New York City Opera in the spring of 1958 could compete with Barber's *Vanessa* in maturity and finesse of musical expression and in richness of ideas. But hearing so many American works within a short space of time, one was aware of the vigorous ferment in the nation's lyric theatre. Here were to be found a variety of attacks on the problem of form and style; many emotional attitudes, as reflected in libretto and music; increasing freedom and skill in setting the English language, from that of Shakespeare to the shrewish tirade of a common middle-class wife of today; and a gratifying sense of opera as theatre, in which the music was not allowed to drown the libretto's dramatic effectiveness in an over-assertive score.

The season opened on 3 April with Douglas Moore's *The Ballad of Baby Doe* (libretto by John Latouche), concerning the domestic troubles and financial ruin that overcame Horace Tabor, Colorado silver king in the late nineteenth century. A factual character, his declining years are traced amid the pageantry of historical events. Moore's score has overtones of musical comedy and popular balladry, but it is attractive in a bright, pretty manner, and its effective arias demand skilful singers.

Mark Bucci's *Tale for a Deaf Ear* and Leonard Bernstein's *Trouble in Tahiti* formed a double bill about contemporary marital strife and frustration. Both composers wrote their own librettos. Bucci stresses the theme that 'The only death in life is the death of love' in an ironic story involving an abusively quarrelling couple in a miracle. A plot device gives the composer a chance to write three long arias for people singing in Italian, German, and a Scottish brogue. Bucci has a facile bent for melody, and his gift for musical characterisation is fortunately growing subtler, so that *Tale for a Deaf Ear* suggests a bright future for the composer in this field. Bernstein's little work is a satirical, parodistic, jazzy, and light musical treatment of the suburban couple's boredom with each other.

Kurt Weill's *Lost in the Stars* is really a play (Maxwell Anderson's dramatisation of Alan Paton's novel *Cry, the Beloved Country*) with some songs and choruses in the composer's Broadway manner. Its inclusion in the repertoire was puzzling except that it proved the most popular production and had to be given several extra performances.

Vittorio Giannini's *The Taming of the Shrew* (text by the composer and Dorothy Fee after Shakespeare's comedy) is a craftsmanlike score in the opera buffa manner, but a little too heavy, lush and reminiscent of Strauss and Puccini where it should be effervescent.

Marc Blitzstein's *Regina* (libretto by the composer based on Lillian Hellman's play *The Little Foxes*) mixed a popular Broadway theatrical style with more serious and dissonant music in an effort to create an opera out of an Ibsenesque play. Blitzstein failed, but not without composing a few ingratiating set pieces and dramatically vivid scenes.

Gian Carlo Menotti's *The Old Maid and the Thief* and *The Medium* (librettos by the composer) are too well known to need comment—the former a trivial and obvious farce, the latter a still chillingly effective melodrama.

Robert Kurka's *The Good Soldier Schweik* was the only opera to receive its world première in the season, on 23 April (libretto by Lewis Allan based on Jaroslav Hasek's novel). A string of revue-like sketches follow the fortunes of the simple-minded Schweik, who innocently gets in and out of trouble as a soldier in World War I. The work was not quite completed by the composer, who died at the age of thirty-five. Scored only for winds and percussion, it is reminiscent of Stravinsky as it underlines—jauntily or mordantly as the case may be—the action onstage. The vocal writing is choppy and undistinguished except for some plaintive little arias for Schweik.

The season's final production was Carlisle Floyd's *Susannah* (libretto by the composer), which had won a critics' group award for the composer. Its story of a bigoted congregation, an innocent young girl, and a lustful itinerant preacher inspired Floyd into composing scenes of lyric beauty which are not musically original but blend perfectly with his melodramatically effective libretto.

All productions were freshly staged through a generous financial grant from the Ford Foundation. Producers from the Broadway theatre were brought in, and settings varied from the colourfully literal to the imaginatively suggestive. Not all presentations were equally successful, but they were never dull. A large, extremely able company of young singers was headed by such members of the Metropolitan as Martha Lipton, Walter Cassel, and Norman Kelley; by guests such as Claramae Turner; and by regular members of distinction such as Phyllis Curtin.

This was indeed a valuable and engrossing season, which was a great credit to the director of the New York City Opera, Julius Rudel, who had assumed his post only the previous fall. A young Austrian-born conductor who had been with the company for some years, Mr. Rudel took over the reins in October, 1957. He returned to a policy of presenting performances in a freshly traditional fashion, but making sure that these performances were musically honourable. The repertory was safe but well balanced, and the season brought a revived interest from the public, which had been made apathetic by Erich Leinsdorf's old-fashioned, expressionistic, Middle European ideas the previous year.

The repertory offered *Turandot*, Verdi's *Macbeth*, Falla's *La Vida Breve* and *El Amor Brujo*, *The Abduction from the Seraglio*, *Faust*, *La Traviata*, *Madama Butterfly*, *The Merry Widow*, *La Bohème*, *Carmen*, *Susannah*. and *Die Fledermaus*. The singing was often notable, particularly from Irene Jordan, Frances Yeend, Adèle Addison, Phyllis Curtin, Consuelo Rubio, Giuseppe Gismondo, Norman Treigle, and Joshua Hecht. But everyone's attention was caught by the début and subsequent appearances of a young Italian conductor, Arturo Basile, whose sensitivity and stylistic assurance gave new life to the familiar Verdi and Puccini scores.

Aside from *Vanessa* (dealt with at length elsewhere in the *Annual*), the Metropolitan offered three other distinguished new productions during the 1957–8 season. One of them, a revival of Tchaikovsky's *Eugene Onegin* after some three-and-a-half decades, was unveiled before an indifferent opening-night audience, on 28 October. The work itself was too bland for most listeners, including the critics, but in later performances it began to win from the public some of the affection and esteem it deserves. Rolf Gerard had designed an exquisite and atmospheric production, which seemed just right, from the autumnal garden of Madame Larina's country house to the wintry park in St. Petersburg. Peter Brook's direction never called attention to its many ingenuities, only to its dramatic truth and apparent authenticity. A vocally handsome cast included Lucine Amara (Tatiana), Rosalind Elias (Olga), Martha Lipton (Madame Larina), Belen Amparan (Filippyevna), Richard Tucker (Lenski), George London (Onegin), Alessio De Paolis (Triquet), and Giorgio Tozzi (Gremin), and only Miss Amara's characterisation was on the pallid side. A sensible English translation by Henry Reese was easily understood. Dimitri Mitropoulos conducted with his wonted fervour, and he had commissioned Julius Burger, of the Metropolitan's musical staff, to prepare orchestral interludes to bridge scene changes. When it was found out that these were not by Tchaikovsky they were severely criticised in the Press.

Three nights later, on 31 October, the Metropolitan presented its new and eagerly awaited *Don Giovanni*. It was the artistic triumph of the season, perhaps of Mr. Bing's directorship at the Metropolitan. Eugene Berman, the designer, and Karl Bœhm, the conductor, were the principal architects of this production. Berman's settings had at once solidity and mobility; unity and variety; grandeur, colour and ornateness that did not overwhelm. Bœhm's contribution came in the finesseof the orchestral playing, the accurate balance of the vocal and instrumental forces at all times, the curve of intensification that rose as the opera progressed. Herbert Graf's staging had many fresh touches but stayed wisely within the best traditional grounds. The cast was one the Metropolitan could be proud of, with the magnetic, vital Giovanni of Cesare Siepi at its head, Eleanor Steber (Donna Anna), Lisa Della Casa (Donna Elvira), Roberta Peters (Zerlina), Cesare Valletti (Don Ottavio), Giorgio Tozzi (Commendatore), Fernando Corena (Leporello), Theodor Uppman (Masetto).

Mr. Bing invited two Japanese to create the new production of *Madama Butterfly*, Yoshio Aoyama for the staging and Motohiro Nagasaka for the designing. The visual results had the unclouded sharpness of detail that comes with the correct focusing of a lens. The shiny second-act interior, framed in realistic cherry blossoms, was particularly enchanting. Antonietta Stella, who sang in the initial performance on 19 February, and in most of the subsequent ones, carefully followed the stage movement worked out for her without sacrificing any of the Italianate warmth and passion in her singing. Eugenio Fernandi, in his début with the company, sang Pinkerton with a voice that suggested he might become another Del Monaco. Margaret Roggero (Suzuki), Mario Zanasi (Sharpless), and Alessio De Paolis (Goro) were just as valuable members of the cast. Dimitri Mitropoulos conducted different kinds of performances at different times, but frequently treated the score to indiscriminate rhythms and dynamics.

The rest of the season's repertory dominated, as usual, by Italian works, included *Otello*, *Aida*, *La Traviata*, *La Forza del Destino*, *La Bohème*, *Tosca*, *Il Barbiere di Siviglia*, *Lucia di Lammermoor*, *Gianni Schicchi* and *Salome* in a double bill, *Orfeo ed Euridice*, *Samson et Dalila*, *La Périchole*, *Faust*, *Carmen*, *Le Nozze di Figaro*, *Der Rosenkavalier*, *Die Walküre*, *Tristan und Isolde*, and *Parsifal*.

Inge Borkh joined the company to sing one of her specialities, Salome, and Sieglinde. Despite its air of calculation, her Salome was theatrically effective and vocally strong. Gloria Davy, young American Negro soprano, made her début as Aida. Although she had sung the role in Europe, she was not ready for it, and the music was too taxing for her beautiful, but light, lyric voice. Marcella Pobbe was first heard in a late-season *Bohème*. Her rather cool, pretty voice was employed in a modestly affecting impersonation. Marguerite was her only other role.

Grace Hoffman, an American who has sung at Bayreuth and other German opera houses, made an impressive début here as Brangaene, singing most musically and with smooth vocalism.

Faust served as the début role for one of the most intelligent and musianly tenors to sing here for some time—Nicolai Gedda. He also sang Don Ottavio, the tenor in *Rosenkavalier* and Anatol. Flaviano Labò made his début as Don Alvaro in *Forza*. A forceful tenor, gifted with a large voice, he seemed in this and other Italian roles possibly the best of the crop of young Italian tenors the Metropolitan has imported in recent seasons. William Lewis, a young American tenor, had little chance to make any impact when he sang Narraboth in *Salome*.

Two new Italian baritones of about equal merit, and hard to tell apart, were Mario Sereni, first heard as Gérard, and Mario Zanasi, first heard as Germont père.

The new basses were both Americans. William Wilderman, already widely admired for his well-rounded, well-sung characterisations at the New York City Opera, and Ezio Flagello, winner of last year's Metropolitan Auditions of the Air. Mr. Wilderman, made his début as Padre Guardiano and went on to sing a number of roles, from Hunding to the Old Hebrew in *Samson*. Mr. Flagello first disclosed his exceptionally round, mellow voice as the Jailor in *Tosca*. Leoporello was the largest of the many roles he tackled, most of which were small.

Several leading singers were heard in certain roles for the first time at the Metropolitan. Among sopranos: Martha Mödl, as Isolde and Kundry; Mattiwilda Dobbs, as Lucia; Eleanor Steber, as Tosca; Mary Curtis-Verna (the company's chief pinch-hitter), as Tosca, Leonora in *Forza*, Aida, and Donna Anna; Laurel Hurley, as Rosina, Zerlina, Micaëla, and Sophie; Patrice Munsel, as Mimì; Maria Callas, as Violetta; Victoria de los Angeles, as Violetta and Desdemona; Antonietta Stella, as Violetta; Zinka Milanov, as Desdemona; Hilde Güden, as Marguerite and Euridice; Lucine Amara, as Euridice; Brenda Lewis, as Vanessa.

Among mezzo-sopranos and contraltos: Irene Dalis, as Amneris, Brangaene and Fricka; Jean Madeira, as Fricka and Herodias; Regina Resnik, as Marcellina and Herodias; Margaret Roggero, as Marcellina, Annina in *Rosenkavalier*, Berta, and Bersi; Belen Amparan, as Preziosilla and Suzuki.

Among tenors: Ramon Vinay, as Parsifal; Carlo Bergonzi, in seven standard leading roles; Eugenio Fernandi, as Edgardo; Giulio Gari, as Lenski and Narraboth; Norman Kelley, as Herod; Mario Del Monaco, as Samson; Albert Da Costa, as Tristan and Siegmund.

A scene from Werner Egk's 'Der Revisor' in Günther Rennert's production.

THE SEASON
AT STUTTGART

Wolfgang Windgassen as *Rienzi*, Paula Brivkalne as *Irene*, Josef Traxel as *Adriano* in a scene from Wieland Wagner's new production of 'Rienzi'.

Werner Frost

WAGNER AT DRESDEN
A scene from Act I of 'Lohengrin' at the Dresden Staatsoper with Ernst Gruber in the title role and
Brünnhild Friedland as *Elsa*.

PROKOFIEV
OPERA
AT
LEIPZIG

Helga Wallmüller

Two scenes from Prokofiev's 'Betrothal in a Cloister', based on Sheridan's 'The Duenna'.

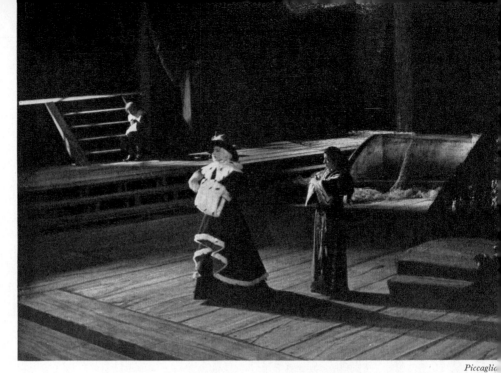

Piccaglia

Act 1, scene 2 of 'Un Ballo in Maschera'. Maria Meneghini Callas as *Amelia*
Giulietta Simionato as *Ulrica*.

THE SCALA, MILAN SEASON

A scene from Hindemith's 'Mathis der Maler'.

Piccagliani

Among baritones and basses: Giorgio Tozzi, as Don Basilio in *Barbiere*, Padre Guardiano, the Old Hebrew in *Samson*; Cesare Bardelli, as Amonasro; Walter Cassel, as Jokanaan; Fernando Corena, as Schicchi; Clifford Harvuot as the Doctor in *Vanessa* and the High Priest in *Samson*.

Max Rudolf, in his last season with the company, added *Barbiere* and *Orfeo* to his conducting assignments. Erich Leinsdorf, returning to the company to take Mr. Rudolf's place in the following season, led *Salome* and *Schicchi* (following Mr. Mitropoulos), and *Figaro*. Mr. Boehm led *Rosenkavalier* as well as *Giovanni*. *Carmen* was assigned to Thomas Schippers and *Faust* to Jean Morel.

The American première of Poulenc's *Les Dialogues de Carmélites* and the San Francisco première of Strauss's *Ariadne auf Naxos* provided the novelty for patrons of the San Francisco Opera, whose opera house celebrated its twenty-fifth birthday. The season was held from 17 September until 24 October, and also included a tour that lasted until 10 November. The element of sensation was provided when Kurt Herbert Adler, general director, found that he had to replace two of his leading sopranos—Maria Meneghini Callas and Antonietta Stella. The latter was forced out for medical reasons, the former was dropped from the roster 'for refusal to fulfil contract obligations', according to an announcement by the company.

The repertory leaned heavily on the Italian side, including such favourites as *Turandot*, *La Traviata*, *A Masked Ball*, *Lucia di Lammermoor*, *Madama Butterfly*, *Tosca*, and *Aida*. Verdi's *Macbeth* was revived, and again given were the successful productions of *Così fan tutte* and *Der Rosenkavalier*. Several Americans made local débuts— Leontyne Price (who was hailed as Aida and the new Prioress in *The Carmelites*), Sylvia Stahlman, Jon Crain, Eugene Tobin, Howard Fried, Robert Merrill, Helen George, and Nan Merriman. Making their operatic débuts in the United States were Rita Streich, Giuseppe Taddei (who was praised especially for his Macbeth), Gianni Raimondi, and Umberto Borghi. The conductor Francesco Molinari-Pradelli also made his American début.

Otello opened the Chicago Lyric Opera's season on 11 October, and, like the Metropolitan Opera, the repertory was singularly unventuresome, stressing strongly the Italian wing. The one novelty was *Adriana Lecouvreur*, which provided a splendid vehicle for Renata Tebaldi. Also performed were *La Bohème*, *Manon Lescaut*, *Cavalleria Rusticana*, *Pagliacci*, *Andrea Chénier*, *La Gioconda*, *Un Ballo in Maschera*, *Tosca*, *Lucia di Lammermoor*, *Don Carlos*. *Mignon* was the only French work, Mozart was represented by *The Marriage of Figaro*, and Wagner was not heard at all. Among the voices new to the company were those of Eileen Farrell, as Gioconda; Anna Moffo, who was a much better Lucia than Mimì, and Boris Christoff, an effective Philip in *Don Carlos*. Of the twenty-nine performances, seventeen were sold out and financially, this was the most successful season and longest (seven weeks) of the company's short history.

Outside of New York, San Francisco, and Chicago, the operatic scene continued to bloom in brief, isolated periods. Fledgling companies of promise exercised their wings in such disparate communities as the wealthy, culturally ambitious city of Dallas, Texas; the colourful South-western town of Santa Fé, New Mexico, and the nation's capital, where some Congressmen still hope to see an opera house built. Full-fledged productions with imported singers of note were to be found, as usual, in Miami, San Antonio, Philadelphia, and similar centres. The vogue for the presentation by symphony orchestras of operas in concert form grew considerably, while the number of opera workshops again increased.

Finally, in New York, the legal hurdles were virtually cleared to erecting the Lincoln Centre of Performing Arts, where a new Metropolitan Opera House will be the focal attraction, and the building should be ready in three years.

*　　　　　*　　　　　*

The production of opera at the Berkshire Music Festival, Tanglewood, Mass., has been an incidental and relatively small feature of this famous institution. Presentations have been in the hands of the faculty and students of the Berkshire Music Centre, a summer school that was opened in July, 1940, as an outgrowth of the festival, then in its seventh year.

However, since the operas given by the centre have usually been novelties or rarely heard works, the productions have won a good deal of attention in American musical circles, despite the semi-professional and sometimes inferior productions.

The opera department of the centre began modestly enough as one element in a five-hour, three-ring Allied Relief Fund Benefit for British Aid, on 16 August, 1940. Scenes from *Aida*, *The Bartered Bride*, *Lohengrin*, and *Rigoletto*, were sung in the smallish Theatre-Concert Hall, where all subsequent productions have been staged.

Boris Goldovsky, the vital and shrewd director of the opera department from the start, conducted Handel's *Acis and Galatea* that same year and Mozart's *Così fan tutte* the following year, with Herbert Graf as stage director. Two performances of *Così* were given in August, 1941, which has become the pattern for these productions since then. The year 1942 brought *The Merry Wives of Windsor*, by Nicolai, in which Mack Harrell was Ford, Mario Lanza (described as 'a talented young tenor') was Fenton, Christine Johnson was Mistress Page, and James Pease was Falstaff.

Because of its distance from metropolitan centres, the Berkshire Festival was discontinued in 1943 and continued on a minimal scale in 1944 and 1945. When both it and the centre were resumed on a full scale in 1946, the opera department went all out with the first American production of Britten's *Peter Grimes*, on 6 August. This was a singularly appropriate work, for it had been commissioned by Serge Koussevitzky, director of the festival and centre, as a memorial to his late wife, and the conductor was on hand to speak at the opening performance. Britten himself flew over for the occasion, and Eric Crozier, original stage director for the London production, collaborated with Frederic Cohen on the staging here. Leonard Bernstein conducted the two student orchestras used in the production, and Hugh Ross had prepared the all-important chorus. Members of the case included William Horne and Joseph Laderoute alternating as Peter Grimes, Frances Yeend and Florence Manning alternating as Ellen Orford, James Pease as Balstrode, Paul Franke and Irene Jordan among other singers.

Among the presentations since that year have been the following:

Mozart's *Idomeneo*, 1947, American première, with Joseph Laderoute, Ann Bollinger, Paula Lenchner, Frank Guarrera.

Rossini's *Il Turco in Italia*, 1948, with James Pease, Adèle Addison, David Lloyd.

Britten's *Albert Herring*, 1949, American première, with David Lloyd, Ellen Faull, James Pease, Manfred Hecht.

Ibert's *Le Roi d'Yvett*, 1950, American première, with Manfred Hecht, Rosalind Elias.

Tchaikovsky's *Pique Dame*, 1951, with David Lloyd, Phyllis Curtin, Eunice Alberts, James Pease, Mac Morgan, Rosalind Elias. (Koussevitzky was to have made his first American appearance as an opera conductor with this production, but he died in June of the same year.)

Mozart's *La Clemenza di Tito*, 1952, American première, with Irene Jordan.

Triple bill of Gluck's *L'Yvrogne Corrigé* (American première), Debussy's *L'Enfant Prodigue*, and Chabrier's *Une Education Manquée*, 1953.

Grêtry's *Richard Coeur-de-Lion*, 1953, with John McCollum, Theresa Green.

Triple bill of Hindemith's *Hin und zurück*, Toch's *The Princess and the Pea*, Vecchi's *L'Amfiparnaso*, 1954.

Copland's *The Tender Land*, 1954, first performance of revised version.

Louis Mennini's *The Rope*, first performance, and Mozart's *Zaide*, 1955. *The Rope* was the first opera commissioned for performance at Tanglewood.

Blacher's *Romeo and Juliet*, Milhaud's *Ariane Abandoned*, Martinu's *Comedy on the Bridge*, 1955.

Lukas Foss's *Griffelkin*, 1956.

Mark Bucci's *Tale for a Deaf Ear*, 1957, first performance.

Promised for 1958 is Rossini's *Count Ory*, in an English version.

THE SEASON IN GERMANY

HORST KOEGLER

As if the German operatic scene had to recover from the immense strains of a season which had been dominated by a whole series of world premières by Henze, Egk, Klebe, Fortner and Schönberg (if one dares to include Zürich in this list), the 1957–8 season was comparatively dull and uninteresting, with publicity focused on internal questions of personal politics rather than on outstanding productions.

At Bayreuth it was Wolfgang Wagner's turn. And just as his former productions had neither the consequence of his brother's Wieland bare austerity nor the courage of breaking away completely from his genial, if somewhat dogmatic approach, so his new *Tristan* was a rather uneven and lame affair. Main interest, however, centred on Wolfgang Sawallisch's cool and detached reading of the score, the elements of which emerged under his scrutinising eye like the object of a vivisection. If this approach represents the typical (anti-) Wagner-conception of the young German generation, who took over after 1945, it came as a sort of shock to most of the listeners, who were not at all prepared for this almost Brechtian (*Verfremdungs*) treatment of one of the most passionate and surging scores of music history. Let down by the director-designer and the conductor, all they could do, was to concentrate on the singing, and there, at least, was much to admire: most of all Birgit Nilsson's supreme, vocally immensely powerful Isolde, Wolfgang Windgassen's well-known Tristan, Grace Hoffman's reliable Brangaene, Hans Hotter's sturdy Kurwenal, and Arnold van Mill's dignified King Marke. Wieland Wagner's controversial *Meistersinger* production from 1956 returned in a slightly revised, much improved form, again conducted by André Cluytens. Sachs was sung by the very elegant Otto Wiener (alternating with Gustav Neidlinger), Stolzing by the overtaxed Josef Traxel, Eva by the incredibly lovely Elisabeth Grümmer, Pogner by Gottlob Frick and Kothner by Toni Blankenheim; while Karl Schmitt-Walter and Gerhard Stolze repeated their successes of the previous year as Beckmesser and David respectively. *Parsifal* and the *Ring* reappeared, of course, on the programme.

At first it seemed as if the flow of new operas would go on. Within one week in

August Munich offered the première of Hindemith's long-awaited *Die Harmonie der Welt* and Salzburg, Rolf Liebermann's Molière-adapted *School for Wives*, which was actually an expansion of the one-act-opera he had been commissioned to write in 1955 by the American Louisville Orchestra Society. This practice of substitute world first-performances of revised operas was to continue through the whole season.

The rather negative reaction to Hindemith's *Die Harmonie der Welt* at the Munich Staatsoper (which makes it very difficult for the work to be performed by any other opera-house—in fact, Bremen certainly would have thought twice before embarking on a production of it, had not the theatre signed the contract with the publishers before the Munich première; astonishingly enough the Bremen production revealed a much more effective work than the Munich première) doomed the whole Munich season. Admittedly this solid, serious and soul-reaching opera, which treats the astronomer Kepler against the background of the Thirty Years' War, is dramatically rather poorly conceived; as a succession of loosely connected single scenes it proceeds at a very leisurely, epic pace, which, ineffective though it seems to be from a purely theatrical point of view, is just what the moralist Hindemith needs for his meditations. Musically the complicated, thick and brassy texture of the score, the substance of which is hidden behind all conceivable contrapuntal devices, is not at all so unrewarding and monotonous as it seems to be at the first hearing. A later performance, which I happened to chance upon, revealed much more subtleties of musical imagination than I had been able to discover at the première. At that time the conducting had been taken over by Meinhard von Zallinger, who succeeded marvellously in making the orchestra sound much more luminously than the composer himself had been able to. Then Karl Schmitt-Walter, too, gave a less stiff and better worked out interpretation in the title-role than Josef Metternich who had created this part. The other roles were still sung by Richard Holm, Kurt Wehofschitz, Marcel Cordes, Lieselotte Fölser and Hertha Töpper.

Certainly the work would have enjoyed more critical acclaim had it been produced as carefully as Munich's Strauss productions; in this case Rudolf Hartmann and Helmut Jürgens delivered only a routine job.

Munich's other new productions included Stravinsky's *Oedipus Rex* (in a production by Heinz Arnold, which ignored most of the composer's scenic instructions, conducted by Ferenc Fricsay, with Ernst Haefliger in the title role), Strauss's *Daphne* (von Zallinger; title role sung by Annelies Kupper), *Un Ballo in Maschera* (Fricsay; Maud Cunitz, Lorenz Fehenberger, Metternich), Egk's *Der Revisor* (with the composer himself as conductor and Richard Holm as Khlestakov) and *Faust* (Lovro von Matacic; Fölser, Fehenberger, Ferdinand Frantz, Metternich). As the last première of the season Fricsay conducted *Figaro*, with which the reconstructed Cuvilliér-Theater was inaugurated on 14 June.

Public disapproval of Fricsay's rare appearances in the pit of the house, of which he is the nominal Generalmusikdirektor, have led to his resignation, and it seems probable now, that Joseph Keilberth who has not renewed his Hamburg contract, will become his successor. Knappertsbusch led some enthusiastically acclaimed performances before the end of the year only to state afterwards that he would not conduct any performance during 1958—which is Munich's much celebrated 800th anniversary year—as a protest against the scandalous delay of the rebuilding of the Nationaltheater. However, as the season 1957–8 comes to its close, it seems as if the Bavarian Parliament has at long last decided to approve of the much discussed plans for the reconstruction of the Nationaltheater, so that the venerable Maestro may return before long.

Stuttgart's main contribution to the new season was, apart from a revival of Othmar Schoeck's *Penthesilea*, which bore the stamp of Günther Rennert and Ferdinand Leitner as directors and Martha Mödl and Eberhard Wächter as singers, a new try-out of Wagner's *Rienzi* under the combined leadership of Wieland Wagner and von Matacic, with Windgassen, Traxel, Neidlinger, Otto von Rohr and Paula Brivkalne in the leading roles. While Wieland's dramaturgical operation of the work was on the whole very successful, his direction suffered from his indecision, whether to tackle the work as the grand opera it is (and as which it must be an aesthetic horror to a man of Wieland's catholic taste) or as a scenic oratorio, with the result that one was alternately amused and bored. Though audience polls at Bayreuth last summer named *Rienzi* as the work people most of all liked to see performed at 'the Green Hill', the Stuttgart test makes it little likely that *Rienzi* will be mounted there during the next few years. During the latter part of the season the Stuttgart Opera was busily engaged in rehearsing and polishing the four productions that will be seen at the 1958 Edinburgh Festival: *Entführung*, *Euryanthe*, *Der Wildschütz* and *Tristan*.

Farther down the Rhine, Darmstadt rediscovered Weill's *Rise and Fall of the State of Mahagonny*, and staged a very creditable performance (the first outside of the English Opera Group) of Britten's *The Turn of the Screw*. Frankfurt continued its course of mostly first-class provincial and a few excellent Solti performances. Among the latter a new *Don Carlos* and *Figaro*, and among the former Gluck's *Iphigénie en Aulide* and a double-bill, consisting of Dallapiccola's *Il Prigionìreo* and Orff's *Die Kluge*. Wiesbaden was able to complete its *Ring* cycle with a *Götterdämmerung*, which was dominated by Karl Liebl as Siegfried, and introduced a new Slovakian folk-opera, *Prince Bajazid*, by the Pressburg composer Jan Cikker. Cologne was not able to fulfil the hopes which had been entertained at the opening of the much discussed new house. But with the appointment of Oskar Fritz Schuh as the new Generalintendant Cologne can certainly become again an important centre of operatic activity.

Düsseldorf-Duisburg's Deutsche Oper-am-Rhein, with its 437 performances during the season, must be one of the busiest opera institutions of the world. That such a large organisation creates its own difficulties, became obvious when the Duisburg citizens revolted against the Düsseldorf operatic government and clamorously asked for a company of their own. Thanks to Generalintendant Dr. Juch's persuasive Viennese trained diplomacy, the argument was settled. And now no divorce will take place. On the whole the season showed a marked stabilisation of Dr. Juch's artistic policy, which will become even more effective when Alberto Erede takes over the whole musical responsibility at the beginning of next season. Outstanding productions during 1957-8 included a new version of Ernst Krenek's *Karl V* (conducted by Reinhard Peters, directed by Heinz Arnold), Liebermann's *School for Wives* (Erede, Leopold Lindtberg—with Anneliese Rothenberger and Kurt Böhme repeating their Salzburg success), Britten's *The Beggar's Opera*, conducted by Peters, Weill's *Der Protagonist*, Wolf-Ferrari's *La Dama Boba*, Strauss's *Arabella* (Erede, Roth), Verdi's *Macbeth* (Erede, Gustaf Gründgens, with Astrid Varnay and Heinz Imdahl as the protagonists) and the start of a new *Ring* production with *Walküre* (Fritz Zaun, Kurt Ehrhadt, with Wiener as Wotan). As the list of soloists given in the appendix shows, the Deutsche Oper-am-Rhein can compete with any other German opera-house in offering its public top-flight singers. Soloists who made marked progress during last season include Hildegard Hillebrecht (an excellent Tosca) and the already mentioned Imdahl and Wiener. The climax of the season was again a week of 'Music Theatre of the 20th Century', where all the contemporary works in the repertory were performed in quick succession.

If Nuremberg and Augsburg, Mannheim and Karlsruhe, Wuppertal and Bonn, Bremen and Hanover (which staged a remarkable production of Janacek's *From the House of Dead*), Kiel (which even embarked on Pfitzner's *Palestrina*) and Lübeck are mentioned only in passing, and other cities not at all, this should not induce one to underrate their mostly very ambitious and often locally very successful undertakings. How well one does to observe closely what is going on there, became obvious once again during the present season when Germany suddenly discovered through the London triumph of Gerda Lammers what a thrilling dramatic soprano the relatively small and often overlooked Cassel Opera possesses in her.

This leaves Hamburg as the last major West German opera-house to be considered. In the second year of Heinz Tietjen's reign a sudden crisis arose about his prospective successor, for Tietjen was only engaged as a sort of 'Caretaker' Intendant, and not a few people were hoping for the return of Rennert. However, as the more influential section of the public was wholly satisfied with Tietjens's solid, skilled, untroublesome artistic policy, his contract seems to have been prolonged for the next few years. One of his main achievements is undoubtedly the fact that he has been able to keep Alban Berg's *Lulu* in the repertory through the whole season. Otherwise he follows a sound, if somewhat unexciting course of repertory completion. The season opened with a new and not completely successful *Fidelio* (Rennert still has some difficulties with the vast new stage, his earlier production on the *Ersatz*-stage was definitely more homogeneous; it was conducted by Leopold Ludwig and sung by Siw Erics-dotter, Ludwig Suthaus and Toni Blankenheim). This was followed by Mozart's newly-adapted *La Finta Giardiniera* (with Erna-Maria Duske and Blankenheim in the leads), Strauss's *Rosenkavalier* (Keilberth, Rudolf Hartmann; Clara Ebers, Helga Pilarczyk, Melitta Muszely, James Pease) and *Frau ohne Schatten* (Ludwig, Otto Ehrhardt; Edith Lang, Helene Werth, Gisela Litz, Metternich, Kurt Ruesche) and Egk's *Der Revisor* (supervised again by Egk himself and Rennert, with Kurt Marschner in the title role). Next came Tietjen's masterstroke: he combined with, of all people, Wieland Wagner, and together they produced a *Lohengrin*, which was immediately hailed as 'the' opera production of the 1957–8 season. And a magnificent, grand-scale performance it was, radiating a classical dignity and authoritativeness, both from the pit, where Tietjen was in complete control of the not so easily handled orchestra, and from the stage, where Wieland achieved a most natural flow of movement without any of the awkward mannerisms which so often mar his Bayreuth productions. With Elisabeth Grümmer, Arturo Sergi, Helene Werth, Caspar Bröcheler and Arnold van Mill the cast had a superb Elsa, a youthful, dashing Lohengrin, a shrill and loud singing Ortrud, an insignificant Telramund and a sonorous Heinrich; if only the roles of Ortrud and Telramund could be re-cast, this might easily become the perfect *Lohengrin* of our time. The remainder of the season saw a mediocre *Otello* (Ludwig, leads sung by Lang, Hans Beirer and Metternich), Meyerbeer's refurbished *Les Huguenots* (Albert Bittner conducting, with Ebers, Ericsdotter, Ruesche, Ernst Wiemann and Sigmund Roth as the soloists) and Liebermann's *School for Wives*.

Lack of reliable information other than titles and casts of works performed compels one to form a very vague idea about the operatic scene in East Germany, which none the less seems very much alive. The two foremost opera houses there are still Dresden and Leipzig, of which the first attracted wider publicity through its productions of Moniuszko's *Halka*, Strauss's *Daphne* and Prokofiev's *Love for Three Oranges*. Leipzig was able to score special successes with Suchon's *Krutnava* and the first German performance of Prokofiev's *Betrothal in a Monastery*. That the repertories of the smaller theatres are not at all so dull and uniform as some people in West Germany are inclined to think, a quick survey of the list of productions will show. 'The bread and butter' operas are often ignored, and one finds, for instance, Dessau's *Die Verurteilung des Lukullus* at the Dresden Landesoper (this is a touring company, which has nothing to do with the Dresden Staatsoper), Alan Bush's *The Men of Blackmoor* at Jena, Mussorgsky's *Khovantshchina* at Altenburg, the same composer's *Fair at Sorotchinsk* at Eisenach, Hindemith's *Cardillac* at Plauen, Auber's *La Muette de Portici* at Dessau, Wagner-Régeny's *Der Günstling* at Weimar and Görlitz, Dvorak's *Rusalka* at Halberstadt and Nordhausen, Handel's *Tamerlano* and *Ottone e Teophano* at Halle, Britten's *The Beggar's Opera* and Cimarosa's *Il Matrimonio Segreto* at Chemnitz (Karl-Marx-Stadt), Gotovac's *Ero the Joker* and Wolf-Ferrari's *Il Campiello* at Zwickau and so on. . . . The list is endless! This leaves only Berlin, which, with its three opera houses (the Deutsche Staatsoper and Komische Oper in East Berlin, and the Städtische Oper in West Berlin), is a source of eternal temptation to every opera-lover, who often cannot make up his mind which performance to attend.

The aim of the Staatsoper seems to have been to strengthen the modern wing of its repertory—with *La Forza del Destino* (conductor: Hans Löwlein, with Helge Roswaenge), *Madama Butterfly* (with Ingeborg Wenglor and Roswaenge) and *Lohengrin*, which is promised for the last days of the season, thrown in for good measure. The season opened with Strauss's *Elektra*, sung at the première by Christel Goltz (who was later replaced by Sigrid Ekkehard), Hedwig Müller-Bütow and Margarete Klose, conducted deafeningly by von Matacic. Later on followed Egk's *Der Revisor*, with Gerhard Stolze repeating his amazingly realistic and marvel-lously sung portrayal of Khlestakov, the role he had created in the rather more elegant production at Schwetzingen; the Berlin performance saw Franz Konwit-schny in the pit. Next came an inadequate production of Suchon's *Krutnava* and a more enjoyable, but not specially subtle performance of Prokofiev's very infective *Betrothal in a Monastery* (which is based on Sheridan's *The Duenna*) with a large cast, out of which Wenglor, Gertraud Prenzlow, Gerhard Stolze, Gerhard Unger and Robert Lauhöfer stood out by the quality of their singing, while von Matacic led the orchestral forces this time with more restraint. The main problem of the Staat-soper is still the lack of really top-flight voices, especially for the more dramatic roles, which makes it extremely difficult to cast the Verdi and Wagner repertory. There exists however a group of younger singers (most of them have already been mentioned here, but Theo Adam, a very fine bass, should not be forgotten) with highly pleasing voices for lighter operas. I am afraid that as long as the Staatsoper continues to consider singers like Maria Corelli, Müller-Bütow, Ekkehard, Gerhard

Frey, Rudolf Gonszar, Gerhard Niese and Heinrich Pflanzl as artists of international calibre, the argument between the Intendant and the critics has little chance of being settled.

At the Komische Oper the first half of the season was completely overshadowed by the event to come: Felsenstein's long expected new production of Offenbach's *Tales of Hoffmann*. There was first a new *Entführung*, a not very exciting performance under the baton of Harold Byrns, starring Sonja Schöner as Constanze. Then Britten's *Albert Herring* (performed several years ago by the Städtische Oper) was revived in a splendidly directed (Joachim Herz), but musically somewhat under-nourished production. The title role was taken by Erwin Wolfarth, and the conductor was Walter Knör. And then, at last, it happened: Felsenstein presented his new version of *Hoffmann*, which uses the original play of the same title by Barbier and Carré, in which Offenbach's musical numbers are fitted in, so that the whole work emerges as originally conceived by Offenbach: as an *opéra comique* with spoken dialogues (and all the recitatives composed after Offenbach's death cut). The clarity and logical development thus won, are amazing, but unfortunately the result has little to do any more with opera, it is a play with just a bit too much incidental music. In his striving for realism, Felsenstein has arrived now at a dead end. As a production it is a marvel of modern stagecraft—actually the technical spell of the working stage supersedes by far what is left of the spell of the music—it is a real *tour de force*. The musical qualities are lagging far behind, but they stand no chance where everything is judged by the standard of realistic credibility. Vaclav Neuman conducted the scraps of music, which had been left over after this procedure of purification. Hoffmann was interpreted by Hanns Nocker; Olympia, Antonia, Giulietta and Stella by Melitta Muszely; Lindorf, Coppelius, Miracle and Daper-tutto all by Rudolf Asmus: the Muse and Nicklausse by Irmgard Arnold. All of them might have been accepted as straight actors; but one cannot hold them personally responsible for the poorness of much of their singing, as they were hardly allowed to sing but had to deliver vocal character-portraits. The whole production will certainly be registered one day as one of the most genial failures of operatic history.

The Städtische Oper continued on its dangerous path, zigzagging between half-hearted successes and near-misses. The impressive list of conductors with whom he had negotiated, was a poor *Ersatz* for Carl Ebert's failure to find a suitable General-musikdirektor for his house. After both Sawallisch and Erede had turned down his offers, the public became gradually aware that the reason for the conductors' unwillingness to come to Berlin might perhaps not be so much any prejudice on their side against the city but rather the terms which Ebert offered them and which must be obviously unacceptable to any conductor with a feeling for self-respect and responsibility. Public indignation rose to feverish heights at the especially poor *Carmen* première (conductor: Heinz Wallberg from Bremen, producer: Carl Ebert, with Elisabeth Grümmer as Micaëla and Sandor Konya as Don José), when a considerable scandal broke loose. In several public statements Ebert tried to sooth the anger of the people, but he must be aware, that the spark of discontent with his régime is by no means extinguished, so that it may burst into flames at the slightest excuse.

The Städtische Oper's main contribution to the Berlin Festival was Weill's *Die Bürgschaft*, an astonishing and majestic, if uneven work, the severely social critical tendency of which was belittled if not actually falsified in the new version, for which Carl Ebert as the producer, Artur Rother as the conductor and Caspar Neher as the librettist and designer were responsible. The production itself was very impressive. Main parts were sung by Joseph Greindl, Tomislav Neralic and Irene Dalis. The following *Iphigénie en Tauride*, which was conducted by Richard Kraus, was rather undistinguished, despite some good singing by Hilde Zadek and Hermann Prey. Then came the event of the season: Verdi's *Falstaff*, which was virtually a Berlin new edition of Ebert's famous Glyndebourne production. This saw Erede in the pit and Neher as designer. The cast was as good as the Städtische Oper could afford, it included among others Elfride Trötschel, Marcel Cordes and Ernst Haefliger, but the surprise was Dietrich Fischer-Dieskau in the title role: humorous, intelligent, well-mannered, vocally relaxed and so completely at ease, that one could think that he was singing in Italian instead of in clumsy German, he was just lovable. Unfortunately this first rank production was followed by the dismal *Carmen*. Next came the revival of Henze's *König Hirsch* in definitely improved form and some weeks later Britten's *Rape of Lucretia* in a performance conducted by Kraus, which was hardly persuasive enough to convince one of the qualities of the work. Things improved a bit at a Mozart week early in June, when the de-luxe-production of Mozart's *Così* (Grümmer, Sieglinde Wagner, Lisa Otto, Haefliger, Herbert Brauer, Lorenzo Alvary, conductor Rother) was restored to the repertory. For the last week of the season a new *Boris* was announced, conducted by Kraus with Greindl and Neralic sharing the title role.

1957-8, CRISIS YEAR IN BRITISH OPERA

BY THE EDITOR

For whatever else the 1957–8 season might be remembered in British operatic history, it will most certainly go down as the year of opera crises. All three of our permanent companies have been shaken to a greater or lesser degree by artistic, financial and organisational troubles.

The first signs of trouble made themselves apparent early last summer (1957) when the Sadler's Wells Trust announced that despite an increased grant from the Arts Council, and the success attendant on the world première of John Gardner's opera, *The Moon and Sixpence*, no further new productions could be undertaken for a year. The immediate reaction to this announcement was one of concern, not only over the financial stability of the theatre, but over its ability to survive; for new productions are, as has truly been said, the life-blood of an opera house.

That the 1957–8 season at Sadler's Wells started off with two new productions was due to an accident. The chorus of the theatre went on strike demanding more pay—so in fact did the chorus of Covent Garden—but whereas the administration of the latter theatre was able to make a compromise with the union representatives, the Sadler's Wells administration dug their heels in and as a result the opening weeks of the season had to be reorganised to include only works which did not employ a chorus—*The Consul*, *Così fan tutte*, *The School for Fathers*, and a triple bill that comprised *Gianni Schicchi* and the two new productions referred to above— Bartok's *Duke Bluebeard's Castle* and Menotti's *The Telephone*.

The Bartok work was well received by the critics and connoisseurs alike, and eventually the larger public responded, and the last performances were packed out. But unfortunately the repertory operas were ill supported during the season, and the revivals of *Samson and Delilah* (Patricia Johnson and Charles Craig), and *Falstaff* (Howell Glynne) rarely attracted capacity audiences. One other work did, Lehárs' *The Merry Widow*.

The Lehár operetta had been planned for production some two or three years ago, and the scenery and costumes were thus already available; that it had not been

148

given when planned was due to difficulties over the copyright which were settled in the meantime. The production of this work brought capacity houses to the Wells, audiences in which many unfamiliar faces were to be seen, and which one hoped contained many potential recruits to opera. So successful was the public response that several scheduled performances of other operas were cancelled and replaced by *The Merry Widow*. And at the time of writing we learn that the production will enjoy a short season in the West End of London in August and September.

But while Lehár might have been causing the Sadler's Wells box office to rejoice, other events were taking place behind the operatic scene which precipitated the greatest operatic crisis this country has so far experienced.

During February the Arts Council and the Treasury argued over every penny that was to be devoted to opera during the financial year 1958–9. With the 'credit squeeze' in operation elsewhere, our financial wizards obviously did not see why the Arts should be treated any differently from industry or the private individual who is unable to persuade his bank manager to grant him an overdraft. A misguided principle when applied to the Arts, and an attitude which one must, it seems, expect always to be displayed by our philistine government when it comes to culture!

By the time the treasury estimates were agreed, and the Arts Council saw exactly how much money it was going to receive, it became obvious that there was not going to be enough money available for both the Sadler's Wells and Carl Rosa Companies to continue to function as in the past. And so on the 28th of February, the Chairman of the Sadler's Wells Trust issued the following statement:

In order to provide the widest possible coverage both in London and in the country, the proposal is now being considered that the Sadler's Wells and Carl Rosa organizations should combine to set up a new trust representative of both bodies. The new trust, with one opera company, would undertake a tour in the autumn of 1958 and a London season in the spring of 1959, followed by a further provincial tour. Should times prove more propitious in the future, it might be possible to return to the position in which two companies can again be maintained. But in the meantime it is hoped that the proposed working arrangements will give the best service possible to the great and ever growing audience of opera lovers and provide the maximum of work for the greatest possible number of artists from both companies.

This was immediately followed by the resignations of Norman Tucker, the Sadler's Wells Director, Stephen Arlen, the theatre's General Manager, and Alexander Gibson, its Musical Director. A few days later, Norman Tucker issued a statement which outlined the scheme he and his colleagues had put forward for the amalgamation of the Wells and Rosa Companies, and which had foundered for the lack of some twenty to thirty thousand pounds.

149

This memorandum on 'Operatic repertoire in London', has so far not been reproduced in full, and I think it should be published. While not agreeing with all its conclusions, and while feeling that the best solution for London is eventually a Covent Garden–Sadler's Wells amalgamation, there is still much of interest in it.

MEMORANDUM ON OPERATIC REPERTOIRE IN LONDON

The question of repertoire has been looming large in the discussions about amalgamation during the last six months and needs airing in order to get rid of misconceptions. It may be useful to set down my own views about the position of Sadler's Wells in this respect. The moment for this is particularly opportune as amalgamation with the Carl Rosa will enable Sadler's Wells to organise its own repertoire to the best effect.

The London public is served as regards repertoire by:—

1. The permanent companies at Covent Garden and Sadler's Wells.
2. Annual visits of the Carl Rosa and Welsh National Opera Companies to Sadler's Wells.
3. The New Opera Company which was formed last year and which looks like becoming a regular visitor to Sadler's Wells.
4. Occasional visiting companies from Continental opera houses to Covent Garden or the Festival Hall.
5. Other visiting companies, e.g. Italian companies, at the Stoll.

It would seem desirable that the various repertoires should be as far as possible complementary, always bearing in mind that some people will go to opera in foreign languages but not in the vernacular and also—an extremely important point—that the audiences of the two metropolitan opera houses are to a large degree distinct. Covent Garden is a descendant of the golden age of opera geared as near as may be to the circumstances of today. Sadler's Wells on the other hand, is a child of the times. It started as a localised venture for a section of the London population and has developed in the course of time into the people's or municipal opera house of London. There is nothing in this development which runs counter to the spirit of the Charter of the Governors of Sadler's Wells. Given the site, the size and the resources of the building, its prices will always be lower than those of the national house at Covent Garden. It follows therefore that a section of the public will always go to Sadler's Wells either because it prefers to see its opera there or because it cannot afford to go, or go often, to the more expensive house or perhaps even because it prefers to spend its available cash on a better seat at Sadler's Wells than could be bought at Covent Garden for the same price.

It is often said that Sadler's Wells should approximate to a Volksoper or Opéra-Comique. This broad comparison stands but it should be remembered that while the operatic tradition on the Continent is of very long standing, in England state encouragement of opera is still in its infancy, and much lost ground has to be made up. This means that one cannot simply superimpose on England a pattern from abroad. The principle that Sadler's Wells should perform the smaller scale operas and Covent Garden the larger scale is clearly sound but must be adapted to the English operatic scene. The one overriding principle is that the repertoire should be as widely based as possible both in order to satisfy the demands of the public and also in order to broaden the public's appreciation of opera. The approach therefore to the classification of repertoires should be flexible rather than rigid.

It is comparatively easy to draw up categories of repertoire suitable for the two houses but some exceptions would have to be made. If Covent Garden is to do all the large scale operas, Verdi, Wagner, etc., then Sadler's Wells should have the Mozart repertoire preserved for it. This is essential to the prestige of the house. It is unlikely, however, that the Musical Director of Covent Garden, whoever he might be at any particular time, would agree to forgo entirely *Don Giovanni* or *The Magic Flute*. I see no difficulty about this provided (i) that it is understood that Sadler's Wells is pre-eminently the Mozart house (ii) *The Magic Flute* and *Don Giovanni* are put into the Covent Garden repertoire by agreement and staggered with any productions at Sadler's Wells of these operas. I am referring here to the permanent seasons at Covent Garden and not to visiting companies from abroad where different principles apply. Similarly, Sadler's Wells by agreement should exceptionally perform a work, e.g. *The Flying Dutchman* of Wagner, which is seldom performed at Covent Garden.

There are several reasons why Sadler's Wells could not live on an exclusive diet of small scale operas:—

1. There are not sufficient box office winners among them.
2. The repertoire for a long time has been built on a broad popular basis and it would take a long time to capitalise a different form of repertoire.
3. English operatic singers are not only trained for the broader repertoire but need it for the development of their careers. A certain element of Verdi, Puccini, and Wagner therefore is necessary.
4. Much more important than any of the above but allied to (1) is the fact that at permanent opera houses the public expects to see a certain amount of the larger scale singing repertoire and these operas do in fact bring in most money to the box office. I suggest therefore that in the same way that Covent Garden may always want to perform certain operas which are the prerogative of Sadler's Wells, so Sadler's Wells should be free to perform certain operas which, ideally, should be staged at Covent Garden. In saying this I am not suggesting that Sadler's Well should duplicate with Covent Garden any longer the popular operas of large scale which Covent Garden contain in their repertoire, e.g., *Trovatore*, *Rigoletto*, *Don Carlos* but that Sadler's Wells should be free to perform certain works which would otherwise not be seen at either house, e.g. *Samson and Delilah*, *Andrea Chénier*, because they fulfil a popular demand and help to broaden the overall repertoire.

The point then arises that a number of popular works such as *Trovatore*, *Faust* (assuming that Covent Garden will do it at some point) are only available for the public at Covent Garden. This is met to an appreciable extent by visits of the Carl Rosa to Sadler's Wells which, under the scheme now under discussion, viz: the original scheme of amalgamation, should be more frequent in future. The Carl Rosa's repertoire is of necessity primarily of a popular character and in future the Carl Rosa would be able to play at Sadler's Wells for eight weeks in the year at least, during which time the particular Sadler's Wells public would be able to see the *Trovatores* and *Rigolettos* which they will no longer be able to see performed by the Sadler's Wells Company itself.

Thus, London could be served with the following categories of repertoire:—

1. Covent Garden. All the large scale operas requiring large choral, orchestral and scenic resources, Mozart within the limits suggested above, and any other suitable works not performed elsewhere.

2. Sadler's Wells. The Mozart and kindred repertoire, operetta, singspiel and a whole range of operas which can be performed with the existing orchestral and scenic resources but not requiring an over-large chorus: in addition, certain operas requiring larger choral resources which could be performed during part of the season by supplementing with the Carl Rosa chorus. No duplication with Covent Garden would arise except within the narrow limits suggested above.
3. Carl Rosa. A predominantly popular repertoire which would be welcomed by the particular Sadler's Wells public for limited seasons of the year, together with the occasional prestige production which again would not involve duplication.
4. The Welsh National Opera Company, which has hitherto mainly concerned itself with presenting large scale works in which their chorus can be best deployed and which cannot be seen elsewhere.
5. The New Opera Company which at present is concentrating on new and mainly English works.
6. Visiting Italian companies performing stock repertoire in Italian and also works like *Lucia* seldom seen in London.

It has been suggested that a proper distinction of the respective repertoires of Covent Garden and Sadler's Wells would only be successful under amalgamation. I do not think that this is so. Given the general acceptance of the above principles, any queries about repertoire could be dealt with by a small committee drawn from the various opera companies with possibly an Arts Council chairman.

Conclusions:—

1. The widest possible repertoire should be presented to the public. It follows from this that duplication should be avoided except within the limits suggested above.
2. The two permanent London companies should within their respective spheres both aim at standards of metropolitan excellence.
3. Sadler's Wells should be a popular opera house in the best sense of the word with a repertoire complementary to Covent Garden on the one hand and to the Carl Rosa on the other.

I suggest that the interests of the public and the future development of opera will best be served in this way.

The storm that broke following the various pronouncements and resignations was unparalleled. The affection with which the Wells is evidently held by the public was never more manifest, and with the Press unanimously behind Mr. Tucker and his colleagues, with protest meetings organised and a 'Save the Wells' movement afoot, a complete *volte-face* took place as far as the Governors of Sadler's Wells were concerned, as the following statement issued on 14 March shows:

The Governors and Trustees of Sadler's Wells met today to consider the future of Sadler's Wells Opera. They wish it to be known how deeply moved they have been by the expressions of affection and support for Sadler's Wells which have been received from all sides.
The Governors have unanimously come to the conclusion that Sadler's Wells shall be preserved and developed, and they have given instructions that plans for next season shall go forward on the basis of a full programme. At the same time, while maintaining and developing the closest

Piccagliani

THE SCALA, MILAN SEASON

Clara Petrella as *Adriana*, Giuseppe di Stefano as *Maurizio* in 'Adriana Lecouvreur'.

THE SCALA, MILAN SEASON

Nicola Rossi-Lemeni as *Thomas à Beckett* in a scene from Pizzetti's new opera, 'Assassinio nella Cattedrale' based on T. S. Eliot's play 'Murder in the Cathedral' which had its world première at the Scala during the season.

Troncone

THE SEASON AT THE TEATRO SAN CARLO, NAPLES

Rosanna Cateri as *Magda*, Giuseppe Gismondo as *Ruggero* in a scene from Act 3 of
Puccini's 'La Rondine'.

THE OPENING OF THE SEASON AT ROME

The curtain call at the end of the first act of 'Norma' with Maria Meneghini Callas, Miriam Pirazzini, Franco Corelli and Giulio Neri.

Below, the curtain call after Anita Cerquetti had taken over the role of *Norma* following Mme. Callas's withdrawal owing to ill health.

Fayer

Wolfgang Windgassen as *Siegfried* in Act 2 of Karajan's new
production of 'Siegfried' at the Vienna Staatsoper.

VIENNA AND ZÜRICH

A scene from the Zürich production of Liebermann's
'Die Schule der Frauen'.

Baur

THE SEASON AT STOCKHOLM

Elisabeth Söderström as the *Governess*, Eva Prytz as *Mrs. Grose*, Sonja Narin as *Flora*, Ingemar Sivebn as *Miles* in 'The Turn of the Screw'. *Bottom left*, Kerstin Meyer as *Dido* and *right*, Set Svanholm as *Aeneas* in 'The Trojans'.

co-operation with the Carl Rosa, Sadler's Wells Opera will retain its separate identity as a metropolitan opera company.

The Governors and Trustees are determined that the money will be raised, and feel sure that the public will wish to contribute and thus ensure that the opera company will come to maturity.

Then, later in the year, A.B.C. Television Limited announced that a grant of £35,000 would be made to Sadler's Wells at the rate of £5,000 a year for the next seven years; this, plus various donations large and small made by members of the public, and the prospect of a grant from the London County Council certainly makes one more hopeful as far as Sadler's Wells is concerned.

The Carl Rosa too went forward with its plans, and although its first London season under the direction of Procter-Gregg was not a financial success, satisfaction was expressed by many people at the improved standards displayed, especially in the orchestral playing.

Unfortunately on 1 July a new crisis broke, when Professor Procter-Gregg, Sir Donald Wolfit (Chairman of the Board), and Alan Bohun, the Secretary, resigned owing to serious disagreement within the board. Procter-Gregg used strong terms in his letter of resignation:

> The motion carried at yesterday's board meeting deprives me of the authority necessary to direct the work of the Carl Rosa Opera Company. I am obliged, therefore, to tender hereby my resignation.
>
> This was, I think, the intention, and is the end, so far as I am officially concerned, of ten months of relentless animosity with which I have been treated since becoming director designate. This treatment, of which in long years of various professional experience, I have never seen the like, I have endured hitherto in the hopes of helping the company to a more secure and prosperous future.
>
> Since taking over I received a proposal of partnership from Sadler's Wells and generous and extensive assistance in all departments, which was the more necessary in view of the dilapidated state in which I found the company's working material.
>
> The friendliest relations, as you know, have been established with Covent Garden and Glyndebourne and we have among other specific benefactions received distinguished kindness from Sir Adrian Boult and been awarded the first broadcast for many years. It would be tragic if the company could not go forward to further developments.
>
> As from to-day, Mr. Chairman, those who are responsible for the state of the company financially, materially, and artistically when I was appointed must be held totally responsible for its future. Of course, what is wanted is a new board and I hereby set a good example by resigning also my membership.

Three further resignations followed, those of Astra Desmond, Norman Allin and Frederick Cox.

While the Carl Rosa and Sadler's Wells faced these serious crises, Covent Garden

H

maintained a long silence. But that august house too became the subject of criticism when, at the end of January, it was announced that Rafael Kubelik was resigning as Musical Director at the end of the 1957–8 season, and that no successor was to be appointed. Rather was Covent Garden going to rely 'for collaboration and advice, on the principal conductors, who will spend some time at Covent Garden each season. During the 1958–9 season Mr. Kubelik will spend four months with the company, and Mr. Rudolf Kempe will spend a similar period at Covent Garden'.

Although this announcement brought a certain amount of comment and criticism from a number of the leading critics, Covent Garden's future was not so much in the news as in previous years. And the generally excellent performances of *Don Carlos* and *Elektra*, the centenary celebrations, the return of Callas, and the other excitements of the summer were such as to leave many people with more benevolent feelings toward our major opera house.

The outstanding event of the year at Covent Garden was undoubtedly the magnificent production of *Don Carlos* by Luchino Visconti, conducted by Carlo Maria Giulini, a truly gifted young Italian operatic conductor, with Gré Brouwenstijn, Fedora Barbieri, Jon Vickers, Tito Gobbi, and Boris Christoff in the leading roles. Not only was this a highly integrated production, but one which completely vindicated Italian grand opera, and restored a great Verdi opera to its rightful place in the repertory.

The other new production of the centenary summer could hardly be called a success. This was a new *Tristan und Isolde* conducted by Kubelik, produced by Christopher West, and with designs by Leslie Hurry. Sylvia Fisher, Irene Dalis, Ramon Vinay, Otakar Kraus and James Pease were the principal singers. After two performances Birgit Nilsson took over the role of Isolde, and sang with an amplitude and beauty of tone that is rare among Wagner singers.

The other great event of the summer was the return of Maria Meneghini Callas, who sang the 'Mad scene' from *I Puritani* in the Centenary Gala on 10 June, and Violetta in five performances of *La Traviata*. Mme. Callas, as always, succeeded in dividing opinions about her interpretation of the role, and she showed once more that she is a consummate mistress of the operatic stage, and one of the few great singing-actresses in operatic history.

Perhaps the greatest vocal discovery of the year was Gerda Lammers, leading dramatic soprano at Cassel, who was engaged last November to replace the indisposed Christel Goltz as Elektra. She immediately proved herself to be one of the greatest singers of the day, and certainly the finest Elektra since Rose Pauly. With Georgine von Milinkovic as Klytemnestra, Hedwig Müller-Bütow as

Chrysothemis, and the excellent Rudolf Kempe conducting, the performances were a triumph for all concerned.

Kempe was once again in charge of the two *Ring* cycles which were given in a special season on their own in September with a mostly familiar cast (Windgassen, Vinay, Witte, Klein, Hotter, Kraus, Böhme, Dalberg, Ilosvay), but with a magnificent new Brünnhilde in Birgit Nilsson and the Bayreuth Fricka, Milinkovic. Three extra performances, one of *Walküre* and two of *Götterdämmerung* brought us Sylvia Fisher's *Walküre* Brünnhilde, Svanholm's and Aldenhoff's Siegfried, and Gottlob Frick's wonderful Hagen.

Glyndebourne's 1958 season introduced only one work to the repertory, Wolf-Ferrari's one-act *Il Segreto di Susanna* which was given as a curtain-raiser to *Ariadne auf Naxos*. There were several new artists though, including the young Spanish mezzo-soprano Teresa Berganza as Cherubino, the Italian soprano Ilva Ligabue as Alice Ford, another Spanish soprano, Consuelo Rubio as Alceste, the French baritone Robert Massard as the High Priest in *Alceste*, the American mezzo Gloria Lane as Baba the Turk in *The Rake's Progress*, the Polish soprano Helga Pilarczyck as the Composer in *Ariadne*, and the German conductor Hans Schmidt-Isserstedt who made a very great impression in his direction of *Figaro*. Among the old hands Geraint Evans was again a fine Falstaff—he also sang Figaro, Richard Lewis was Tom Rakewell, Admetus and Bacchus, and Oralia Dominguez Mistress Quickly. The enchanting Graziella Sciutti returned after too long an absence to sing Nanetta and Susanna; and of course Gui and Pritchard were, as always, the welcome conductors Once again the overall genius and influence of Carl Ebert was manifest throughout the festival.

Visiting companies to Great Britain this last year were few in number. If the season can be reckoned as having begun last September at Edinburgh, then undoubtedly the visit of the Piccola Scala Company from Milan, must be counted as the most important of the lot, with the Callas *Sonnambula* vying with Giorgio Strehler's finished production of *Il Matrimonio Segreto* (Sciutti, Ratti, Carturan, Alva, Badioli, Calabrese, conductor Sanzogno) for first place in the public's favour. Nearly as much interest was displayed by the public in *L'Elisir d'Amore* (Carteri and Scotto, Di Stefano and Monti, Fioravanti, Corena; conductor Gavazzeni) and Rossini's seldom-played *Il Turco in Italia*.

To the Theatre Royal, Drury Lane in London, in February and March came an Italian Company organised by Sandor Gorlinsky with a repertory of eight operas: *Guglielmo Tell* (the first performance in London since before the First War), *L'Elisir d'Amore*, *La Forza del Destino*, *Andrea Chénier* (the first for more than twenty-five years), *Turandot*, *L'Amico Fritz*, and *I Pescatori di Perle*—otherwise *Les Pêcheurs de*

Perles. The company included some excellent new singers, some not so good, and several old friends, like the conductors Tullio Serafin and Vincenzo Bellezza, the tenor Tagliavini, the mezzo Ebe Stignani, the charming young Renata Scotto, and the powerful Giangiacomo Guelfi. The loud-voiced Mario Filippeschi was heard as Manrico and Arnold, and the stylist Alvinio Misciano as Fritz. The season did not live up to the promise of the similar one organised by Mr. Gorlinsky in the early summer of 1957 at the Stoll Theatre.

There was also an interesting short season in July (1958) by the Opera de Camera of Buenos Aires, who gave two double bills at Sadler's Wells, which comprised Telemann's *Pimpinone* and Hindemith's *Hin und Zuruck*, and Galuppi's *Il Filosofo di Campagna* and Cimarosa's *Il Maestro di Capella*.

Also at Sadler's Wells there was another season by the New Opera Company. Besides repeating their last summer's success, *A Tale of Two Cities* by Arthur Benjamin, they gave the English première of Egk's *Der Revisor* and Menotti's *The Unicorn, The Gorgon and The Manticore*, and revived Vaughan Williams's *Sir John in Love*. Attendances were poor, and the season ended with a deficit of some £5,000.

Schools, colleges, amateur and semi-professional societies once again enlivened the year by producing works that were well off the beaten track such as *La Juive, La Gazza Ladra, The School for Wives, Carmina Burana, Fedora, Der Corregidor, Ernani* and *Rienzi*. But perhaps the most interesting of the school activities were the Lotte Lehmann Master Classes, sponsored by the admirable Opera School and its Principals Joan Cross and Anne Wood. Besides bringing back to London a revered and loved opera singer, these classes demonstrated the serious shortage that exists in this country of teachers really versed in the tradition of European opera giving. And that of course is, with a shortage of money, the key to our whole operatic future.

THE OPERA HOUSES OF THE WORLD

Their Artists and Repertoires, 1957-8

Listing works performed and artists appearing. Works written to English, Flemish, French, German, Italian, Portuguese and Spanish texts are given their original titles, but all other works are given English titles. The name of the composer is only given in the case of a new or unfamiliar opera, and only then the *first time* it is listed. It will be noticed that the names of certain singers appear with more than one company; in the case of Germany certain artists have joint contracts with more than one house; and most artists appear at the five or six leading theatres during the course of the season. The names of the conductors are listed alphabetically, but in the German theatres the first two conductors named are the Generalmusikdirektor and the first Kapellmeister; where there is no Generalmusikdirektor the first name is that of the first Kapellmeister.
*Indicates that the opera was a new production during the season.

AUSTRIA

GRAZ. STADTTHEATER
Director: André Diehl
REPERTORY

Aida, Bettelstudent, Boris Godunov*, Campiello (Wolf-Ferrari), Don Giovanni, Entführung aus dem Serail*, Fidelio, Fledermaus, Forza del Destino, Gianni Schicchi*, Hänsel und Gretel*, Madama Butterfly, Matrimonio Segreto, Mona Lisa (Schillings), Notre Dame (Schmidt), Nozze di Figaro, Orfeo*, Pagliacci*, Palestrina, Parsifal, Rigoletto, Salome, Tiefland*, Tosca, Trovatore, Turandot*, Undine*, Zar und Zimmermann, Zauberflöte.

ARTISTS

Dorit Hanak, Dagmar Hartl, Gertraud Hopf, Margit Kobeck, Maria Kouba, June Linden, Kerttu Metsälä, Friedl Pöltinger, Eleanor Schneider, Erika Schubert, Waltraud Schwind, Olga Voll.
Robert Charlebois, Wolfgang Etterer, Alexander Fenyves, Paul Graf, Dino Halpern, Stephen Harbach, Hans Helm, Helmut Ibler, Erich Klaus, Hans Krotthammer, Gerhard Soucek, Raymond Wolansky, Wolfram Zimmermann.

CONDUCTORS

Gustav Cerny, Maximilian Kojetinsky, Miltiades Caridis.

KLAGENFURT. STADTTHEATER
Director: Philipp Zeska
REPERTORY

Cenerentola, Faust*, Fledermaus, Fliegende Holländer, Rigoletto, Wildschütz.

ARTISTS

Farah Afiatpour, Betty Kopler, Mi Romboy, Hilde Vadura.
Helmut Conradt, Theo Knapp, Bruno Krebs, Zdenko Richter, Karlheinz Schmidt, Heinrich Schubert, Fred Schulz-Holz.

CONDUCTORS.

Wolfgang Schubert, Karl Horst Wichmann.

GUEST ARTISTS during the season included:
Leonie Rysanek; Walter Berry, Frederick Guthrie, Waldemar Kmentt, Paul Schöffler, Karl Terkal.

LINZ. LANDESTHEATER
Intendant: Fred Schroer
REPERTORY

Abu Hassan*, Barbiere di Siviglia, Beggars' Opera (Britten), Consul, Flut (Blacher), Xerxes (Handel)*, Wildschütz.*

ARTISTS

Fritzi Bauer, Getrud Burgsthaler, Ingrid Flemming, Meta Gallus, Margit Gara, Yvette Matta, Elisabeth Ranic.
Emo Cingl, Paul Conrad, Franz Glawatsch, Claus Hennecke, Erich Klimesch, Alfons Kral Otto Lagler, Albert Messany, Siegfried Schantl.

CONDUCTORS

Siegfried Meik, Leopold Mayer, Michael Hutterstrasser.

SALZBURG. LANDESTHEATER
Director: Fritz Klingenbeck
REPERTORY

Carmen*, Evangelimann, Martha*, Rossini in

Neapel (Paumgartner)*, Traviata*, Widerspenstigen Zähmung* (Goetz), Wiener Blut*, Zarewitsch*, Zauberflöte.

ARTISTS
Eva Comployer, Ditta Diesl, Brigitte Georgi,
Eva Görner-Kosmas, Hanny Löser, Greta Runa,
Joan Volek.
Fritz Bischof, Joschy Eberle, Adi Fischer,
Robert Granzer, Wolfgang Hackenberg, Hubert
Hofmann, Beppo Louca, John Reynolds, Rudolf
Rock, Heinz Rohn.

CONDUCTORS
Gustav Wiese, Josef Nigl, Richard Helliger.

GUEST ARTISTS
Mimi Coertse; Murray Dickie.

VIENNA. STAATSOPER AN DER RING
Director: Herbert von Karajan
REPERTORY
Aida, Ariadne auf Naxos, Bohème, Carmen,
Carmina Burana and Catulli Carmina, Contes
d'Hoffmann, Don Carlos, Don Giovanni, Elektra,
Falstaff, Fidelio, Frau ohne Schatten, Madama
Butterfly*, Manon Lescaut, Mathis der Maler*,
Meistersinger von Nürnberg, Nozze di Figaro*,
Oedipus Rex*, Otello, Palestrina, Rigoletto,
Rosenkavalier, Salome*, Siegfried*, Sturm (Frank
Martin), Tannhäuser, Tosca*, Traviata, Tristan
und Isolde, Turandot, Walküre, Wozzeck,
Zauberflöte.
And in the Redoutensaal: Barbiere di Siviglia,
Cosi fan Tutte, Entführung aus dem Serail, Nozze
di Figaro, Revisor (Egk).

ARTISTS
Rosette Anday, Polly Batic, Ruthilde Boesch,
Dagmar Braun-Hermann, Inge Borkh, Lisa Della
Casa, Mimi Engela-Coertse, Anny Felbermayer,
Dorothea Frass, Christel Goltz, Gertrud Grob-
Prandl, Elisabeth Grümmer, Hilde Güden, Judith
Hellwig, E. Höbarth, Elisabeth Höngen, Sena
Jurinac, Margarita Kenney, Erika Köth, Hilde
Konetzni, Vilma Lipp, Aase Nördmo-Lövberg,
Emmy Loose, Christa Ludwig, Jean Madeira,
Liselotte Maikl, Ira Malaniuk, Carla Martinis,
Georgine von Milinkovic, Marta Mödl, Birgit
Nilsson, Maria Reining, Traute Richter, Hildegard
Rössel-Majdan, Marta Rohs, Anneliese Rothen-
berger, Leonie Rysanek-Grossmann, Lotte
Rysanek, Gerda Scheyrer, Irmgard Seefried, Berta
Seidl, Margarete Sjöstedt, Elisabeth Sobota, Teresa
Stich-Randall, Rita Streich, Herta Töpper, Ljuba
Welitsch, Lore Wissmann, Hilde Zadek.
Herbert Alsen, Theo Baylé, Walter Berry, Franz
Bierbach, Kurt Böhme, Hans Braun, Oskar
Czerwenka, Anton Dermota, Murray Dickie,
Karl Dönch, Otto Edelmann, Kurt Equiluz,
Eugenio Fernandi, Karl Friedrich, Gottlob Frick,
Jao Gibin, Josef Gostic, Josef Greindl, Frederick
Guthrie, Hans Hopf, Hans Hotter, Edmond
Hurshell, August Jaresch, Alfred Jerger, Karl
Kamann, Peter Klein, Waldemar Kmentt, Endre
Koreh, Erich Kunz, Karl Liebl, George London,
Max Lorenz, Rudolf Lustig, Duncan MacLeod,
Viktor Madin, Erich Majkut, Josef Metternich,
Hugo Meyer-Welfing, Alfred Muzzarelli, Gustav
Neidlinger, Tomislav Neralic, Ljubomir
Pantscheff, Julius Patzak, Alfred Poell, Harald
Pröglhöf, Helge Roswaenge, Marjan Rus, Rudolf
Schock, Ottakar Schöfer, Paul Schöffler, Hans
Schweiger, Friedrich Sperlbauer, Gerhard Stolze,
Ludwig Suthaus, Laszlo Szemere, Karl Terkal, Eugen
Tobin, Hermann Uhde, Adolf Vogel, Eberhard
Wächter, Karl Weber, Ludwig Weber, William
Wernigk, Wolfgang Windgassen, Giuseppe Zam-
pieri, Ivo Zidek, Wolfgang Zimmer.

CONDUCTORS
Herbert von Karajan, Karl Böhm, Michael
Gielen, Heinrich Hollreiser, Berislav Klobucar,
Josef Krips, Rudolf Moralt.

GUEST ARTISTS during the season included:
Farah Afiatpour, Nassja Berowska-Heger, Lillian
Benningsen, Anna Maria Canali, Fiorenza Cos-
sotto, Gigliola Frazzoni, Dorit Hanak, Grace
Hoffman, Ilse Hollweg, Maria Kinas, Lenora
Lafayette, Colette Lorand, Hanna Ludwig, Elsa
Matheis, Anna Moffo, Leontyne Price, Eli sabeth
Schwarzkopf, Marianne Schech, Renata Scotto,
Giulietta Simionato, Arlene Slater-Stone, Renata
Tebaldi, Claire Watson, Helene Werth.
Luigi Alva, Philip Curzon, Guiseppe di Stefano,
Renato Ercolani, Nicola Filacuridi, Carlo Forti,
Zdenek Gjaurov, Tito Gobbi, Carlos Guichandut,
Walter Kreppel, Gastone Limarelli, Eugenia
Lorenzi, Rolando Panerai, Mario Petri, Aldo
Protti, Gianni Raimondi, Michel Roux, Karl
Schmitt-Watter, Enzo Sordello, Tomaso Spataro,
Richard Tucker, Arnold van Mill, Jon Vickers,
Raymond Wolansky, Nicola Zaccaria.

GUEST CONDUCTORS
Glauco Curiel, Gianandrea Gavazzeni, Joseph
Keilberth, Rudolf Kempe, Dimitri Mitropoulos,
Georg Szell, Antonino Votto.

VIENNA. STAATSOPER IN DER VOLKSOPER
Intendant: Franz Solmhofer

REPERTORY
Bettelstudent, Dona Francisquita*, Evangelimann, Fledermaus, Graf von Luxemburg, Hänsel und Gretel, Land des Lächelns, Martha*, Nabucco*, Nacht in Venedig, Orphée aux Enfers*, Rigoletto, Vizeadmiral*, Vogelhändler, Walzertraum, Wiener Blut, Zar und Zimmermann, Zigeunerbaron.

ARTISTS
Sonja Draksler, Hedy Fassler, Erika Feichtinger, Emmy Funk, Henny Herze-Pernerstorfer, Maria Kowa, Else Liebesberg, Sonja Mottl, Esther Rethy, Elisabeth Sobota, Christiane Sorell.

Theo Baylé, Rudolf Christ, Gale Doss, Norbert Ecker, Eduard Fritsch, Per Grunden, Walter Höfermayer, August Jaresch, Fritz Krenn, Erich Kuchar, Fred Liewehr, Klaus Löwitsch, Friedrich Nidetsky, Erwin Nowaro, Gottfried Nowak, Alois Pernerstorfer, Alexander Pichler, Kurt Preger, Herbert Prikopa, Marjan Rus, Ottokar Schöfer, Emil Siegert, Hans Strohbauer, Karl Weber, Wolfgang Zimmer.

CONDUCTORS
Franz Bauer-Theussl, Anton Paulik, Wilhelm Schönherr, Paul Walter.

GUEST ARTISTS during the season included many members of the Staatsoper ensemble and:
Valerie Bak, Demmer, Libuse Domanínská, Herta Freund, Christine Görner, Hilde Koch, Küppers, Adèle Leigh, Elsa Matheis, Dagmar Rosikova, Eleanor Schneider.

Peter Harrower, Zdenek Kroupa, Helmut Meinokat, Peter Minich, Eric Sundquist, Raymond Wolansky.

Argeo Quadri.

BELGIUM
BRUSSELS. THEATRE ROYAL DE LA MONNAIE
Director: Joseph Rogatschewsky

REPERTORY
Amelia al Ballo, Barbiere di Siviglia, Beggars' Opera (Britten)*, Bohème, Boris Godunov, Carmen, Carmina Burana*, Cavalleria Rusticana, Céphale et Procris, Cheminau (Leroux), Don Carlos, Don Juan de Manara (Tomasi), Education Manquée (Chabrier), Faust*, Fledermaus, Iphigénie en Tauride, Kluge*, Macbeth (Bloch)*, Madama Butterfly, Manon, Pagliacci, Pêcheurs de Perles, Pelléas et Mélisande, Samson et Dalila, Rigoletto,

Roi d'Ys, Telephone, Thyl de Flandre (Chailley)* (World Première), Tosca, Traviata, Walküre, Werther.

ARTISTS
Michele Auber, Micheline Cortois, Gilberte Danlée, Lui-Li Fei, Diane Lange, Helene Masset, Mlle. Pascal, Maryse Patris, Ysel Poliart, Jacqueline Vallière, Huberte Vecray.

Francis Andrien, Jacques Bouet, Bjarne Buntz, Gilbert Dubuc, Pierre Fischer, Guy Fouché, Germain Ghislain, Robert Gouttebroze, Huc-Santana, Jean Laffont, Robert Lilty, René Lits, Jean Marcor, Monsieur Paul, Monsieur Pestiaux, Jacques Piergyl, Michel Trempont, Pol Trempont, Robert Vernay, Tadeuz Wierzbicki.

CONDUCTORS
Maurice Bastin, Frits Celis, René Defossez, Robert Wagner.

GUEST ARTISTS during the season included:
Victoria de los Angeles, Simone Couderc.
The 1957 Bayreuth Company for *Walküre*.

GHENT. KONINKLIJKE OPERA
Director: Constant Meillander

REPERTORY
Aida, Andrea Chénier, Ballo in Maschera, Barbiere di Siviglia, Bohème, Bride of the Sea (Blockx), Carmen, Cavalleria Rusticana, Consul, Don Carlos*, Elisir d'Amore, Faust, Favorita, Fidelio, Fledermaus, Forza del Destino*, Jongleur de Notre Dame, Lucia di Lammermoor, Madama Butterfly, Manon, Mignon, Noces de Jeannette, Pagliacci, Parsifal, Rigoletto, Tiefland*, Tosca, Traviata, Trovatore, Turandot*, Walküre*.

ARTISTS
Geri Bruninx, Tina Claus, Mia Clein, Mimi Daemars, Yola de Gruyter, Marie Liétard, Dina Norman, Josette Sulmonte, Lucy Tilly, Simonne van Parijs, Renée Varly.

Stany Bert, Lucien Cattin, Jules de Mulder, Francis de Paep, Robert Derville, Felix Giband, Lode Le Moine, Jean Massink, Antonio Nardelli, Richard Plumat, Raymond Rossius, Jan Verbeeck, John Vissers, Roger Willems.

CONDUCTORS
Maurice de Prêter, Maurits Veremans, Luigi Martelli, Jef Nachtergaele.

GUEST ARTISTS during the season included:
Marian Balhant, Mina Bolotine, Gré Brouwenstijn, Rachel Carlay, Gina Carrera, Lucienne Delvaux, Irma de Keukeleire, Gina Elmese, Christiane Gruselle, Jany Will.

Giorgio Algorta, Doro Antonioli, Gino Bechi, Francois de Lathouwer, Georges Goda, Ugo Novelli, Luigi Pontiggia, Carlo Tagliabue, Tony Vanderheyden, Antonio Zola.

CZECHOSLOVAKIA
BRATISLAVA. NÁRODNÉ DIVADLO
REPERTORY
Bartered Bride, Bohème, Boris Godunov, Carmen, Count Bajazid (Cikker), Dalibor*, Devil and Kate (Dvořák), Don Carlos, Don Giovanni, Eugene Onegin, Faust, Fliegende Holländer, Fra Diavolo, Gelo (Andrašovan)*, Juro Jánošík (Cikker), Krutnava (Katrina) (Suchon), Madama Butterfly, Nozze di Figaro, Otello*, Rigoletto, Rosenkavalier*, Rusalka, Tosca, Traviata.

ARTISTS
Margita Česanyiová, Dita Gabajová, Janka Gabčová, Olga Hanáková, Nina Hazuchová, Anna Hornungová, Zita Hudcová-Fresová, Mária Hubová, Stefania Hulmanová, Tatjana Masariková, Marta Meierová, Anna Prosencová-Hrusovská, Helena Schützová, Mária Slotíková, Božena Suchánková.

Alexander Baránek, Stanislav Benačka, Ján Blaho, Stefan Gabriš, Imrich Gál, Ján Hadraba, František Hájek, Bohuš Hanák, Stefan Hoza, Frano Hvastija, Ferdinand Krčmář, Andrej Kucharský, Juraj Martvoň, Václav Nouzovský, Gustáv Papp, Karol Sekèra, Emil Schütz, František Šubert, Boris Šimanovský, Juraj Wiedermann.

CONDUCTORS
Tibor Frešo, Gerhard Auer, Juraj Schöffer.

BRNO. STÁTÍN DIVADLO
REPERTORY
Aida, Barbiere di Siviglia*, Bartered Bride, Bridegrooms (Fischer)*, Carmen, Cunning Little Vixen*, Dalibor, Devil's Wall, Don Carlos, Don Giovanni, Duenna (Prokofieff)*, Eugene Onegin, Fidelio, Freischütz, From the House of the Dead*, Jacobin, Jan Hus (Horký)*, Jenufa, Kiss, Krútňava, Libuše, Madama Butterfly, Makropulos Affair (Janáček) Mr. Brouček's Excursions (Janáček)*, Nozze di Figaro, Prince Igor, Rigoletto, Rosenkavalier, Rusalka, Samson et Dalila*, Šárka (Janáček)*, Tosca*, Two Widows.

ARTISTS
Tatjana Arsenina, Kveta Belanová, Helena Buroanová, Sonja Červená, Míla Ledererová, Jarmila Lenská, Libuše Lesmanová, Alena Nováková, Jarmila Palivcová, Jindra Pokorná, Marie

Steinerová, Cecilie Strádalová, Jadwiga Wysoczanská.

Vladimír Bauer, Boris Čechovský, Jindřich Doubek, Géza Fišer, Václav Halíř, Eduard Hrubeš, Imrich Jakubek, Jaroslav Jaroš, Antonín Jurečka, Josef Kejř, Jiří Kozderka, Zdeněk Kroupa, František Kunc, Antonín Pelc, František Roesler, Zdeněk Soušek, Vlastimil Šíma, Gustav Talman, Jaroslav Ulrych.

CONDUCTORS
František Jílek, Václav Nosek, Jiří Pinkas.

OLOMOUC. DIVADLO OLDŘICHA STIBORA
REPERTORY
Aida, Bartered Bride, Bohème, Cunning Little Vixen, Golden Cockerel, Kiss, Madama Butterfly, Marta*, Psohlavci (Kovařovic)*, Roméo et Juliette, Rusalka, Salome, Theatre behind the Gate (Martinů)*, Turandot*, Zar und Zimmermann*.

ARTISTS
Jarmila Bošínová, Marie Hůrská, Růžena Jelínková, Hana Konvalinková, Jitka Krupová, Milada Marková, Božena Ministrová, Vlastimila Ployharová, Božena Stoegrová.

František Bartůněk, Josef Hladík, Otto Kubín, Vladimír Ott, Karel Petr, Jan Pleticha, Jaroslav Sobota, Vladimír Stropnický, František Šifta, Josef Šulista, Alois Tesař, Konrád Tuček, Josef Vogl.

CONDUCTORS
Iša Krejčí, František Preisler, Adolf Vozka.

OSTRAVA. STÁTÍN DIVADLO
REPERTORY
Bartered Bride, Bohème, Brandenburgs in Bohemia, Carmen, Cunning Little Vixen, Dalibor, Decembrists*, Devil's Wall, Ero the Joker, Faust, Fidelio, Fliegende Holländer, Freischütz*, Jenufa*, Kiss, Krútňava, Madama Butterfly, Queen of Spades, Rigoletto, Rusalka, Secret*, Šárka, Traviata*, Zar und Zimmermann*.

ARTISTS
Marie Burešová, Zdeňka Diváková, Vèra Heroldová, Bohumila Jechová, Ludmila Komancová, Vèra Nováková, Dagmar Průšová, Alice Spohrová, Milada Šafránková, Bronislava Taufrová, Helena Zemanová, Eva Zikmundová.

Jan Hlavsa, Jiří Hèrold, František Janda, Dalibor Jedlička, Rudolf Jusa, Rudolf Kasl, Jaroslav Kachel, Čenek Mlčak, Miloslav Nekvasil, Richard

Novák, Jiří Pavlíček, Lubomír Procházka, Karel Průša, Radoslav Svozil, Jiří Wooth, Slavomír Zerdzicki.

CONDUCTORS
Josef Vincourek, Mirko Hanák, Josef Kuchinka, Josef Staněk.

PLZEŇ (PILSEN). DIVADLO J. K. TYLA
REPERTORY
Aida*, Ballo in Maschera, Bartered Bride, Bohème, Carmen*, Dalibor, Devil and Kate*, Faust, Flames (Hanuš), Gambler (Prokofiev)*, Gianni Schicchi, Jacobin, Jenufa, Katya Kabanova*, Kiss, Libuše*, Lohengrin, Malířský nápad (Artist's whim) (Zich), Nozze di Figaro, Queen of Spades, Rusalka, Secret, Tosca, Two Widows, Vespri Siciliani.

ARTISTS
Libuše Bláhová, Hana Böhmová, Amalie Glembková, Jitka Jůzková, Valeria Kvapilová, Libuše Neubarthová, Věra Soukupová, Anna Stodolová, Miloslava Šeflová, Blanka Vecková, Věra Vlčková.
Josef Beneš, Jiří Berdych, Oldřich Černoch, Karel Harvánek, Jaroslav Honžik, Josef Hořický, Zdenek Jankovský, Jaroslav Kantor, Karel Křemenák, Jiří Novotný, Oldrich Spisar, Zdeněk Šnaiberg.

CONDUCTORS
Bohumír Liška, Dr. Karel Vasata, Albert Rosen.

PRAGUE. NÁRODNÍ DIVADLO (NATIONAL THEATRE)
REPERTORY
Aida*, Barbiere di Siviglia, Bartered Bride, Boleslav 1st. (Vomáčka)*, Brandenburgs in Bohemia, Bride of Messina (Fibich), Brothers Karamasoff (Jeremiáš)*, Carmen, Cosi fan tutte, Count Bajazid (Cikker)*, Cunning Little Vixen, Dalibor, Devil and Kate, Devil's Wall, Don Giovanni, Dráteník (Škroup), Eugene Onegin, Eva, Faust, Fidelio, From the House of the Dead*, Honza's Kingdom (Ostrčil)*, In the Well (Blodek), Jacobin, Jenufa, Katya Kabanova, Kiss, Krútňava, Libuše, Madama Butterfly, Makropulos Affair, Meistersinger*, Nozze di Figaro, Peasant a Rogue, Prince Igor, Queen of Spades, Rigoletto, Rusalka, Šárka (Fibich), Secret, Tannhäuser, Tsar Saltan*, Two Widows, Zvíkovský rarášek (Imp of Zvikov) (Novák).

ARTISTS
Milada Čadikovičová, Ludmila Červinková, Jaroslava Dobrá, Libuše Domanínská, Miloslava Fidlerová, Ludmila Hanzalíková, Eva Hlobilová, Zdenka Hrnčířová, Štěpánka Jelínková, Milada Jirásková, Sylvie Kodetová, Marta Krásová, Věra Krilová, Marcela Lemariová, Ivana Mixová, Milada Musilová, Marie Ovčačíková, Jarmila Pechová, Štefa Petrová, Marie Podvalová, Jaroslava Procházková, Štěpánka Štěpánová, Milada Šubrtová, Helena Tattermuschová, Marie Tauberová, Drahomíra Tikalová, Vlasta Urbanová, Marie Veselá, Jaroslava Vymazalová.
Rudolf Asmus, Václav Bednář, Karel Berman, Beno Blachut, Josef Celerin, Jaroslav Gleich, Eduard Haken, Lubomír Havlák, Josef Heriban, Jaroslav Horáček, Vladimír Jedenáctík, Rudolf Jedlička, Jiří Joran, Karel Kalaš, Přemysl Kočí, Viktor Kočí, Jan Konstantin, Oldřich Kovář, Josef Křikava, Miloš Linka, Ladislav Mráz, Zdeněk Otava, Jaroslav Rohan, Jan Rožánek, Jiří Schiller, Jaroslav Stříška, Theodor Šrubař, Antonín Švorc, Hanuš Thein, Jaroslav Veverka, Bohumír Vích, Josef Vojta, Rudolf Vonásek, Antonín Votava, Antonín Zlesák, Ivo Žídek.

CONDUCTORS
Jaroslav Vogel, Zdeněk Chalabala, Jaroslav Krombholc, Robert Brock, Zdeněk Folprecht, Bohumil Gregor, Václav Kašlík, Karel Nedbal, František Škvor, Jan Hus Tichý.

FRANCE
BORDEAUX. GRAND THEATRE
Director: Roger Lalande
REPERTORY
Aida, Attaque du Moulin (Bruneau), Bohème, Carmen, Contes d'Hoffmann, Don Carlos*, Don Quichotte, Faust, Guillaume Tell, Hérodiade, Huguenots, Lakmé, Madama Butterfly, Manon, Mireille, Mozart (Guitry) Numance, Pêcheurs de Perles, Rigoletto, Tannhäuser, Tosca, Traviata, Trovatore, Werther, Zauberflöte.

ARTISTS
Isabelle Andreani, J. Barrès, Geori Boué, Jacqueline Brumaire, Christine Cloez, Simone Couderc, Renée Doria, Denise Duval, Franca Duval, F. Eckart, Andrée Esposito, Monique Florence, Andrée Grandjean, Christine Harbell, Suzanne Joyol, Raymonde Lapeyre, Françoise Louvay, Adrienne Miglietti, Janine Panis, Jane Rinella, Huguette Rivière, Denise Scharley, Janette Vivalda.
M. Alicia, J.-L. Bacque, Roger Barsac, Maurice Blondel, Jean Borthayre, Roger Bourdin, Georges Bouvier, Paul Cabanel, Xavier Depraz, Jacques

Doucet, Pierre Fleta, Guy Fouché, François Gatto, Julien Haas, Ch. Hebreard, Henry Legay, Adrien Legros, José Luccioni, Libero de Luca, Raymond Malvasio, Richard Martell, Henri Medus, Ken Neate, J. Pomarez, Jacques Sullivan, Georges Vaillant, Robert Vernay.

CONDUCTORS
Roger Gayral, George Sebastian.

GUEST ARTISTS during the season included: C. Ferrario, Hildegard Hillebrecht, Grace Hoffman, Erika Köth, Adriana Lazzarini.

Hans Beirer, Achille Braschi, Anselmo Colzani, Josef Greindl, Ernst Häfliger, Heinz Imdahl, Benno Kusche, Arnold Van Mill, Antonio Zerbini. Leopold Ludwig, Peter Maag.

MULHOUSE. THEATRE MUNICIPAL
Administrator: Louis Schneider

REPERTORY
Ballo in Maschera, Consul, Faust, Fragonard (Pierné), Hulla (Marcel Samuel-Rousseau)*, Pelléas et Mélisande, Queen of Spades, Samson et Dalila, Thaïs, Tristan und Isolde.

ARTISTS
Monique Daphnis, Jacqueline Delbray, Lucienne Delvaux, Andrée Esposito, Monique Florence, Liliane Francou, Geneviève Gallo, Odette Lhost, Jacqueline Lussas, Annette Martineau, Monique de Pondeau, Emilienne Ranson, Odette Renaudin.

Franck Almero, Bernard Alvi, Etienne Bernard, Gerard Boireau, Dominique Devercors, André Dran, François Etienne, René Fabre, Marc Gazal, Roger Guerdy, Henri Gui, Marcel Harter, Claude Hector, Marcel Huylbrock, Roland Leonar, Denis Poujol, Jacques Sullivan, René Terrasson, Maurice Vaubrey, Jean Vilary, Zbyslaw Wozniak.

CONDUCTOR
Paul Jamin.

PARIS. THEATRE NATIONAL DE L'OPERA
Director: M. E. Bondeville

REPERTORY
Aida, Damnation de Faust, Dialogues des Carmélites*, Don Giovanni, Faust, Fliegende Holländer, Heure Espagnole, Indes Galantes, Jeanne au Bûcher, Martyre de Saint Sebastien, Otello, Rigoletto, Roméo et Juliette, Rosenkavalier, Samson et Dalila, Siegfried, Tannhäuser, Traviata, Tristan und Isolde, Walküre, Zauberflöte.

PARIS. THEATRE NATIONAL DE L'OPERA-COMIQUE
Director: François Agostini

REPERTORY
Barbiere di Siviglia*, Bohème, Carmen, Cavalleria Rusticana, Ciboulette, Contes d'Hoffmann, Cosí fan tutte, Eugene Onegin, Lakmé, Louise, Madama Butterfly, Manon, Mignon, Mireille, Nozze di Figaro, Pagliacci, Pêcheurs de Perles*, Poule Noire (Rosenthal) Tosca, Werther.

ARTISTS
Most artists are under joint contract for both the Paris Opera Houses, which are administered by Georges Hirsch under the Réunion des Théâtres Lyriques Nationaux, and are therefore listed together:
Claude Allard, Isabelle Andréani, Martha Angelici, Liliane Berton, Jacqueline Brumaire, Jacqueline Broudeur, Bonny-Pellieux, Denise Boursin, Georgette Camart, Christiane Castelli, Jacqueline Cauchard, Ines Chabal, Paulette Chalanda, Simone Clery, Jeannine Collard, Régine Crespin, Lyne Cumia, Susanne Darbans, Gisèle Desmoutiers, Renée Doria, Jacqueline Dufranne, Denise Duval, Janine Fourrier, Christiane Gayraud, Rita Gorr, Andrèa Guiot, Elise Kahn, Jeanne Lefève, Susanne Lefort, Jacqueline Lucazeau, Alyette Melvat, Janine Micheau, Solange Michel, Berthe Monmart, Léna Pastor, De Pennafort, Nadine Renaux, Jane Rhodes, Odette Ricquier, Mado Robin, Suzanne Sarroca, Jeanne Segala, Geneviève Serrés, Denise Scharley, Georgette Spanellys, Rosa Van Herck.

Raymond Amande, Louis Arnoult, René Bianco, Ernest Blanc, Jean Borthayre, Gustave Botiaux, Gérard Chapuis, Charles-Paul, Edmond Chastenet, Marcel Clavère, Xavier Depraz, Henri Doublier, José Fagianelli, Paul Finel, Michel Forel, Charles Fronval, Pierre Froumenty, Roger Gardes, Frederic Gibert, Julien Giovanetti, Jean Giraudeau, Raoul Gourgues, Huc-Santana, Edouard Kriff, Jean-Pierre Laffage, Robert Lamander, Albert Lance, José Luccioni, Jacques Mars, Robert Massard, Max-Conti, Henri Medus, Ken Neate, Louis Noguera, Georges Noré, Dimitar Ouzounov, André Pactat, André Philippe, Tony Poncet, Louis Rialland, Raphael Romagnoni, Camille Rouquetty, Michel Roux, Pierre Savignol, Gérard Serkoyan, Georges Vaillant, Alain Vanzo, René Verdière.

CONDUCTORS
René Blot, Pierre Dervaux, Louis Fourestier, George Sebastian, Albert Wolff.

GUEST ARTISTS during the season included: Paula Brivkalne, Astrid Varnay; Hans Beirer, Alfons Herwig, Josef Greindl, Paul Kuen, Alois Pernerstorfer, Sigurd Björling, Otto Wiener, Otto von Rohr. Hans Knappertsbusch.

TOULOUSE. THEATRE DU CAPITOLE
General Director: Louis Izar
REPERTORY

Amahl*, Boris Godounov, Carmen, Education Manquée*, Falstaff, Fedora, Halka, Heure Espagnole, Manon Lescaut, Medium*, Mozart (Hahn)*, Nabucco, Orfeo, Platée*, Poule Noire (Rosenthal)*, Roi David (Honegger)*, and a complete Ring Cycle by artists of Bayreuth, Berlin and Vienna.

ARTISTS

Vivette Barthelemy, Geori Boué, Jacqueline Brumaire, Inès Chabal, Simone Couderc, Denise Duval, Lina Gerry, Rita Gorr, Michèle Jensous, Nicole Jolivalt, Raymonde Lapeyre, Monique Linval, Josette Menchon, Claudia Noves, Marysé Patris, Clara Petrella, Marie Powers, Huguette Rivière Consuelo Rubio, Suzanne Sarroca, Annick Simon, Janette Vivalda, Paulette Viel.

Carlo Bergonzi, Pierre Blanc, Henry Bonnoure, Serge Breonce, Paul Cabanel, Xavier Depraz, Jacques Doucet, Frank Eckart, Lionel Elsen, Gérald Etienne, Paul Finel, Lorenzo Gaetani, Robert Geay, Jean Giraudeau, Jean Gray, Julien Haas, Roger Hieronimus, Jacques Jansen, Henri Legay, Richard Martell, Marcel Merkes, Bernard Rety, Michel Roux, Gerard Souzay, Jacques Sullivan, Jean Tezenas, Arnold van Mill.

CONDUCTORS

Robert Herbay, Paul Ethuin.

GERMANY

AACHEN-STADTTHEATER
Generalintendant: Paul Mundorf
REPERTORY

Ballo in Maschera*, Don Carlos, Don Pasquale, Eugene Onegin*, Hänsel und Gretel*, Meistersinger von Nürnberg*, Si j'etais roi, Tosca*, Waffenschmied*, Zauberflöte.

ARTISTS

Carla Balzer, Franzi Berger, Elisabeth Bjurquist, Sylvia Carlisle, Rommy Lennartz, Jutta Meyfarth, Margit Oexle, Anna Palo, Barbara Pfitzenreiter, Gabriele Treskow, Jutta Vosgerau.

Marion Alch, Martin Elsholz, Kurt Essich, Winand Esser, Kurt Joussen, Ado Kemper, Rudolf Knoll, Carl Kronenberg, Konrad Kuska, Rudolf Lustig, Walter Maurer, Walter Schürmann, Hansjoachim Worringen.

CONDUCTORS

Wolfgang Sawallisch, Wilhelm Pitz, Johannes Graichen, Wilhelm Sautter, Alfred Walter.

AUGSBURG. STADTTHEATER
Generalintendant: Hans Meissner
REPERTORY

Ariadne auf Naxos, Bohème, Brücke von San Luis Rey (Reutter)*, Carmen, Don Giovanni*, Fidelio*, Idomeneo, Irische Legende, Lustigen Weiber von Windsor*, Martha, Meistersinger von Nürnburg, Nozze di Figaro, Prigioniero*, Queen of Spades*, Revisor*, Tannhäuser, Tosca*, Walküre*, Zar und Zimmermann.

ARTISTS

Renata Fack, Friederike Kirchweger, Beatrix Laqua, Marion Lippert, Elizabeth Löw-Szöky, Waltraud Möller, Hilde Nicoll, Gunnel Ohlson, Aennelie Schwarz-Baumbach, Leopoldine Sunko Hildegard Walter, Norma Willmann.

Hugh Beresford, Svetozar Drakulic, Dr. Hans Ducrue, John Robert Dunlap, Helmut Graml, Theo Herrmann, Karl Hundertmark, Anton John, Hans Kagel, Willy Krings, Willy Kubesch, Walter Mauckner, Günther Morbach, Jerney Plahuta, Gerhard Schott.

CONDUCTORS

Anton Mooser, Christoph Stepp, Max Hahn, Heinrich Hirsch, Klaus Pawasser.

GUEST ARTISTS

Ursula Jurisch, Anna Fiege, Hildegard Jonas, Randolf Symonette, Dolf Zeller.

BERLIN. DEUTSCHE STAATSOPER
Intendant: Max Burghardt
REPERTORY

Aida, Arabella, Betrothal in a Cloister (Prokofiev)*, Cavalleria Rusticana, Così fan tutte, Don Giovanni, Elektra*, Entführung aus dem Serail, Eugene Onegin, Fidelio, Forza del Destino*, Frau ohne Schatten, Götterdämmerung, Günstling (Wagner-Régény) Halka, Hexe von Passau (Gerster), Incoronazione di Poppea (Monteverdi), Iphigénie en Aulide, Jenufa, Krutnava (Katrena) (Suchow)*, Lohengrin*, Madama Butterfly*

Meistersinger, Pagliacci, Prince Igor, Revisor*, Rheingold, Siegfried, Tosca, Traviata, Tristan, Trovatore, Walküre, Wozzeck.

ARTISTS

Elisabeth Aldor, Gisela Behn, Maria Corelli, Clara Ebers, Sigrid Ekkehard, Marianne Fischer, Brunnhild Friedland, Gertrud Grob-Prandl, Esther Hilbert, Ruth Keplinger, Irmgard Klein, Margarete Klose, Christa Lehnert, Liselotte Losch, Inge-Maria Lossau, Hildegard Lüdtke, Anneliese Müller, Hedwig Müller-Bütow, Adelheid Müller-Hess, Melitta Muszely, Sylvia Pawlik, Gertraud Prenzlow, Margot Risa, Erna Roscher, Christa Schrödter, Gertrud Stilo, Ilona Weber-Papenthin, Jutta Vulpius, Ingeborg Wenglor.

Martin Abendroth, Theo Adam, Pieter van den Berg, Karl-Heinz Berndt, Heinz Braun, Hans Dunker, Gerhard Frei, Eugen Fuchs, Rudolf Gonszar, Walter Grossmann, Günter Gützlaff, Karl-Olof Johansson, Hilbert Kahl, Julius Katona, Robert Lauhöfer, Helmut Meinokat, Gerhard Niese, Heinrich Pflanzl, Kurt Rehm, Walter Stoll, Gerhard Stolze, Manfred Schmidt, Günther Treptow, Gerhard Unger, Kay Willumsen, Erich Witte, Hans-Heinz Wunderlich.

CONDUCTORS

Franz Konwitschny, Lovro von Matacic; Hans Löwlein, Horst Stein.

GUEST ARTISTS during the season included:
Paula Baumann, Helene Braun, Alicja Dankowska, Diana Eustrati, Hedwig Fichtmüller, Franziska Friedländer, Christel Goltz, Lütowa, Frl. Nerius, Poliwonova, Maria Tauberova, Ria Pohl-Urban.

Frans Andersson, Heinz Braun, Ferdinand Bürgmann, Sebastian Feiersinger, Siegfried Fischer, Fokin, Karl-Ludwig Gottshall, Ernst Grüber, Ludwig Hofmann, Hiolski, Dalibor Jedlicka, Kasak, Marion Kouba, Kurt Liebl, Pavel Lissitsian, Hans Löbl, Max Lorenz, Hans-Joachim Lukat, Werner Müller, Herald Neukirch, Paprocki Popoff, Christian Pötzsch, Martin Ritzman, Herbert Rössler, Helge Roswaenge, Karl Schmitt-Walter, Kurt Seipt, Hans-Joachim Sonntag, Josef Traxel, Klaus Wendt, Erich Zimmermann.

Arthur Apelt, Oscar Danon, Werner Egk, Zdzislaw Gorzynski, Robert Heger, Hans Knappertsbasch, Vilmos Komor, Leonidas Zoras.

BERLIN. KOMISCHE OPER.
Intendant: Walter Felsenstein

REPERTORY

Albert Herring*, Bartered Bride, Contes

d'Hoffmann*, Cunning Little Vixen, Devil and Kate, Donne Curiose, Entführung aus dem Serail, Manon Lescaut, Tiefland, Zar und Zimmermann, Zauberflöte.

ARTISTS

Irmgard Armgart, Irmgard Arnold, Eva-Maria Baum, Lydia Dertil, Ena Timm-Döhle, Marianne Dorka-Knör, Sigrid Ekkehard, Camilla Kallab, Melitta Muszely, Gertraud Prenzlow, Ursula Richter, Anny Schemm, Hanna Schmoock, Elvira Scholz, Sonja Schöner, Clementine von Shuch, Jutta Vulpius, Emilie Walter-Sacks, Brunhilde Wenzel.

Frans Andersson, Rudolf Asmus, Georg Baumgartner, Wolf von Beneckendorff, Erich Blasberg, Josef Burgwinkel, Wilhelm-Walther Dicks, Werner Enders, Hermin Esser, Ferry Grüber, Karl-Friedrich Hölzke, Manfred Jungwirth, Hilbert Kahl, Richard Kogel, Hellmuth Kreuzer, Uwe Kreyssig, Werner Missner, Kurt Mülhardt, Gerhard Niese, Hans Nocker, Karl Paul, Ralph Peters, Hans Reinmar, Martin Ritzmann, Herbert Rössler, Martin Rosen, Sigmund Roth, Willy Sahler, Arwed Sandner, Erwin Wohlfahrt.

CONDUCTORS

Vaclav Neumann, Robert Hanell, Harold Byrns, Herbert Guthan, Karl-Fritz Voigtmann, Vilmos Knör.

GUEST ARTISTS during the season (besides artists from the Deutsche Staatsoper) included:
Brigette Kretschmer, Dora Zschille, Siegfried Rudolf Frese, Krassmann.

BERLIN. STÄDTISCHE OPER
Intendant: Carl Ebert

REPERTORY

Amahl and The Night Visitors, Ballo in Maschera, Bohème, Bürgschaft (Weill) (World Première of New Edition)*, Capriccio, Carmen*, Contes d'Hoffmann, Comte Ory, Cosi fan Tutte, Don Carlos, Don Pasquale, Falstaff*, Fliegende Holländer, Freischütz, Götterdämmerung, Idomeneo, Iphigénie en Tauride*, Jenufa, Katya Kabanova, König Hirsch (Henze), Meistersinger von Nürnberg, Nabucco, Nozze di Figaro, Oberon, Otello, Parsifal, Rape of Lucretia*, Rheingold, Rigoletto, Salome, Siegfried, Tannhäuser, Tosca, Tristan und Isolde, Walküre, Zar und Zimmermann, Zauberflöte.

ARTISTS

Sari Barabas, Irma Beilke, Irene Dalis, Ingeborg Exner, Elisabeth Grümmer, Helga Hildebrand, Nora Jungwirt, Hedi Klug, Erika Köth, Heidi

Krall, Gloria Lane, Renate Laude, Vera Little, Alice Oelke, Lisa Otto, Helga Pilarczyk, Nada Puttar, Leonie Rysanek, Ursula Schirrmacher, Marlies Siemeling, Sieglinde Wagner, Helene Werth, Hilde Zadek.

Theo Altmeyer, Hans Beirer, Herbert Brauer, Leopold Clam, Marcel Cordes, Dietrich Fischer-Dieskau, William Forney, Walter Geisler, Josef Greindl, Ernst Haefliger, Claude Heater, Alfons Herwig, Fritz Hoppe, John van Kesteren, Robert Koffmane, Karl Kohn, Sandor Konya, Helmut Krebs, Ernst Krukowski, Roland-Dietrich Kunz, Wilhelm Lang, Anton Metternich, Tomislav Neralic, Hanns Heinz Nissen, Hanns Pick, Hermann Prey, Peter Roth-Ehrang, Carl-Friedrich Schubert, Ludwig Suthaus, Martin Vantin, Lawrence Winters, Oswald Zowislok.

CONDUCTORS
Artur Rother, Richard Kraus, Wolfgang Martin, Hans Lenzer.

GUEST ARTISTS during the season included:
Ingrid Bjoner, Inge Borkh, Siw Ericsdotter, Madlon Harder, Hildegard Hillebrecht, Lore Hoffmann, Gertrude Hutter, Gladys Kuchta, Colette Lorand, Ira Malaniuk, Carla Martinis, Martha Mödl, Hedwig Müller-Bütow, Marianne Schech, Ria Pohl-Urban, Gisela Vivarelli, Walburga Wegner, Herta Wilfert.

Bernd Aldenhoff, Carlos Alexander, Lorenzo Alvary, Lothar Brüning, Anton de Ridder, Gottfried Fehr, Sebastian Feiersinger, Ernst Gutstein, Hans Hopf, Heinz Imdahl, Alfred Köhl, Herold Kraus, Walter Kreppel, Benno Kusche, Fritz Lehnert, Karl Liebl, Peter Markwort, Bernhard Minetti, Herbert Schachtschneider, Erich Winkelmann, Theo Zilliken, Erich Zimmermann; Alberto Erede, Jascha Horenstein, Walter Kämpfel, Rudolf Kempe, Berislav Klobucar, Märzendorfer, Peter Maag, Otto Matzerath, Heinz Günther Wallberg, Silvio Varviso.

BONN. THEATER DER STADT
Intendant: Karl Pempelfort

REPERTORY
Aida*, Entführung aus dem Serail*, Fledermaus, Freischütz*, Gianni Schicchi*, Orfeo*, Pagliacci*, Revisor*, Rosenkavalier, Rusalka*, Tristan und Isolde*, Trovatore, Zar und Zimmermann*, Zauberflöte.

ARTISTS
Yvonne Ciannella, Elfriede Pfleger, Tamara Pilossian, Gertrude Schretter, Patricia Hyde Thomas.

Jean Alofs, Fritz Berger, Jakob Engels, Karlheinz Euler, James McCraken, Werner Riepel, Kenneth Stevenson, Heinz Stöver.

CONDUCTORS
Peter Maag, Hans Göhre, Theodor Scheer, Eduard Reger, Heribert Beissel.

BREMEN. THEATER DER FREIEN HANSESTADT
Generalintendant: Albert Lippert

REPERTORY
Bohème, Boris Godunov, Campanello*, Cavalleria Rusticana, Così fan tutte*, Dalibor*, Don Pasquale, Fledermaus, Harmonie der Welt, (Hindemith)*, Lohengrin*, Macbeth*, Pagliacci, Parsifal, Postillon de Longjumeau, Rita* (Donizetti), Salome, Schule der Frauen*, Trovatore, Undine*, Waffenschmied.

ARTISTS
Irmgard Huber, Edith Kertesz, Hanna Kistner, Irmgard Meiners, Lore Paul, Ursula Reichart, Adelheid Schwenke, Liselotte Thomamüller, Erika Wien.

Fritz Bramböck, Caspar Bröcheler, Ernst Ebeling, Fritz Grumann, Heinz Hoppe, Heinz Kahlstorf, Franz Klug, Georg Koch, Gert Mechoff, Hans Paweletz, Paul Pokorny, Phillip Sack, Hugo Sieberg, Alfred Scheibner, Fritz Schlegel, Theodor Schlott.

CONDUCTORS
Heinz Wallberg, Helmut Wuest, Hans Kast, Paul Hindemith (guest).

GUEST ARTISTS
Christa Maria Ziese, Herbert Charlier.

BREMERHAVEN. STADTTHEATER
Intendant: Hans Herbert Pudor

REPERTORY
Boris Godunov*, Gianni Schicchi*, Peter Grimes*, Postillon de Longjumeau, Revisor*, Rigoletto*, Schwarze Peter*, Tristan und Isolde*, Zar und Zimmermann.

ARTISTS
Eva Acker, Irmgard Graustein, Christine Hartwich, Margarete Katz, Erica Pilari, Annelotte Schubert-Behr, Lilli Volkert.

Hans Basseng, Rudolf Bautz, Rudolf Bechtold, Otto Flack, Hans Hassen, Jack Hölzers, Karl Hans Jäger, Fred Kypta, Bert Rohrbach, Axel Rolfshammer, Alfred Rupp-Weygel, Victor Talbot, Walter Vertrit.

CONDUCTORS
Hans Kindler, Hermann Wetzlar, Ulrich Hesse.

GUEST ARTIST
Howard Vandenberg.

BRUNSWICK. STAATSTHEATER
Generalintendant: Hermann Kühn

REPERTORY
Aida*, Bohème, Campiello, Don Carlos, Entführung aus dem Serail*, Forza del Destino*, Freischütz, Lohengrin, Matrimonio Segreto, Rodelinda, Wozzeck*, Zaubergeige*.

ARTISTS
Lore Eckhardt, Herrat Eicker, Wilma Funken, Gertie Kleiber, Gerda Lampe, Edith Menzel, Lise Sorrell, Lisel Sturmfels, Gerda Wismar.
William Blankenship, Jean Cox, Joachim Herzberg, Herbert Heidrich, Max Kerner, Carl Momberg, Hermann Nothnagel, Rolf Polke, Hanns Schaeben, Karl-Heinz Vosgerau.

CONDUCTORS
Arthur Grüber, Heinz Zeebe, Kurt Teichmann.

GUEST ARTISTS
Gladys Kuchta, Birgit Nilsson, Anneliese Rothenberger, Astrid Varnay; Walter Beissner, Herbert Fliether, Gerd Nienstedt, Rudolf Soyka, Rudolf Schock.

CASSEL. STAATSTHEATER
Intendant: Herman Schaffner

REPERTORY
Alceste*, Ariadne auf Naxos*, Bohème, Campanello, Cardillac*, Cavalleria Rusticana*, Daphne, Entführung aus dem Serail, Eugene Onegin*, Medium*, Nozze di Figaro, Pagliacci*, Rigoletto*, Schule der Frauen*, Schwarze Peter (Norbert Schultze)*, Two Widows (Smetana)*.

ARTISTS
Dagmar Behrendt, Erika Brill, Carin Carlsson, Christa Degler, Christa Emde, Inge Fontin, Gladys Kuchta, Gerda Lammers, Lisa Penting, Elfriede Podhajecki, Ellen Pfitzner, Ingrid Steger, Irene Walter.
Hermann Blasig, Heinz Brinks, Josef Ellmauer, Horst Euler, Werner Franz, Günther George, Christian Gollong, Rolf Heide, Egmont Koch, Aage Poulsen, Rudi Schippel, Martin-Matthias Schmidt, Kurt Schüffler, Kurt Söhning, Andre Tessonneau, Horst Wilhelm.

CONDUCTORS
Paul Schmitz, Willy Krauss, Rudolf Ducke, Hans Schaffrath, Erwin Born.

GUEST ARTISTS
Gertie Charlent, Helen Laird; Jean Cox, Karl Heinze Euler, Louis Roney, Hugo Sieberg.

CHEMNITZ (KARL-MARX STADT) STADTISCHE THEATER
Intendant: Paul Herbert Freyer

REPERTORY
Amelia al Ballo, Bohème*, Così fan tutte, Donne Curiose, Fliegende Holländer, Katja Kabanova*, Mazeppa, Si j'etais Roi*, Tabarro, Waffenschmied, Der Widerspenstigen Zähmung, Zauberflöte.

ARTISTS
Elly Doerer, Helga Maria Fiedler, Gisela Geusch, Renate Härtel, Urusual Handrick, Lilo Kirmse, Jolanthe Koziel, Irmgard Kunze-Becker, Eveline Wenzel.
Lothar Burkhardt, Gerhard Eisenmann, Heinz Kraayvanger, Alfred Krohn, Rolf Kühne, Heinz Linke, Ludwig Pasztor, Eckehartd Pohl, Adolf Savelkouls, Hans Schellenberger, Heinrich Zell.

CONDUCTORS
Walter Stoschek, Siegfried Franze, Walter Heymann.

COLOGNE. GROSSES HAUS
General Intendant: Herbert Maisch

REPERTORY
Aida, Barbiere di Siviglia, Bluthochzeit (Fortner), Boris Godunov, Carmen, Contes d'Hoffmann, Così fan tutte, Dialogues des Carmélites, Entführung aus dem Serail, Fidelio, Fliegende Holländer, Italiana in Algeri*, Lustigen Weiber von Windsor*, Nozze di Figaro, Oberon, Orphée aux Enfers*, Parsifal, Rake's Progress, Rodelinda*, Rosenkavalier*, Trovatore, Turandot*, Wildschütz, Zauberflöte.

ARTISTS
Rita Bartos, Irmgard Gerz, Charlotte Hoffmann-Pauels, Emmy Lisken, Sylva Maurick, Irmgard Meinig, Käthe Möller-Siepermann, Helene Petrich, Else Veith, Hildegunt Walther, Walburga Wegner.
Herbert Bartel, Robert Blasius, Ernst Grathwol, August Griebel, Gerhard Gröschel, Martin Häusler, Heiner Horn, Felix Knäpper, Gerhard Nathge, Wilhelm Otto, Russel Roberts, Heinz Seifert, Karl Schiebener, Alexander Schoedler, Albert Weikenmeier.

CONDUCTORS
Otto Ackermann, Wolfgang von der Nahmer, Siegfried Köhler, Tibor Szöke, Heribert Esser.

GUEST ARTISTS during the season included:
Mimi Aarden, Lillian Benningsen, Anne Bol-
linger, Yvonne Ciannella, Martha Deilen, Sigrid
Ekkehard, Siw Ericsdotter, Ingeborg Exner,
Ingeborg Felderer, Elisabeth Grümmer, Hilde
Güden, Inge Helmreich, Ilse Hollweg, Elfriede
Hingst, Grace Hoffman, Hannelore Kuhse,
Ursula Lippmann, Colette Lorand, Doris Lorenz,
Käthe Maas, Veronika Marcant, Ira Malaniuk,
Melitta Muszely, Marcella Reale, Eva Maria
Rogner, Romana Rombach, Gladys Spector,
Liane Synek, Ria Urban, Gisella Vivarelli,
Westhoff, Erika Wien.

Marion Alch, Walther Baldauf, Walter Berry,
Anton Dermota, Johannes Elteste, Hasso Eschert,
Sebastian Feiersinger, Rudolf Francl, Alfred
Höbarth, Richard Holm, Hans Hopf, Heinz
Hoppe, Heinz Imdahl, Karl Kohn, Josef Metter-
nich, Victor Remsey, Arno Schellenberg, Wilhelm
Schirp, Karl Schmitt-Walter, Kurt Schüffler,
David Thaw, Erich Winkelmann.

Josef Rosenstock, Günther Wand.

DARMSTADT. LANDESTHEATER
Intendant: Gustav Rudolf Sellner
REPERTORY
Arabella*, Aufstieg und Fall der Stadt
Mahogany (Weill)*, Bluthochzeit, Gianni
Schicchi*, Orfeo, Tabarro*, Tiefland*, Trova-
tore*, Turn of the Screw*, Zauberflöte.

ARTISTS
Renate Bochow, Margarethe Cornell, Martha
Geister, Leonore Glückmann, Irene Gut, Ursula
Lippmann, Charlotte Raab, Hella Rosenthal,
Dorothea von Stein.

Günther Ambrosius, Ludwig Boder, Otto
Boettcher, James Gettys, Willi Hauer, Alexander
Helfmann, Aribert Kammann, Franz Köth,
Wilhelm Krings, Georg Littasy, George Maran,
Heinz Prybit.

CONDUCTORS
Hans Zanotelli, Richard Kotz (guest), Helmut
Franz.

DESSAU. LANDESTHEATER
Intendant: Willy Bodenstein
REPERTORY
Carmen, Eugene Onegin*, Fliegende Holländer,
Götterdämmerung, Halka*, Lohengrin, Madama
Butterfly, Manon Lescaut*, Meistersinger von
Nürnberg, Muette de Portici, Rheingold, Rienzi,
Rusalka, Siegfried, Si j'etais Roi, Sly (Wolf-
Ferrari), Tannhäuser, Tristan und Isolde,
Trovatore, Walküre, Zauberflöte.

ARTISTS
Erna Bellmann, Anny Dörr, Ina Fassbaender,
Urusla Freudenberg, Magdalena Güntzel, Emmy
Prell, Thea Schmitt-Keune, Käte Senrewald.

Walter Allner, Willy Böhrig, Emil Fritz,
Günther Fröhlich, Matthias Klein, Kurt Reinhardt,
Oscar Schimoneck, Walter Schmidt, Hans Steudel,
Richard Surek, Adalbert Waller, Norbert Wolde-
Kindermann.

CONDUCTORS
Heinz Röttger, Roland Wambeck.

GUEST ARTISTS
Alicja   Dankowska,   Vilma   Fichtmüller,
Katherina Nicolai, Traute Richter; Arthur Bard,
Albin Fechner, Sebastian Feiersinger, Rudolf
Gonszar, Karl-Ludwig Gottschall, Theodor
Horand, Josef Joviczym, Arthur John, Marion
Kouba, Robert Lauhöfer, Karl Liebl, Henryk
Lukaszek, Helmut Schindler, Kay Willumsen;
Zdzislaw Gorzynski, Hans Löwlein.

DETMOLD. LANDESTHEATER
Intendant: Otto Will-Rasing
REPERTORY
Aida*, Barbier von Bagdad*, Bohème, Don
Pasquale, Mathis der Maler*, Matrimonio
Segreto*, Parsifal*, Turandot*.

ARTISTS
Edith Brodersen, Dorothy Fisher, Gisella
Knabbe, Anita Krauss, Helga Merkl, Siglinde
Müller, Edith Ostendorf, Gerda Reerink,
Katharina Walewski, Gerda Wonner.

Ferdinand Erdtmann, Felix Fleckenstein, Pom-
peo Greotti, Paul-Vincent Gunia, Walter Hofer,
Kurt Lucas, Hans Mitsch-Roeder, Helmuth Otto,
Franz Ringler, Helmuth Schickedanz, Leo
Schmidt-Hernals, Gotthardt Schubert, Ludwig
Schwarz.

CONDUCTORS
Paul Sixt, Ernst Waigand, Erich Mewes,
Herbert Finne.

DORTMUND. OPERNHAUS
Intendant: P. Walter Jacob
REPERTORY
Aida*, Barbiere di Siviglia, Bartered Bride*,
Donna Urracca* (Malipiero), Donne Curiose*
(Wolf-Ferrari), Fidelio, Fliegende Holländer*,
Liebesverbot (Wagner), Lohengrin, Meistersinger,
Nana (Gurlitt)* (World Première), Nozze di
Figaro*, Yü Nu (Die Tochter des Bettlerkönigs)

(Riede)* (World Première), Vogelhändler, Zar und Zimmermann.

ARTISTS

Inge Detlefsen, Herta Fischer, Victoria Gassner, Maria Lacorn, Charlotte Mantler, Marta de Marco, Margarete Mühlenbeck, Gerhild Siegel.

Karl Heinz Armaan, Hermann Deist, Rudolf Fiebelkorn, Harry Fleck, Georg M. Furtmair, Ernst Günther, Kunibert Hildebrand, Gerhard Kleinen, Leonhard Päckl, Hektor Plüss, Will Ribbert, Erhard Riemer, Willi Schmidt, Phil Stork, Axel Therfenn.

CONDUCTORS

Rolf Agop, Hellmuth Günter.

GUEST ARTISTS

Ingrid Becker-Schillings, Hedi Klein, Lenora Lafayette, Liselotte Schäfer-Risse; Kurt Dittrich.

DRESDEN. STAATSOPER
Generalintendant: Heinrich Allmeroth

REPERTORY

Aida, Albert Herring, Ariadne auf Naxos, Barbiere di Siviglia, Bartered Bride, Bohème, Carmen, Contes d'Hoffmann, Cosi fan tutte, Daphne*, Don Carlos, Don Giovanni, Donne Curiose*, Entführung aus dem Serail, Fidelio, Fliegende Holländer, Freischütz, Halka*, Im Sturm (Chrennikow), Kluge, Lohengrin*, Love for Three Oranges*, Lucio Silla (Mozart), Madama Butterfly, Meistersinger, Nozze di Figaro, Orfeo, Revisor*, Rheingold*, Rosenkavalier, Salome, Si j'etais Roi, Tiefland, Tristan und Isolde, Trovatore, Walküre.

ARTISTS

Maria Alexander, Hermi Arnbros, Elenore Elstermann, Liselotte Enck, Sieglinde Feise, Brünnhild Friedland, Ruth Glowa-Burkhardt, Siegrid Griessbach, Inger Karén, Ingrid Kielmann, Angela Kolniak, Ruth Lange, Eva-Maria Linke, Ilse Ludwig, Elizabeth Reichelt, Helena Rott, Ingeborg Weiss, Dora Zschille.

Theo Adam, Kurt Böhme, Siegfried Rudolf Frese, Helmut Goldmann, Karl-Ludwig Gottshall, Ernst Gruber, Erich Händel, Karl-Friedrich Hölzke, Gerd Hösel, Manfred Huebner, Hellmuth Kaphahn, Johannes Kemter, Werner Liebing, Hans Löbel, Wolfgang Markgraf, Harald Neukirch, Hans-Georg Nowotny, Karl Paul, Christian Pötsch, Arno Schellenberg, Helmut Schindler, Gerhard Stolz, Ference Sxönyi, Fred Teschlov, Karl Heinz Thomann, Manfred Wolf.

CONDUCTORS

Lovro von Matacic, Wilhelm Schleuning, Rudolf Neuhaus, Engel Epplee, Joachim Freyer, Siegfried Kurz.

GUEST ARTISTS

Jordawna, Edith Kemety, Ruth Kepplinger, Kossena Kirowa, Annelies Kupper, Pillatzke, Marianne Radev, Ingeborg Wenglor, Christa Maria Ziese.

Sebastian Feiersinger, Max Lorenz, Anton Metternich, Kurt Rösinger, Oscar Schiminck, Wolfgang Windgassen.

Prof. Heinz Bongart, Gerhard Lenssen, Kurt Masur, Kurt Striegler, Leonidas Zoras.

DUSSELDORF-DUISBURG
DEUTSCHE OPER AM RHEIN
Generalintendant: Hermann Juch

REPERTORY

Arabella*, Ariadne auf Naxos, Beggars' Opera (Britten), Bernauerin (Orff)*, Carmen*, Don Carlos, Don Pasquale*, Elektra, Falstaff, Fidelio, Fledermaus, Fliegende Holländer*, Karl V (Krenck)* (World Première of new edition), Macbeth*, Makropoulos Affair (Janacek), Meistersinger von Nürnberg*, Nacht in Venedig*, Nozze di Figaro, Parsifal, Räuber (Klebe), Rosenkavalier, Schule der Frauen*, Siegfried, Die Strasse* (Weill), Tosca*, Tristan und Isolde, Trovatore, Vedova Scaltra*, (Wolf-Ferrari), Walküre*, Wildschütz, Zar und Zimmermann, Zauberflöte.

ARTISTS

Valerie Bak, Kitsa Damassioti, Martha Deisen, Vilma Georgiou, Christel Goltz, Hildegard Hillebrecht, Ilse Hollweg, Karen Kadwig, Eva Kaspar, Margarita Kenny, Eta Köhrer, Ingeborg Lasser, Hanna Ludwig, Helen Mané, Elfie Mayerhofer, Waltraud Ossendorf, Ingrid Paller, Anneliese Rothenberger, Sigrid Schmidt, Elisabeth Schwarzenberg, Dorothea Siebert, Ruth Siewert, Astrid Varnay, Hilde Zadek.

Kurt Böhme, Walter Beissner, Willi Brokmeier, Rudolf Christ, Philip Curzon, Karl Diekmann, Karl Dönch, Wilhelm Ernest, Hans Esser, Helmut Fehn, Sebastian Feiersinger, Rudolf Francl, Kurt Gester, Thomas Hemsley, Alfons Holte, Hans Hopf, Heinz Imdahl, Anton Imkamp, Manfred Jungwirth, Ernst Kozub, Herold Kraus, Hugo Kratz, Walter Kreppel, Benno Kusche, Fritz Ollendorff, Josef Prehm, Wilhelm Schäfer, Sanders Schier, Rudolf Schock, Paul Späni, Randolph Symonette, Otto Wiener, Erich Winkelmann.

CONDUCTORS

Alberto Erede, Fritz Zaun, Karl Böhm, Arthur

Toth Laszlo

OPERA AT BUDAPEST

Erich Witte, guest artist
from Berlin, as *Otello*.

Ersi Hazy as *Antonia*,
Georg Radnay as *Dr.
Miracle* in 'Les Contes
d'Hoffmann'.

NEW OPERA AT
THE BOLSHOI THEATRE

Two scenes from Sheba-
lin's 'The Taming of the
Shrew' which had its pre-
mière at the Bolshoi
Theatre during the 1957-8
season.

Bolshoi

Grüber, Friedrich Brenn, Richard Peters, Arnold Quennet, Robert Schaub.

GUEST ARTISTS
Lucie Klüfer, Rosa di Giorgio, Christiana Dalamangas, Franco Inglesias, Otmar Suitner, Hermann Uhde.

ESSEN. BÜHNEN DER STADT
Intendant: Karl Bauer

REPERTORY
Aida, Alceste*, Arabella*, Don Giovanni, Fidelio, Gianni Schicchi, Lohengrin, Manon Lescaut, Pagliacci, Parsifal, Peter Grimes*, Tosca, Waffenschmied, Zauberflöte, Zaubergeige.

ARTISTS
Tilla Briem, Doris Feld, Käthe Graus, Helene Millauer, Hilla Oppel, Hilde Plaschke, Trude Roesler, Gladys Spector, Anni Student, Ruth Tietzel.
Hans-Walter Bertram, Gerd Block, Herbert Fliether, Willi Friedrich, Timo Jacobs, Julius Jüllich, Karl-Heinz Lippe, Wilhelm Lückert, Erwin Röttgen, Walter-Reinhold Schaefer, Herbert Schachtschneider, Heinrich Semmelrath, Günter Treptow, Xaver Waibel, Leonardo Wolovsky, Hugo Zinkler.

CONDUCTORS
Gustav König, Paul Belker, Hans Ehrnsperger, Valentin Huber, Wolfgang Drees.

FRANKFÜRT (am Main). GROSSES HAUS
Intendant: Harry Buckwitz

REPERTORY
Aida, Ariadne auf Naxos, Ballo in Maschera, Barbiere di Siviglia, Bartered Bride, Bohème, Carmen, Columbus (Egk), Contes d'Hoffmann, Così fan tutte*, Don Carlos*, Entführung aus dem Serail, Eugene Onegin, Fanciulla del West*, Fledermaus, Fliegende Holländer, Forza del Destino, Gianni Schicchi, Hänsel und Gretel, Iphigénie en Aulide*, Italiana in Algeri*, Kluge*, Madama Butterfly, Matrimonio Segreto, Nozze di Figaro, Orfeo, Prigioniero (Dallapiccola)*, Prozess (v. Einem)*, Rigoletto, Rosenkavalier, Tabarro, Tannhäuser, Traviata*, Wildschütz, Zauberflöte.

ARTISTS
Annie Delorie, Marit Isene, Irma Keller, Colette Lorand, Irene Salemka, Anny Schlemm, Erika Schmidt, Elisabeth Verlooy, Coba Wackers, Claire Watson, Marlise Wendels, Barbara Wittelsberger, Rosl Zapf.

Theo Adam, Andreas Camillo Agrelli, Carl Ebert, Rudolf Gonszar, Ernst Gutstein, Ernst Kozub, Walter Kreppel, Willy Müller, Emil Seidenspinner, Arturo Sergi, Georg Stern, Ludwig Welter, Oskar Wittazscheck, Willi Wolff, Kurt Wolinski.

CONDUCTORS
Georg Solti, Felix Prohaska, Wolfgang Rennert, Gerd Heidger, Karl Klauss.

GUEST ARTISTS during the season included:
Maria Corelli, Siw Ericsdotter, Ingeborg Felderer, Sylvia Fisher, Hertha Fischer, Ingeborg Friedrich, Ina Gerhein, Irmgard Gerz, Eva Görner-Kosmas, Madelon Harder, Marta Helm, Hedda Heusser, Hildegard Hillebrecht, Heidi Krall, Marion Lippert, Hanni Mack, Irmgard Meinig, Kathrein Mietzner, Hedwig Müller-Bütow, Dora Palludan, Lore Paul, Helga Pilarczyk, Gladys Spector, Sylvia Staklmann, Gisella Vivarelli, Herta Wilfert.
Carlos Alexander, Gunther Ambrosius, Walter Beissner, Kurt Böhme, Frans Crass, Cesare Curzi, Hans Dahman, Fred Dalberg, Walter Deissner, Ratko Delorko, Dezoe Ernster, Sebastian Feiersinger, Ferdinand Frantz, Gerhard Frei, Heinz Friedrich, Gustav Grefe, Ernst Gruber, Horst Gunther, Heine Horn, Laszlo Jambor, Julius Jüllich, Karlheinz Kahlstorf, Peter Lagger, Rupert Lauhöfer, Fritz Ollendorff, Rolf Polke, Vladimir Ruzdak, Kurt Sablotzke, Karl Schmitt-Walter, Norman Scott, Heinz Seifert, Walter Schreemann, David Thaw, Josef Traxel, Willibald Vohla, Gerd Wienstedt, Leonardo Wolowsky; Hans Zanotelli.

GELSENKIRCHEN. STÄDTISCHE BÜHNEN
Generalintendant: Gustav Deharde

REPERTORY
Contes d'Hoffmann*, Dantons Tod (von Einem)*, Elisir d'Amore*, Fanciulla del West*, Fidelio*, Heure Espagnole*, Manon Lescaut, Martha*, Rape of Lucretia, Revisor*, Simone Boccanegra*.

ARTISTS
Helma Arens, Annemarie Dölitzsch, Maria Helm, Marilyn Horne, Marie-Jeanne Marchal, Meta Ober, Ursula Peters, Inge Sichermann, Trude Stemmer, Gudrun Schmidt, Ingeborg Ziersch.
Erich Benke, Josef Connotte, Herbert Drechsler, Richard Erdmann, Elfego Esparza, Walther Finkelberg, Otto Heppenheimer, Hans Lättgen, Kurt Meinhardt, Werner Nesseler, Gerd Nienstedt, Ludwig Renko, Hermann Schnok, Theo

Strosyk, Ernst August West, Albert Zell, Fritz Zipper, Fritz Zöllner.

CONDUCTORS

Ljubomir Romansky, Theo Mölich, Julius Asbeck, Richard Heime (guest).

HAGEN. STÄDTISCHE BÜHNEN
Intendant: Hermann Werner

REPERTORY

Arabella*, Barbiere di Siviglia*, Bartered Bride*, Bohème*, Freischütz*, Iphigénie en Tauride*, Macbeth*, Madama Butterfly, Schüle der Frauen*, Tristan und Isolde*, Trovatore.

ARTISTS

Katharina Bütow, Irmgard Dahlke, Jutta Franc, Monika Grünheid, Emma-Klara Kirchner, Geneviève Marson, Käthe Munter, Ursula Prokop, Ingeborg Weiss, Mara Wernheim.

Kaspar Bargon, Jos Borelli, Walter Buckow, Peps Graf, Georg Kloss, Hans Loose, Hans-Joachim Lukat, Peter Meven, Helmut Raetsch, Fritz Ranglack, Hans Reischl, Gerd Rödiger, Karl Sablotzke, Hansdieter Sundermann, Kenk Voshart, Willem van der Sluijs.

CONDUCTORS

Berthold Lehmann, Walther Meyer-Giesow, Heinrich Bender.

GUEST ARTISTS

Paula Baumann, Elisabeth Höngen, Anny Schlemm, Ruth Siewert, Astrid Varnay, Lore Wissmann; Gunther Baldauf, Ratko Delorko, Walter Geisler.

HALLE. LANDESTHEATER
Intendant: Fritz Dietz

REPERTORY

Campanello*, Freischütz, Poro (Handel), Queen of Spades*, Rita (Donizetti)*, Radamisto, Rosen-kavalier*, Ottone, Re di Germania (Handel)*, Tannhäuser*, Tamerlano, Tosca*, Turandot.

ARTISTS

Edith Bach, Charlotte Berthold, Jutta Bohnen-kano, Philine Fischer, Margarete Herzberg, Irene Tzschoppe.

Rolf Apreck, Kurt Hübenthal, Siegfried Joachim, Werner Kraft, Ralph Walter Otto, Walter Richter-Dührss, Wolfgang Sommer, Franz Stumpf, Reiner Suss.

CONDUCTORS

Horst-Tanu Margraf, Ernst Schwazzmann, Olaf Koch.

HAMBURG. STAATSOPER
Intendant: Heinz Tietjen

REPERTORY

Aida, Ballo in Maschera, Barbiere di Siviglia, Barbier von Bagdad, Bohème, Boris Godunov, Capriccio, Così fan tutte, Don Carlos, Don Pasquale, Falstaff, Fidelio*, Fledermaus, Fliegende Holländer, Frau ohne Schatten*, Finta Giar-diniera*, Götterdämmerung, Huguenots*, Lohen-grin*, Lulu, Manon Lescaut, Otello*, Revisor*, Rheingold, Rosenkavalier*, Salome, Schule der Frauen*, Siegfried, Trovatore, Walküre, Wildschütz, Wozzeck, Zauberflöte.

ARTISTS

Margarete Ast, Oda Balsborg, Lisa Bischop Erna-Maria Duske, Clara Ebers, Siw Ericsdotter Elisabeth Grümmer, Lore Hoffmann, Maria von Ilosvay, Hilde Marie Keim, Edith Lang, Gisela Litz, Christa Ludwig, Martha Mödl, Melitta Muszely, Helga Pilarczyk, Anny Schlemm, Erna Schlüter, Cvetka Soucek, Ria Urban, Elfriede Wasserthal, Helene Werth.

Mathieu Ahlersmeyer, Hans Beirer, Toni Blankenheim, Caspar Bröcheler, Ratko Delorko, Herbert Fliether, Jürgen Förster, Walter Geisler, Fritz Göllnitz, Horst Günter, Theo Herrmann, Heinz Hoppe, Hans Hotter, Sandor Konya, Fritz Lehnert, Kurt Marschner, Helmut Melchert, Josef Metternich, Arnold van Mill, Georg Mund Karl Otto, James Pease, Wilhelm Pfendt, Hermann Prey, Sigmund Roth, Kurt Ruesche, Vladimir Ruzdak, Eugene Tobin, Ernst Wiemann. Lawrence Winters.

CONDUCTORS

Leopold Ludwig, Josef Keilberth, Albert Bittner, Wilhelm Brückner-Rüggeberg, Hans Zanotelli, Günter Hertel.

GUEST ARTISTS during the season included:

Anne Bollinger, Christa-Maria Degler, Hilde Güden, Gladys Kuchta, Hanna Kistner, Lenora Lafayette, Helena Millauer, Anneliese Rothen-berger, Erika Schmidt, Liane Synek, Elfriede Trötschel, Astrid Varnay, Maria-Ilona Walewska, Erika Wien; Kurt Böhme, Herbert Brauer, Wilhelm Ernest, Herbert Fliether, Josef Gostic, Fritz Grumann, Alfons Herwig, Richard Holm, Walter Kreppel, Ernst Krukowski, Benno Kusche, Adolf Meyer-Bremen, Arturo Sergi, Gerhard Stolze, Howard Vanderburg, Willibald Vohla, Curt Wolowsky; Werner Egk, Josef Keilberth, Hugo Sieberg, Luitgard Singer, Josef Rosenstock.

HANOVER. LANDESTHEATER
Intendant: Kurt Ehrhardt

REPERTORY
Aida, Arabella, Bartered Bride, Bohème, Carmina Burana, Cavalleria Rusticana, Così fan tutte, Don Carlos, Fidelio*, Fliegende Holländer, Forza del Destino, Frau ohne Schatten, Freischütz*, House of the Dead*, Italiana in Algeri, Giulio Cesare (Handel)*, Madama Butterfly*, Martha, Meistersinger von Nürnberg, Nozze di Figaro, Orfeo, Pagliacci, Peter Grimes, Revisor*, Rigoletto, Schule der Frauen*, Siegfried, Simone Boccanegra*, Tannhäuser, Tosca, Waffenschmied, Walküre.

ARTISTS
Margarete Berg, Lilo Buckup, Annemarie Ehlert, Ursula Gust, Gertrude Hutter, Lore Lamprecht, Elisabeth Pack, Ruth-Margret Pütz, Wilma Schmidt, Hanna Scholl, Milly Stolle-Garvens, Elfriede Weidlich, Ursula Wendt, Herta Wilfert.

Bernd Aldenhoff, Carlos Alexander, Bert Bessmann, Gerard Clair, Franz Crass, Alfred Frey, Eberhard Gässler, Walter Geisler, Donald Grobe, Otto Köhler, Ernst Sandleben, Walter Schnesmann, Willy Schönweiss, Condi Siegmund, Hubert Weindel, Theo Zilliken.

CONDUCTORS
Johannes Schüler, Ernst Richter, Wolfgang Trommer, Gerhard Steeger, Jacob Franck.

GUEST ARTISTS
Hannelore Backrass, Maria Bowoden, Gina Campelli, Sigrid Ekkehard, Ingeborg Felderer, Hedwig Fichtmüller, Maria Hall, Margarita Kenney, Gladys Kuchta, Jutta Meyfarth, Elisabeth-Marie Schreiner, Marion Siess.

Matthieu Ahlersmeyer, Toni Blankenheim, Hermann Blasig, Fritz Bramböck, Marcel Cordes, Wilhelm Ernest, Albrect Meyerolbersleben, Gerhard Nienstedt, Fritz Ollendorf, Wilhelm Patsche, Oskar Röhling, Theodor Schlott, Hermann Winkler, Franz Xaver Zach.

KARLSRUHE. BADISCHES STAATSTHEATER
Intendant: Paul Rose

REPERTORY
Alceste (Gluck)*, Don Giovanni*, Fliegende Höllander*, Forza del Destino*, Lustigen Weiber von Windsor, Nabucco, Nozze di Figaro, Peter Grimes*, Rigoletto*, Rosenkavalier*, Schneewittchen (Schubert)*, Tiefland*, Waffenschmied*, Zigeunerbaron.

ARTISTS
Paula Baumann, Eva Bober, Grete Holm, Renate Gutmann, Helene Kirsten, Ingeborg Koch, Lieselotte Lorenz, Ingeborg Möckel, Anke Naumann, Gudrun Nierich, Hannelore Wolf-Ramponi.

Wilhelm Felden, Willi Försterling, Albert van Haasteren, Erwin Hodapp, Hans Hofmann, Robert Kiefer, Eric Marion, Eugen Ramponi, Anton de Ridder, Heinz Erich Schanze, Alfred Schmutzer-George, Antonio Tedeski, Raimundo Torres, Hubert Türmer, Georg Völker, Rudolf Werner.

CONDUCTORS
Alexander Krannhals, Walter Born, Frithjoff Haas.

GUEST ARTISTS
Greta Holm, Nora Jungwirt; Scipio Colombo, Hans Kaart, Fritz Ollendorff, Mathias Schmidt, Frans Vroons, Helge Roswaenge, Zbyslaw Wozniak.

LEIPZIG. OPERNHAUS
Intendant: Johannes Arpe

REPERTORY
Aida, Ballo in Maschera, Betrothal in a Cloister (Prokofiev)*, Bohème, Carmen, Cavalleria Rusticana*, Contes d'Hoffmann, Così fan tutte*, Don Carlos, Entführung aus dem Serail, Fliegende Holländer, Krutnava (Katrena) (Eugen Suchon)*, Kluge, Lohengrin*, Madama Butterfly, Meistersinger von Nürnberg, Nozze di Figaro, Otello, Pagliacci*, Prinzessin auf der Erbsa (Toch), Queen of Spades, Rosenkavalier*, Rusalka, Salome, Tannhäuser, Tosca*, Trovatore, Turandot, Verurteilung des Lukullus (Dessau), Waffenschmied, Wildschütz, Zauberflöte.

ARTISTS
Maria Crooner, Hannelore Diehn, Marianne Dorsch, Marianne Dreefs, Ursula Engert, Elfriede Götze, Elsie Hesse, Sigrid Kehl, Ingeborg Kollmann, Maria Lenz, Elisabeth Rose, Lilo Vollrath, Katrin Wölzl, Christa Maria Ziese.

Lothar Anders, Jiri Bar, Rolf Bräunlich, Ferdinand Bürgmann, Wolf Eckert, Hermann Esser, Helmut Eyle, Manfred Geithe, Ernst Gruber, Alfred Herzog, Theodor Horand, Wilhelm Klemm, Hans Krämer, Rainer Lüdecke, Paul Reinecke, Hasso Schmidt, Hans-Peter Schwarzbach, Kurt Seipt, Guntfried Speck, Georg Wegener.

CONDUCTORS
Helmut Seydelmann, Heinz Fricke, Klaus Tennstedt, Alfred Willert.

GUEST ARTISTS
Eleonore Elstermann, Katja Georgiewa, Lilo Kirmse, Kossena Kirowa, Maria Matyas, Anna Remundu.

Alfred Krohn, Ludowicos Kurusopulos, Pavel Lissizian, Konstantin Pascalio, Dimiter Usunow; Günter Blumhagen, Arwid Jansons, Vilmos Komor, Herr Nellessen, Ude Nissen, Herr Wallat, Leonidas Zoras.

LÜBECK. BÜHNEN DER HANSESTADT GROSSES HAUS
Intendant: Christian Mettin
REPERTORY
Arlecchino*, Barbiere di Siviglia, Carmen*, Carmina Burana*, Eugene Onegin, Faust*, Fliegende Holländer, Gianni Schicchi*, Oedipus Rex (Stravinsky)*, Orfeo*, Quattro Rusteghi*, Tiefland*, Wildschütz*.

ARTISTS
Wedda Barnstorff, Magda Egressy, Waltraut Habicht, Litsa Liotsi, Setty Nagel, Janice Roche, Regina Toepper, Edith Vogt-Thieke, Anneliese Welge.

August-Wilhelm Ernst, Heinrich Froschhauser, Hans-Heinrich Hagen, Herbert Klomser, Hans-Otto Kloose, Gustav Köysti, Georg Lorant, Robert Obendahl, Georg Rehkemper, Hermann Rohrbach, Hermann Runge, Heinz Schickel, George Schnapka, Fritz Wenzel.

CONDUCTORS
Christoph von Dohnanyi, Walter Schumacher, Fritz Arndt, Martin Zummach.

MAINZ. STÄDTISCHES THEATER
Intendant: Siegfried Nürnberger
REPERTORY
Brücke von San Luis Rey (Reutter)*, Elektra*, Faust*, Fliegende Holländer, Forza del Destino, Italiana in Algieri*, Let's make an Opera (Britten)*, Lohengrin, Madame Favart (Offenbach), Manon Lescaut*, Perlenhemd (Kauffmann)*, Rigoletto*, Schwanda the Bagpiper*, Turandot*, Zarewitsch, Zaubergeige.

ARTISTS
Sigrid Claus, Nelde Clavel, Elisabeth Friedmann, Lucie Klüfer, Helen Laird, Gerda Schepplen, Ilse Stadelhofer, Gretl Tonndorf.

Erich Eckhard, Olav Eriksen, Werner Gerhardt, Giselbert Kassel, Klaus Kirchner, Franz Mazura, Walter Meiser, Hans Pink, Peter Sand, Richard Zimmermann.

CONDUCTORS
Karl Maria Zwissler, Albert Grünes, Hans Hilsdorf.

GUEST ARTIST
Gerda Lammers.

MANNHEIM. NATIONALTHEATER
Intendant: Hans Schüler
REPERTORY
Ariadne auf Naxos, Barbier von Bagdad, Carmen, Elektra*, Entführung aus dem Serail, Fledermaus, Freischütz, Heimkehr (Mihalovici), Lustige Witwe*, Madama Butterfly, Manon Lescaut*, Meistersinger von Nürnberg*, Nozze di Figaro*, Parsifal, Postillon de Longjumeau, Schule der Frauen*, Des Simplicius Simplicissimus Jugend (Hartmann), Tannhäuser*, Turandot*, Wozzeck*, Zaubergeige.

ARTISTS
Erika Ahsbahs, Eva-Maria Görgen, Irma Handler, Edith Jaeger, Petrina Kruse, Ingrid Ladwig, Hedwig Müller-Bütow, Herta Schmidt, Arlene Slater-Stone, Gladys Spector, Elisabeth Thoma, Irene Ziegler.

Kurt Albrecht, Günther Baldauf, Karl Bernhöft, Fred Dalberg, Hasso Eschert, Hans Günter Grimm, Heinrich Hölzlin, Jakob Rees, Hans Rössling, Kurt Schneider, Thomas Tipton, Willibald Vohla, Willi Wolff.

CONDUCTORS
Herbert Albert, Karl Fischer, Eugen Hesse, Joachim Popelka, Hans Klugmann.

GUEST ARTISTS during the season included:
Gertrud Jahoda, Inge Maurer.
Arthur Bard, Kurt Böhme, Cornelius Hom, Ernst Kozub, Bruno Manazza, Louis Roney. Richard Laugs.

MUNICH. BAYERISCHE STAATSOPER
Intendant: Rudolf Hartmann
REPERTORY
Aegyptische Helena, Aida, Ariadne auf Naxos, Ballo in Maschera*, Barbiere di Siviglia, Bluebeard's Castle, Bohème, Capriccio, Così fan tutte, Daphne*, Elektra, Entführung aus dem Serail, Faust*, Fidelio, Fliegende Holländer, Frau ohne Schatten, Freischütz, Giulio Cesare, Götterdämmerung, Hänsel und Gretel*, Harmonie der Welt (Hindemith) (World Première)*, Khowantchina, Kluge, Lohengrin, Lucia di Lammermoor, Lustigen Weiber von Windsor, Meistersinger von Nürnberg, Mond, Nozze di Figaro, Oedipus Rex*, Otello,

Parsifal, Revisor*, Rheingold, Rigoletto, Rosenkavalier, Salome, Siegfried, Tosca, Walküre, Wozzeck, Zauberflöte, Zaubergeige*.

ARTISTS

Emmy Argauer, Sari Barabas, Irmgard Barth, Lilian Benningsen, Inge Borkh, Lisa Della Casa, Anastasia Chrest, Maud Cunitz, Antonie Fahberg, Liselotte Fölser, Ina Gerhein, Erika Köth, Annelies Kupper, Elisabeth Lindermeier, Birgit Nilsson, Cäcilie Reich, Leonie Rysanek, Marianne Schech, Rosl Schwaiger, Elisabeth Söderström, Gerda Sommerschuh, Hanny Steffek, Hertha Töpper.

Bernd Aldenhoff, Kurt Böhme, Walther Carnuth, Marcel Cordes, Otto Edelmann, Kieth Engen, Lorenz Fehenberger, Ferdinand Frantz, Gottlob Frick, Richard Holm, Hans Hopf, Karl Hoppe, Hans Hotter, Adolf Keil, Franz Klarwein, Josef Knapp, Benno Kusche, Paul Kuen, Friedrich Lenz, Josef Metternich, Hans Hermann Nissen, Karl Ostertag, Albrecht Peter, Max Proebstl, Karl Schmitt-Walter, August Seider, Josef Simandy, Fritz Uhl, Howard Vandenburg, Kurt Wehofschitz, Georg Wieter, Rudolf Wünzer.

CONDUCTORS

Ferenc Fricsay, Hans Knappertsbusch, Robert Heger, Meinhard von Zallinger, Kurt Eichhorn, Werner Egk, Eugen Jochum, Josef Keilberth, Christoph Stepp, Janos Kulka, Erich Bönner.

GUEST ARTISTS during the season included: Elisabeth Grümmer, Sena Jurinac, Frl. Lattenbauer, Elisabeth Löw-Szöky, Colette Lorand, Viktoria Marcant, Hilde Nicoll, Hella Ruttowski, Lore Wissmann, Claire Watson; Karl Kohn, Walter Kreppel, Rudolf Christ, Karl Otto, Robert Edenhöfer; Rudolf Kempe; Lovro von Matacic.

(The rebuilt Cuvilliéstheater was due to open during the summer of 1958.)

(During June there were performances by a company from Rome of Tosca, Madama Butterfly and Manon Lescaut with Gigliola Frazzoni, Stefania Malagu, Magda Olivero, Gabriella Tucci; Franco Corelli, Gino Calo, Anselmo Colzani, Eugenio Fernandi, Melchiorre Luise, Enzo Mascherini, Paolo Washington; Franco Capuana.)

MÜNSTER. STÄDTISCHE BÜHNEN
Intendant: Leon Epp

REPERTORY

Così fan tutte*, Dantons Tod, Elektra*, Fliegende Holländer, Kluge*, Meistersinger von Nürnberg*, Mond*, Tosca*, Traviata*, Trovatore*.

ARTISTS

Karin Brinkmann, Maria Graf, Christa Holt-

meier, Hanna Kitzinger, Anne Pfirschinger, Renate Salinger, Renate Sörrensen, Friedl Teller, Lisa Walter.

Hans Feder-Feldern, Gerard Groot, Siegfried Haertel, Albrecht Meyerolbersleben, Willy van Hese, Emil Müller, Kurt Reinhold, Bodo Schier, Peter Struwe, Konny Thoss, Fritz Wellmann, Pieto Wudtke-Braun.

CONDUCTORS

Robert Wagner, Georg Reinwald, Helmut Wessel-Therhorn, Otto Kleinhammes.

NÜRNBERG—FÜRTH. OPERNHAUS
Generalintendant: Karl Pschigode

REPERTORY

Ariadne auf Naxos*, Barbiere di Siviglia*, Bartered Bride*, Bohème, Carmen*, Don Carlos*, Faust*, Fidelio, Giulio Cesare, Götterdämmerung, Des Kaisers neue Kleider (Lofer), Manon, Martha, Meistersinger von Nürnberg, Revisor*, Rheingold, Rigoletto, Romeo und Julia (Sutermeister), Siegfried*, Des Simplicius Simplicissimus Jugend (Hartmann), Kleine Stadt (Lehner), Tosca, Walküre, Wildschutz*, Wozzeck*, Zauberflöte.

ARTISTS

Anny Coty, Gretel Hartung, Kathryn Harvey, Gerda Hensel, Hildegard Jonas, Sonja Knittel, Emmy Löbel, Elisabeth Müllauer, Hella Ruttkowski, Lotte Schädle, Elisabeth Schärtel, Liselotte Schmidt, Gerda Schopenhauer, Eva Vossen, Barbara Wittkowski.

Arthur Bard, Jonny Born, Manfred Capel, Cesare Curzi, Willi Domgraf-Fassbaender, Sebastian Feiersinger, Georg Goll, Alfons Graf, Alfred Hanus, Hanns Hoffmann, Max Kohl, Robert Licha, Karl Mikorey, Hermann Sandbank, Willy Schmid-Scholven, Kurt Leo Sourisseaux, Alfred Stein, Albert Vogler, Leonardo Wolovsky, Mino Yahia.

CONDUCTORS

Erich Riede, Max Loy, Konrad Peter Mannert, Otto Dinnebier, Adam Rauh, Edgar Schmidt-Bredow.

GUESTS

Gisella Vivarelli, Jacob Engels, Heinz Imdahl, Josef Traxel.

OLDENBURG. STAATSTHEATER
Intendant: Ernst Dietz

REPERTORY

Flut (Blacher), Madama Butterfly, Manon Lescaut*, Nozze di Figaro*, Orfeo*, Revisor*, Rigoletto, Schweigsame Frau* (Richard Strauss),

Schwarze Spinne (Sutermeister), Tristan und Isolde*.

ARTISTS

Greetje Burbach, Johanna Görschler, Maria Kristie, Lene Lund, Linde Rehs, Elisabeth Reich.

Robert Ahlersmeyer, Wolfgang Frey, Guiseppe Masina, Franz Müksch, Franz Pacher, Franz Rarisch, August Sander, Arturo Scalorbi, Franz Xaver Zach, Walter Korth (guest).

CONDUCTORS

Karl Randolf, Heinz Rockstroh, Walter Strauss, Friedrich Wilhelm Karras.

SAARBRÜCKEN. STADTTHEATER
Intendant: Günther Stark

REPERTORY

Boris Godunov, Capriccio, Don Carlos, Don Giovanni, Elisir d'Amore, Fra Diavolo, Revisor*, Rheingold, Turandot, Waffenschmied.

ARTISTS

Helene Fuchs, Gertrud Jahoda, Brunhilde Knack, Waltraud Krieg, Ruth Löser, Susanne Muser, Gretl Schmidek, Hanna Wolters.

Albert Gammon, Cornelius Hom, Rudi Horstmann, Walter Koller, Philipp Rasp, Gottfried Riedner, Michael de Rochel, Otto Rousche, Phil Sona, Ralph Telasko, Johannes Trefny, Alex v. Wachtmeister.

CONDUCTORS

Phillip Wüst, Carl Johannsson, Alfred Leder, Hans-Peter Backhaus, Johannes Pütz.

STUTTGART. WÜRTTEMBERGISCHE STAATSTHEATER
Generalintendant: Walter Erich Schäfer

REPERTORY

Aida, Ballo in Maschera, Bartered Bride, Bohème, Carmen, Cavalleria Rusticana, Clemenza di Tito, Comoedia de Christi Resurrectione (Orff), Così fan tutte, Don Carlos, Entführung aus dem Serail*, Euryanthe, Fledermaus, Fliegende Holländer, Forza del Destino, Götterdämmerung, Jephta (Händel), Lustigen Weiber von Windsor, Manon Lescaut, Martha, Meistersinger von Nürnberg, Mond*, Nozze di Figaro, Orfeo, Otello, Pagliacci, Penthesilea (Othmar Schoeck)*, Revisor*, Rheingold, Rienzi*, Rosenkavalier, Salome*, Siegfried, Tosca, Tristan und Isolde*, Turandot, Undine, Volpone (Francis Burt—world première)*, Walkure, Wildschütz*, Wozzeck, Wunderinsel (Schubert) (First performance of new edition)*, Zar und Zimmermann, Zauberflöte.

ARTISTS

Paula Bauer-Paul, Margarethe Bence, Paula Brivkalne, Trude Eipperle, Res Fischer, Grace Hoffman, Ellinor Junker-Giesen, Sieglinde Kahmann, Paula Kapper, Maria Kinas, Paula Lechner-Schmidt, Martha Mödl, Olga Moll, Hetty Plümacher, Liselotte Rebmann, Friederike Sailer, Lore Wissmann.

Hubert Buchta, Heinz Cramer, Engelbert Czubok, Gustav Grefe, Stefan Kosso, Fritz Linke, Barry McDaniel, Gustav Neidlinger, Hans Günter Nöcker, Alfred Pfeifle, Otto von Rohr, Eugene Tobin, Josef Traxel, Wolfgang Windgassen, Fritz Wunderlich.

CONDUCTORS

Ferdinand Leitner, Rolf Reinhardt, Josef Dünnwald, Wilhelm Seegelken, Heinz Mende.

GUEST ARTISTS during the season included:

Irmgard Barth, Inge Borkh, Gré Brouwenstijn, Suzanne Danco, Hilde Güden, Danise Ilitsch, Friederike Kirchweger, Ingeborg Lasser, Vilma Lipp, Elisabeth Löw-Szöky, Ira Malaniuk, Carla Martinis, Stina Britta Melander, Ruth-Margret Pütz, Gertrude Roesler, Leonie Rysanek, Anna Tassopulos, Gisella Vivarelli.

Carlos Alexander, Lorenzo Alvary, Frans Andersson, Toni Blankenheim, Hans Blessin, Anton Dermota, Lorenz Fehenberger, Franz Glawatsch, Ernst Gutstein, Walter Hagner, Heinrich Hölzlin, Paul Kuen, George London, Fritz Ollendorf, Julius Patzak, Ernst Albert Pfeil, Karl Schmitt-Walter, Stefan Schwer, Frithjof Sentpaul, Gerhard Stolze, Gerhard Unger, Willibald Vohla, Eberhard von Wächter, Kurt Wehofschitz, Alexander Welitsch.

Werner Egk, Lovro von Matacic, Carl-Maria Zwissler.

(A company from Rome visited Stuttgart during the Spring and gave performances of *Tosca*, *Madama Butterfly*, and *Manon Lescaut* with Gigliola Frazzoni, Stefania Malagu, Magda Olivero, Gabriella Tucci; Franco Corelli, Gino Calo, Anselmo Colzani, Eugenio Fernandi, Melchiorre Luise, Enzo Mascherini, Paolo Washington; Franco Capuana.)

WEIMAR
DEUTSCHES NATIONALTHEATER
Intendant: Karl Kayser

REPERTORY

Barbiere di Siviglia, Carmen, Don Giovanni, Eugen Onegin, Freischütz*, Gianni Schicchi, Günstling (Wagener-Regeny)*, Kluge, Manon

Lescaut*, Meistersinger, Men of Blackmoor, Nozze di Figaro, Parsifal, Tannhäuser.

ARTISTS

Annelore Bley, Rosel Dyballa, Dietlinde Kuckelt, Katherina Nicolai, Käthe Retzmann, Sigrid Ruppert, Lisbeth Schmidt-Glänzl, Christiane Petersen, Ingrid Thom.

Werner Atzdrot, Josef Hattemer, Kurt Köhler, Ernst Kranz, Xaver Mang, Franz Neder, Josef Oblertz, Kurt Rösinger, August Schmidt, Franz Schmidt-Baitzen, Hanns-Herbert Schulz, Gerd Schwalbe, Konrad Stopp, Alfred Wroblewski.

CONDUCTORS

Gerhard Pflüger, Hans-Heinrich Schmitz.

WIESBADEN. HESSISCHES STAATSOPER
Intendant: Friedrich Schramm

REPERTORY

Aida, Barbiere di Siviglia, Contes d' Hoffmann*, Così fan tutti*, Count Bajazid* (Jan Cikker), Don Pasquale*, Fidelio*, Freischütz, Götterdämmerung*, Hospa* (Paul Burkhard) (world première), Madama Butterfly, Orfeo*, Siegfried, Simone Boccanegra*, Tannhäuser, Traviata*, Der Widerspenstigen Zähmung, Zar und Zimmermann*, Zauberflöte*.

ARTISTS

Inge Ahrends, Hannelore Backrass, Helga Baller, Marianne Dorka, Margot Fischer, Anita Förderer, Maria Hall, Margarethe Knauff, Trude Kortegast, Ilsa Lehnert, Margarethe Lüddecke, Katrein Mietzner, Erna-Maria Müller, Lotte Munziger, Susanne Muser, Melitta Schaeffer, Margot Streubel, Liane Synek, Lois Toman.

Karl Acher, Reinhold Bartel, Kurt Bausch, Hans Beck, Ewald Böhmer, Dolf Dolz, Josef Ellmauer, Karl Engel, Heinz Friedrich, David Garen, Fabio Giongo, Josef Hanke, Klaus Hennig, Wilhelm Horne, Viktor Hospach, Werner Jonas, Richard Kogel, Peter Lagger, Frank-Rüdiger Leonhard, Karl Liebl, Gerhard Misske, Hubertus Moeller, Leo Ohnhaus, Rolf Sander, Gerhard Schubert, Hans Schwarze, Hans Heinz Steinbach, Lothar Weber, Rudi Weiss, Heinz Zur Buchen.

CONDUCTORS

Arthur Apelt, Ludwig Kaufmann, Horst-Dietrich Schock, Bernhard Stimmler.

GUEST ARTISTS

Stina Britta Melander, Helga Mietzner, Camilla Williams, Maria Wolkowsky, Russel Roberts.

The May Festival included performances by companies from Italy and Jugoslavia.

WUPPERTAL. OPERNHAUS
Generalintendant: Helmut Henrichs

REPERTORY

Ballo in Maschera, Boulevard Solitude*, Daphne*, Dido und Aeneas, Don Pasquale*, Freischütz, Fidelio, Forza del Destino*, Hänsel und Gretel, Lohengrin, Des Simplicius Simplicissimus Jugend*, Zar und Zimmermann*, Zauberflöte*.

ARTISTS

Monique Berghmans, Ingrid Bjoner, Henny Ekström, Else Fischer, Angela Kotthoff, Adelheid Krämer, Doris Lorenz, Käthe Maas, Helma Reich, Ursula Stamm, Odile Sittard, Emilie Walter-Sachs.

Willi Gesell, Otto Heuer, Herbert Görsch, Karl Hartleb, Alfred Hüsgen, Ronald Jackson, Walter Jenckel, Franz Kessel, Fritz Lang, Georg Nowak, George Paskuda, Willi Paulsen, Louis Roney, Herbert Schachtschneider, Hermann Scheuing, Hans Schmalenberg, Michael Schubert, Fritz Uhl, Erich Weckbrodt, Karl Wolfram, Eduard Wollitz.

CONDUCTORS

Hans Georg Ratjen, Hartmut Klug, Johann Andreas Lang, Hans Wolfgang Schmitz, Christian Vöchting.

GREAT BRITAIN

LONDON. ROYAL OPERA HOUSE
General Administrator: David Webster
Musical Director: Rafael Kubelik

REPERTORY

Aida*, Ballo in Maschera, Bohème, Carmen, Contes d'Hoffmann, Dialogues des Carmélites*, Don Carlos*, Elektra, Götterdämmerung, Jenufa, Meistersinger von Nürnberg, Nozze di Figaro, Otello, Peter Grimes, Rheingold, Rigoletto, Siegfried, Tosca, Traviata, Tristan und Isolde*, Trojans, Walküre.

ARTISTS

Noreen Berry, Joan Carlyle, Edith Coates, Marie Collier, Veronica Dunne, Lauris Elms, Sylvia Fisher, Edna Graham, June Grant, Una Hale, Adèle Leigh, Elsie Morison, Constance Shacklock, Amy Shuard, Jeanette Sinclair, Joan Sutherland, Josephine Veasey, Jean Watson.

David Allen, Robert Allman, Owen Brannigan, Rhydderch Davies, William Dickie, Edgar Evans, Geraint Evans, James Johnston, David Kelly, Otakar Kraus, Michael Langdon, John Lanigan, Ronald Lewis, Raymond Nilsson, Peter Pears, Forbes Robinson, Joseph Rouleau, John Shaw,

David Tree, Dermot Troy, Jon Vickers, Jess Walters.

CONDUCTORS

Edward Downes, Alexander Gibson, Rafael Kubelik, John Matheson, John Pritchard, Emanuel Young.

GUEST ARTISTS during the season included:

Fedora Barbieri, Gré Brouwenstijn, Irene Dalis, Gerda Lammers, Edith Lang, Elisabeth Lindermeier, Hedwig Müller-Bütow, Maria Meneghini Callas, Birgit Nilsson, Regina Resnik, Margherita Roberti, Marianne Schech, Marion Studholme, Blanche Thebom, Maria von Ilosvay, Georgine von Milinkovic, Eugenia Zareska.

Kurt Böhme, Boris Christoff, Scipio Colombo, Albert da Costa, Frederick Dalberg, Gottlob Frick, Walter Geisler, Tito Gobbi, Carlos Guichandut, Hans Hotter, Oreste Kirkop, Peter Klein, Albert Lance, James Pease, Arturo Sergi, Marco Stefanoni, Set Svanholm, Robert Thomas, Richard Tucker, Hermann Uhde, Cesare Valletti, Ramon Vinay, Wolfgang Windgassen, Erich Witte, Mario Zanasi; Carlo Maria Giulini, Rudolf Kempe, Nicola Rescigno.

TOUR: (Towns visited during provincial tour:— Manchester and Oxford.)

GUEST ARTIST

Gita Denise.

GUEST CONDUCTOR

Raymond Leppard.

LONDON. SADLER'S WELLS
Director: Norman Tucker

REPERTORY

Bluebeard's Castle*, Bohème, Consul, Don Pasquale, Falstaff, Fidelio, Gianni Schicchi, Hänsel and Gretel, Lustige Witwe*, Martha, Moon and Sixpence (Gardner), Nozze di Figaro, Quattro Rusteghi (School for Fathers), Samson et Dalila, Suor Angelica, Tabarro, Telephone*, Tosca, Traviata, Trovatore, Zauberflöte.

ARTISTS

June Bronhill, Victoria Elliott, Elizabeth Fretwell, Patricia Howard, Ava June, Patricia Johnson, Judith Pierce, Anna Pollak, Marjorie Shires, Joan Stuart, Marion Studholme.

Harold Blackburn, Owen Brannigan, Stanley Clarkson, Charles Craig, Denis Dowling, Kenneth Fawcett, Howell Glynne, John Hargreaves, Raimund Herincx, Rowland Jones, Gwent Lewis, William McAlpine, Alberto Remedios, Thomas Round, Frederick Sharp, David Ward.

CONDUCTORS

Richard Austin, Bryan Balkwill, Edric Cundell, Marcus Dods, Alexander Gibson, Leon Lovett, Leo Quayle, Rudolf Schwarz, Vilem Tausky. (Towns visited on tour included: Aberdeen, Bournemouth, Bristol, Coventry, Dundee, Edinburgh, Glasgow, Leeds, Newcastle, Oxford.)

GUEST ARTISTS during the season included:

Edith Coates, Patricia Baird, Joyce Gartside, Edna Graham, Helen Hillier, Adèle Leigh, Marion Lowe, Marjorie Shires, Amy Shuard; John Kentish, Eric Shilling.

LONDON.
THEATRE ROYAL. DRURY LANE.
ITALIAN OPERA SEASON 1958
Artistic Director: Italo Milani

REPERTORY

Amico Fritz, Andrea Chénier, Forza del Destino, Pêcheurs de Perles, Sonnambula, Guillaume Tell, Trovatore, Turandot.

ARTISTS

Mariella Angioletti, Clara Betner, Sonia Croci, Emilina da Vito, Onelia Fineschi, Carmen Lucchetti, Nicoletta Panni, Odilia Rech, Anna Maria Rovere, Renata Scotto, Luciana Serafini, Ebe Stignani, Laura Zannini.

Ezio Achilli, Antonio Annaloro, Gino Bechi, Gino Calò, Mario Ferrara, Mario Filippeschi, Augusto Frati, Lorenzo Gaetani, Gian Giacomo Guelfi, Alvinio Misciano, Paolo Pedani, Luigi Pontiggia, Guerrando Rigiri, Lorenzo Sabatucci, Ugo Savarese, Guiseppe Savio, Ferruccio Tagliavini, Roberto Turrini.

CONDUCTORS

Vincenzo Bellezza, Henry Krips, Tullio Serafin, Manno Wolf-Ferrari.

GLYNDEBOURNE FESTIVAL OPERA
Artistic Director: Carl Ebert
General Manager: Moran Caplat

REPERTORY

Alceste, Ariadne auf Naxos, Comte Ory, Falstaff, Nozze di Figaro, Rake's Progress, Segreto di Susanna*.

ARTISTS

Lucine Amara, Sari Barabas, Teresa Berganza, Fernanda Cadoni, Tamara Chumakova, Mary Costa, Jacqueline Delman, Oralia Dominguez, Mary Illing, Gloria Lane, Ilva Ligabue, Pilar Lorengar, Elsie Morison, Helga Pilarczyk, Consuelo Rubio, Graziella Sciutti, Monica Sinclair, Rita Streich, Josephine Veasey.

Heinz Blankenburg, Mario Borrielo, Mario Carlin, Hugues Cuenod, Xavier Depraz, André Dorval, Geraint Evans, David Franklin, Gwyn Griffiths, Thomas Hemsley, David Holman, John Holmes, David Kelly, John Kentish, Otakar Kraus, Richard Lewis, Robert Massard, Juan Oncina, Duncan Robertson, Michel Roux, Marco Stefanoni, Mihaly Szekely, Dermot Troy, David Ward, Frederick Westcott, Dennis Wicks, Harold Williams.

CONDUCTORS

Vittorio Gui, Hans Schmidt-Isserstedt, Paul Sacher, John Pritchard; Peter Gellhorn, Bryan Balkwill.

(The company also visited Paris in May, and performed *Le Comte Ory* and *Falstaff*.)

CARL ROSA COMPANY
(tours United Kingdom)
Director: (1957) *Mrs. H. B. Phillips*
Director: (1958) *Prof. H. Procter-Gregg*

REPERTORY

Barbiere di Siviglia, Bartered Bride*, Benvenuto Cellini, Carmen, Cavalleria Rusticana, Contes d'Hoffmann, Don Giovanni, Faust, Manon Lescaut, Pagliacci, Rigoletto.

ARTISTS

Julia Bouttell, Nancy Creighton, Gita Denise, Margaret Elkins, Joyce Goodwin, Glenice Halliday, Doreen Murray, Margaret Nisbett, Estelle Valery.

William Aitken, Eduardo Asquez, Donald Campbell, Ronald Evans, John Holmes, Edwin Jepps, John Lawrenson, Kevin Miller, John Heddle Nash, Stanislav Pieczora, Brychan Powell, Joseph Satariano, Ernest Thomas, Joseph Ward, Frederick Wood.

CONDUCTORS

James Robertson, Bryan Balkwill, Edward Renton, Anthony Addison.

GUEST ARTISTS

Victoria Elliott, John Stuart; Charles Craig, James Johnston, John Hargreaves.

GUEST CONDUCTORS

Sir Adrian Boult, Arthur Hammond.
(Towns visited during the 1957-8 season were: Bradford, Brighton, Liverpool, London (Sadler's Wells Theatre, Streatham Hill Theatre, Golders Green Hippodrome) Norwich, Nottingham, Peterborough, Sheffield, Southampton, Southsea, Wolverhampton.)

WELSH NATIONAL OPERA COMPANY
(Season in Cardiff)

REPERTORY

Barbiere di Siviglia, Lombardi, Mefistofele, Nabucco, Rigoletto, Traviata.

ARTISTS

Phyllis Ash-Child, Joyce Barker, Zoe Cresswell, Anne Edwards, Margaret Elkins, Heather Harper, Patricia Kern, Patti Lewis, Doreen Murray, Ruth Packer, Lilian Prosser-Evans, Jean Stevens, Marion Studholme, Elizabeth Tovey. Elwyn Adams, Hervey Alan, Paul Asciak, John Carolan, Vivian Davies, William Dickie, Bryan Drake, Tano Ferendinos, Robert Gard, Howell Glynne, Alfred Hallett, John Hargreaves, Raimund Herincx, Leonard John, Roderick Jones, Michael Langdon, Walter Midgley, David Parker, Tegwyn Short.

CONDUCTORS

Warwick Braithwaite, Charles Groves.

ITALY

BARI. TEATRO PETRUZZELLI

REPERTORY

Ballo in Maschera, Barbiere di Siviglia, Carmen, Cavalleria Rusticana, Madama Butterfly, Norma, Pagliacci.

ARTISTS

Anita Caminada, Maria Caniglia, Anita Corridori, Nora de Rosa, Miciko Hirajama, Caterina Mancini, Dora Minarchi, Franca Ottaviani, Miriam Pirazzini, Gabriella Tucci.

Rodolfo Azzolini, Achille Braschi, Salvatore Catania, Bruno Cioni, Mario del Monaco, Renato Gavarini, Amerigo Gentilini, Tito Gobbi, Angelo Marchiandi, Walter Monachesi, Andrea Mongelli, Carlo Perucci, Giuseppe Taddei, Ferruccio Tagliavini.

CONDUCTORS

Arturo Basile, Vincenzo Marini, Alfredo Simonetto, Ottavio Ziino.

BERGAMO. TEATRO DONIZETTI
Sovrintendente: Birdo Missiroli

REPERTORY

Andrea Chénier*, Manon Lescaut*, Maria di Rohan*, Nuova Euridice (Roberto Lupi) (world première)*, Requiem per Elisa (Hazon) (world première)*.

ARTISTS

Maria Bertolini, Loretta di Lelio, Gigiola Frazzoni, Renata Heredia, Adriana Martino, Clara

Petrella, Giuseppina Salvi, Roma Sitran, Laura Zannini, Luisana Zerbini.

Domenico Begani, Virgilio Carbonari, Anselmo Colzani, Franco Corelli, Gino del Signore, Guglielmo Ferrara, Giulio Fioravanti, Giorgio Giorgetti, Silvio Maionica, Rinaldo Pelizzoni, Giacinto Prandelli, Franco Ricciardi, Nello Romanato, Teodoro Rovetta, Ugo Savarese, Vito Susca, Niko Tagger.

CONDUCTORS
Adolfo Camozzo, Umberto Cattini, Oliviero de Fabritiis, Ettore Gracis, Roberto Lupi.

BOLOGNA. TEATRO COMUNALE

REPERTORY
Allamistakeo (Viozzi)*, Bohème, Canto del Cigno* (Chailly), Faust, Guerra* (Renzo Rossellini), Guglielmo Tell, Nabucco, Queen of Spades, Siegfried.

ARTISTS
Anna Lia Bazzani, Luciana Bertolli, Rosa Bini, Anita Biolchini, Rosanna Carteri, Rina Corsi, Lucia Danieli, Gigliola De Giorgi, Gigliola Frazzoni, Gianna Galli, Dora Gatta, Maria Luisa Gavioli, Paola Mantovani, Magda Olivero, Gianna Pederzini, Lola Pedretti, Margherita Roberti, Renata Scotto, Ruth Siewert, Chritiane Sorell, Gabriella Tucci, Jeda Valtriani, Edda Vincenzi, Helene Wert.

Giorgio Algorta, Antonio Annaloro, Hans Beirer, Franco Bordoni, Franco Calabrese, Enrico Campi, Mauro Carbonoli, Antonio Cassinelli, Athos Casarini, Dino Dondi, Eugenio Fernandi, Piermiranda Ferraro, Mario Filippeschi, Gilberto Fogli, Giorgio Giorgetti, Giangiacomo Guelfi, Nicolai Gjaurov, Endré Koreh, Ferdinando Lidonni, Gastone Limarilli, Silvio Majonica, Dino Mantovani, Kurt Marchner, Ferruccio Mazzoli, Vittorio Pandano, Alois Pernerstorfer, Antonio Pirino, Gianni Raimondi, Franco Ricciardi, Ivan Sardi, Paul Schoeffler, Guiseppe Taddei, Nicola Tagger, Ivo Vincò, Mario Zanasi, Antonio Zerbini.

CONDUCTORS
Franco Capuana, Felice Cillario, Armando La Rosa Parodi, Leopold Ludwig, Francesco Molinari Pradelli, Angelo Questa.

BRESCIA. TEATRO GRANDE

REPERTORY
Bohème, Pagliacci, Sonnambula, Suor Angelica, Tosca, Trovatore.

ARTISTS
Gianna d'Angelo, Paula Mantovani, Edda Melchiorri, Anna Moffo, Lola Pedretti, Gabriella Tucci, Jeda Valtriani.

Aldo Bertocci, Umberto Borsò, Plinio Clabassi, Antonio Galiè, Giampiero Malaspina, Enzo Mascherini, Saturno Maletti, Carlo Perucci, Aldo Protti, Santafè, Ferruccio Tagliavini, Franco Taino, Danilo Vega, Enzo Vezzosi.

CONDUCTORS
Danilo Belardinelli, Nino Verchi, Ottavio Ziino.

CAGLIARI. TEATRO MASSIMO

REPERTORY
Domanda di Matrimonio (Chailly), Italiana in Algeri, Malata Immaginario, Manon Lescaut, Segreto di Susanna, Turandot.

ARTISTS
Fernanda Cadoni, Dora Gatta, Ilva Ligabue, Carla Martinis, Anna Moffo, Vera Montanari, Antonietta Pastori, Anna Maria Rota.

Umberto Borsò, Sesto Bruscantini, Vito de Taranto, Gianni Iaia, Agostino Lazzari, Paolo Montarsolo, Paolo Pedani, Antonio Pirino, Afro Poli, Giorgio Onesti.

CONDUCTORS
Giuseppe Antonicelli, Ettore Gracis, Emidio Tieri.

CATANIA. TEATRO MASSIMO BELLINI
Sovrintendente: Arturo Appio

REPERTORY
Barbiere di Siviglia, Cavalleria Rusticana*, Francesca da Rimini, Iris*, Pantea (Lizzi)*, Prince Igor*, Sonnambula*, Tosca.

ARTISTS
Maria Teresa Bertasi, Rina Corsi, Maria Curtis Verna, Gianna d'Angelo, Gigliola Frazzoni, Elvira Galassi, Luisa Malagrida, Maria Teresa Mandalari, Luisa Maragliano, Giuditta Mazzoleni, Elena Mazzoni, Maria Noè, Clara Petrella, Dina Piccini, Marisa Pintus, Miriam Pirazzini, Marcella Pobbe, Giuliana Raimondi, Margherita Roberti, Bruna Ronchini, Maria Scolaro, Eugenia Vaiani.

Raffaele Ariè, Gaetano Bardini, Ettore Bastianini, Bruno Carmassi, Antonio Cassinelli, Plinio Clabassi, Giuseppe Di Stefano, Renato Ercolani, Ferrando Ferrari, Piero Guelfi, Flaviano Labò, Dante Mari, Alfredo Mariotti, Saturno Meletti, Alvinio Misciano, Carmelo Mollica, Valiano Natali, Rolando Panerai, Mirto Picchi, Vico Polotto, Luigi Pontiggia, Giuseppe Taddei, Sergio Tedesco, Nino Valori.

CONDUCTORS

Franco Capuana, Umberto Cattini, Mario Parenti, Gabriele Santini, Oscar Massa.

COMO. TEATRO SOCIALE

REPERTORY

Cenerentola, Gianni Schicchi, Guerra, Maestro di Musica, Traviata.

ARTISTS

Sandra Baruffi, Ketty Fernandez, Gianna Pederzini, Elda Ribetti, Renata Scotto, Giulietta Simionato.

Renato Capecchi, Virgilio Carbonari, Sesto Bruscantini, Giulio Fioravanti, Alfredo Kraus, Melchiorre Luise, Nicola Monti, Camillo Righini, Niko Tagger.

CONDUCTORS

Argeo Quadri, Angelo Questa.

GENOA. TEATRO CARLO FELICE

REPERTORY

Bohème, Boris Godunov, Don Pasquale, Fiammiferraia (Veretti), Fliegende Holländer, Guerra, Luisa Miller, Segreto di Susanna, Sonnambula.

ARTISTS

Mariella Adani, Mariella Angioletti, Sofia Bandin, Giannella Borelli, Rosanna Carteri, Gabriella Carturan, Lucia Danieli, Oralia Dominguez, Magda Olivero, Vittoria Palombini, Eugenia Ratti, Renata Scotto, Giuliana Tavolaccini, Silvana Zanolli.

Carlo Badioli, Alfredo Bienchini, Umberto Borghi, Sesto Bruscantini, Franco Calabrese, Miroslav Cangalovic, Plinio Clabassi, Eugenio Fernandi, Piermiranda Ferraro, Giovanni Fioani, Enzo Guagni, Hans Hofmann, Prust Kozol, Nicola Monti, Tomislav Neralic, Gino Orlandini, Mirto Picchi, Nico Polotto, Marco Stefanoni, Niko Tagger, Ivo Vinco, Paolo Washington.

CONDUCTORS

Franco Capuana, Umberto Cattini, Alceo Galliera, Alexander Krannhals, Bruno Rigacci.

LEGHORN. (LIVORNO) TEATRO GOLDONI

REPERTORY

Amica (Mascagni), Fanciulla del West, Suor Angelica, Traviata.

ARTISTS

Elisabetta Barbato, Rosanna Carteri, Lydia Coppola, Gigliola Frazzoni, Adriana Lazzarini, Lola Pedretti, Lucia Rivolta, Marta Rotondi.

Gino Belloni, Alberto Ciulli, Anselmo Colzani, Franco Corelli, Mario Frosini, Bruno Gentilini, Piero Guelfi, Alfredo Kraus, Dino Montovani, Angelo Mercuriali, Ugo Novelli, Salvatore Puma, Enzo Sordello.

CONDUCTOR

Argeo Quadri.

MILAN. TEATRO ALLA SCALA

Sovrintendente: Antonio Ghiringhelli

REPERTORY

Abu Hassan*, Adriana Lecouvreur, Amfiparnaso (Vecchi)*, Anna Bolena, Assassinio nella Cathedrale (Pizzetti)* (world première), Ballo in Maschera*, Buona Figliuola (Piccinni), Cappello di Paglia di Firenze (Rota), Comte Ory*, Cunning Little Vixen*, Elisir d'Amore, Enfant et les Sortilèges*, Häusliche Krieg (Schubert)*, Heure Espagnole*, Lohengrin*, Madama Butterfly, Mathis der Maler*, Mefistofele, Mignon*, Nabucco*, Orfeo, Pirata* (Bellini), Porta Divisoria (Carpi)* (world première), Stone Guest*, Turco in Italia, Walküre*.

ARTISTS

Mariella Adani, Mariella Angioletti, Fedora Barbieri, Vivette Barthelemy, Aureliana Beltrami, Jeanne Berbié, Teresa Berganza, Bianca Maria Berini, Freda Betti, Cesy Broggini, Jacqueline Brumaire, Rosanna Carteri, Gabriella Carturan, Biancamaria Casoni, Christiane Castelli, Rina Cavallari, Floriana Cavalli, Anita Cerquetti, Fiorenza Cossotto, Lucia Danieli, Anna de Cavalieri, Marcella de Osma, Nora de Rosa, Gigiola Frazzoni, Elisabetta Fusco, Christiane Gayraud, Leyla Gencer, Sena Jurinac, Ilva Ligabue, Stefania Malagu, Luisa Mandelli, Lida Marimpietri, Malfalda Masini, Edith Martelli, Maria Meneghini Callas, Nan Merriman, Françoise Ogeas, Antonietta Pastori, Mirella Parutto, Pinuccia Perotti, Clara Petrella, Marcella Pobbe, Teresa Querol, Elvina Ramella, Eugenia Ratti, Margherita Roberti, Graziella Sciutti, Renata Scotto, Giulietta Simionato, Giuliana Tavolaccini, Angela Vercelli, Silvana Zanolli.

Francesco Albanese, Luigi Alva, Carlo Badioli, Ettore Bastianini, Erminio Benatti, Jean Christophe Benoit, Aldo Bertocci, Sesto Bruscantini, Franco Calabrese, Enrico Campi, Dario Caselli, Antonio Cassinelli, Michele Cazzato, Athos Cesarini, Eraldo Coda, Anselmo Colzani, Franco Corelli, Adolfo Cormanni, Gino de Lilla, Mario del Monaco, Paul Dernne, Giuseppe di Stefano, Dino Dondi, Jacques Doucet, Constantine Ego, Ferrando

Ferrari, Nicola Filacuridi, Giulio Fioravanti, Carlo Forti, Carlo Franzini, Carlo Gasperini, Alfredo Giacomotti, Salvatore Gioia, Giorgio Giorgetti, Enzo Guagni, Franco Iglesias, Silvio Maionica, Dino Mantovani, Robert Massard, Angelo Mercuriali, Alvinio Misciano, Giuseppe Modesti, Leonardo Monreale, Paolo Montarsolo, Nicola Monti, Giuseppe Morresi, Ugo Novelli, Juan Oncina, Mario Ortica, Rolando Panerai, Luciano Panzeri, Rinaldo Pellizzoni, Mirto Picchi, Franco Piva, Gianni Poggi, Aldo Protti, Lino Puglisi, Gianni Raimondi, Franco Ricciardi, Nicola Rossi Lemeni, Luigi Rumbo, Cesare Siepi, Mario Spina, Marco Stefanoni, Giuseppe Taddei, Giorgio Tadeo, Vittorio Tatozzi, Giuseppe Valdengo, Ivo Vincò Gustave Wion, Nicola Zaccaria, Giuseppe Zampieri, Antonio Zerbini.

GUESTS

The Company of the Vienna State Opera in *Die Walküre* included: Rosette Anday, Judith Hellwig, Christa Ludwig, Jean Madiera, Birgit Nilsson, Hilda Roessel-Majdan, Martha Röhs, Leonie Rysanek, Lotte Rysanek, Gerda Scheyrer, Margarethe Sjoestedt, Gottlob Frick, Hans Hotter and Ludwig Suthaus.

CONDUCTORS

Gianandrea Gavazzeni, Herbert von Karajan, Nino Sanzogno, Antonino Votto.

MODENA. TEATRO COMUNALE

REPERTORY

Lucia di Lammermoor, Manon Lescaut, Queen of Spades, Trovatore.

ARTISTS

Lucia Danieli, Gianna d'Angelo, Gigliola Frazzoni, Gianna Pederzini, Lola Pedretti, Margherita Roberti, Renata Scotto.

Aldo Bertocci, Dario Caselli, Dino Dondi, Piero Miranda Ferraro, Eugenio Fernandi, Mario Filippeschi, Giovanni Foiani, Ferdinando Li Donni, Cesare Masini-Sperti, Ugo Novelli, Vittorio Pandano, Ivan Sardi.

CONDUCTORS

Francesco Molinari-Prandelli, Mario Parenti, Nello Santi.

NAPLES. TEATRO SAN CARLO

Sovrintendente: Pasquale di Constanza

REPERTORY

Abstract Opera (Blacher)*, Adriana Lecouvreur*, Bohème (Leoncavallo)*, Carmen, Così fan tutte, Forza del Destino, Gianni Schicchi, Herz (Anton Webern)*, Hin und Zurück (Hinde-mith)*, Jura (Gavino Gabriel)* (world première), Linda di Chamounix*, Mas'aniello (Jacopo Napoli)*, Medea) Canonica)*, Mort de Socrate (Satie)*, Nerone (Boito)*, Norma, Rondine, Siegfried, Suor Angelica, Tabarro, Tosca, Trovatore*, Vortice (Rossellini) (world première)*.

ARTISTS

Nelly Adamante, Leonore Antonacci, Teresa Apolei, Fedora Barbieri, Teresa Berganza, Vera Biondi, Anna Maria Borrelli, Vittoria Buccini, Rosanna Carteri, Anita Cerquetti, Mara Coleva, Lydia Coppola, Olga Costanzo, Stella Costas, Marina Cucchio, Anna De Cavalieri, Iole De Maria, Teresa Destito, Anna Di Stasio, Oralia Dominguez, Pina Esca, Valeria Escalar, Conchita Figuera, Res Fischer, Olimpia Gentile, Marie Luise Gerlach, Rina Gigli, Edith Hantzesche, Ellinor Junker-Giesen, Adriana Lazzarini, Laura Macario, Vera Magrini, Luise Malagrida, Maria Teresa Mandalari, Mafalda Masini, Ursula Menert, Tina Merola, Sofia Mezzetti, Neda Monte, Lidia Nerozzi, Rosetta Noli, Alda Noni, Fiorell Ortis, Ellinor Palme, Clara Petrella, Dina Piccini, Miriam Pirazzini, Marcella Pobbe, Giulietta Pulissi, Tina Quagliarella, Gisella Richter, Anna Maria Roccato, Valeria Roselli, Hildegard Ruthegers, Lari Scipioni, Carla Schlean, Carol Smith, Nerina Stabile, Antonietta Stella, Teresa Stich Randall, Maja Sunara, Pia Tassinari, Renata Tebaldi, Astrid Varnay, Palmira Vitali Marini, Vera Vogna.

Francesco Albanese, Giorgio Algorta, Alfredo Allegro, Theo Altmeyer, Lorenzo Alvary, Giovanni Amodeo, Antonio Annaloro, Gianni Avolanti, Ettore Bastianini, Donald Bell, Massino Bison, Mario Borriello, Gerd Brenneis, Renato Capecchi, Mariano Caruso, Antonio Casagrande, Antonio Cassinelli, Carlo Cava, Gennaro Chiocca, Mario Cioffi, Plinio Clabassi, Anselmo Colzani, Franco Corelli, Francesco Cotogno, Armando Dadò, Mino della Porta, Mario Del Monaco, Piero de Palma, Gustl Dierkers, Mario Famiglietti, Mino Fanelli, Sergio Feliciani, Enzo Feliciati, Ferrando Ferrari, Nicola Filacuridi, Mario Filippeschi, Curzio Felmi, Augusto Frati, Mario Frozini, Renato Gavarini, Salvatore Gioia, Giuseppi Gismondo, Francesco Glori Carooci, Giangiacoma Guelfi, Ulfried Gunther, Fritz Linke, Horst Lunoff, Guido Malfatti, Alfredo Mariotti, Giulio Mastrangelo, Ferruccio Mazzoli, Giuseppe Modesti, Walter Monachesi, Giovanni Napoleone, Gustav Neidlinger, Juan Oncina, Giorgio Onesti, Luigi Palatucci, Luigi Paolillo, Mario Petri, Osvaldo Petricciuolo, Mirto Picchi, Antonio

Pomposelli, Carlo Portaluppi, Aldo Protti, Gianni Raimondi, Jose Ramon, Angelo Rossi, Antonio Sacchetti, Silvio Santarelli, Gino Sarri, Gino Sinimberghi, Mario Sorrentino, Gerhard Stolze, Manuel Spatafora, Reiner Suchsdorf, Vito Susca, Giuseppe Taddei, Ferruccio Tagliavini, Lino Telesco, Giuseppe Valdengo, Gaetano Valentini, Enzi Viaro, Ramon Vinay, Wolfgang Windgassen, Oswald Zowielok.

CONDUCTORS

Vincenzo Bellezza, Franco Capuana, Oliviero de Fabritiis, Alessandro Derevitzky, Ferdinand Leitner, Francesco Molinari Prandelli, Angelo Questa, Ugo Rapalò, Mario Rossi, Hermann Scherchen, Tullio Serafin, Paul Strauss.

PALERMO. TEATRO MASSIMO
Sovrintendente: Simone Cuccia

REPERTORY

Aida, Domanda di Matrimonio*(Chailly), Elisir d'Amore, Enfant et les Sortilèges*, Fanciulla del West*, Fedora*, Fliegende Holländer, Mefistofele, Norma*, Oedipus Rex*, Pagliacci, Pirata*, The Old Maid and the Thief (Menotti).

ARTISTS

Maria Caniglia, Maria Cannizzaro, Rosanna Carteri, Anita Cerquetti, Maria Curtis Verna, Lucia Danieli, Laura Didier, Loretta Di Lelio, Jolanda Gardino, Dora Gatta, Maria Luisa Gavioli, Mafalda Micheluzzi, Maria Noè, Rosetta Noli, Alda Noni, Magda Olivero, Nicoletta Panni, Giulietta Simionato, Jane Stuart Smith, Maja Sunara, Jeda Valtriani.

Luigi Alva, Mario Assen, Enrico Campi, Renato Capecchi, Mariano Caruso, Athos Cesarini, Leonardo Ciriminna, Anselmo Colzani, Franco Corelli, Franco Cotogno, Gaetano Crinzi, Giuseppe Di Stefano, Pietro Ferrara, Agostino Ferrin, Giulio Fioravanti, Dino Formichini, Amedeo Graziano, Giangiacomo Guelfi, Alfredo Kraus, Rino Le Cicero, Angelo Loforese, Guido Malfatti, Guido Mazzini, Giuseppe Micucci, Ugo Miraglia, Giuseppe Modesti, Mirto Picchi, Aldo Protti, Paul Schoeffler, Lari Scipioni, Cesare Siepi, Manuel Spatafora, Giuseppe Taddei, Ferruccio Tagliavini, Giuseppe Vertechi, Ivo Vinco.

And for *L'Enfant et les Sortilèges:*

Annik Simon, Janine Micheau, Hélène Bouvier, Agnes Disney, Marcelle Croizier, Matilde Riva, Bernard Plantey, Julien Haas, Charles Clavensy, Gerard Friedmann.

CONDUCTORS

Franco Capuana, Umberto Cattini, Franco Ghione, Jonel Perlea, Gianfranco Rivoli, Tullio Serafin, Ottavio Ziino.

PIACENZA. TEATRO MUNICIPALE

REPERTORY

Bohème, Ernani, Faust, Pagliacci, Raggio di Sole (Martini), Traviata.

ARTISTS

Aureliana Beltrami, Raffaella Ferrari, Mirella Fregni, Rina Malatraši, Claudia Parada, Carmen Piccini, Anna Maria Rota.

Doro Antonioli, Piero Miranda Ferraro, Remo Jori, Gastone Limarelli, Cesare Masini-Sperti, Gianni Poggi, Aldo Protti, Gianni Raimondi, Ivo Vincò, Paolo Washington, Mario Zanasi.

CONDUCTORS

Renzo Martini, Mario Parenti, Nello Santi, Ottavio Ziino.

REGGIO EMILIA. TEATRO MUNICIPALE

REPERTORY:

Carmen, Faust, Forza del Destino, Gianni Schicchi, Lucia di Lammermoor, Manon Lescaut, Medium*, Pagliacci, Simone Boccanegra, Suor Angelica, Tabarro, Tristan und Isolde, and (by the Teatro Comunale di Bologna) Queen of Spades.

ARTISTS

Fedora Barbieri, Maria Bertolini, Elsa Camellini, Anna-Maria Canali, Anita Corridori, Sonia Croci, Gianna d'Angelo, Raffaella Ferrari, Pilar Lorengar, Dora Minarchi, Vera Montanari, Elena Nicolai, Magda Olivero, Augusta Oltrabella, Margherita Panni, Claudia Parada, Franca Sacchi, Margherita Roberti, Anna Maria Rovere.

Antonio Annaloro, Doro Antoniolo, Raffaela Ariè, Effire Bastianini, Gino Belloni, Anselmo Colzani, Franco Corelli, Eugenio Ferrandi, Renato Gavarini, Tito Gobbi, Piero Guelfi, Gianni Iaia, Flaviano Labo, Gastone Limarilli, Melchiorre Luise, Aurelio Oppicelli, Attilio Paterlini, Paolo Pedani, Aldo Protti, Iginio Riccò, Romano Roma, Nicola Rossi-Lemeni, Lorenzo Sabatucci, Felice Schiavi, Tommaso Spataro, Mariano Stabile, Roberto Turrini, Enzo Viaro, Carlo Zampighi.

CONDUCTORS

Oliviero de Fabritiis, Franco Ghione, Wolfgang Martin, Franco Patane, Ermanno Wolf-Ferrari, Ottario Ziino.

ROME. TEATRO DELL'OPERA
Sovrintendente: Constantino Parisi

REPERTORY

Adriana Lecouvreur, Bohème (Puccini), Boris Godunov, Dialogues des Carmélites*, Don Carlos, Freischütz, Gianni Schicchi, Lucia di Lammermor, Madama Butterfly, Madame Bovary (Pannain)*, Norma, Pagliacci, Parsifal, Quattro Rusteghi, Rigoletto, Tesoro (Napoli) (world première)*, Werther.

ARTISTS

Elisabetta Barbato, Fedora Barbieri, Silvana Bazzoni, Silvia Bertona, Rita Bezzi Breda, Giannella Borelli, Fernanda Cadoni, Anna Maria Canali, Rosanna Carteri, Anita Cerquetti, Santa Chissari, Nini Colombo, Rina Corsi, Gianna D'Angelo, Lucia Danieli, Nara Demarista Bacci, Nietta De Robertis, Nora De Rosa, Loretta Di Lelio, Ofelia Di Marco, Maria Eira, Gina Ercole, Onelia Fineschi, Valeria Fiocchi Escalar, Myriam Funari, Dora Gutta, Rina Gigli, Maria Huder, Ornella Jachetti, Ada Landi, Anna Leonelli, Juanita Llosa Porras, Pina Malgarini, Caterina Mancini, Anna Marcangeli, Lydia Marimpietri, Maria Mazza, Maria Meneghini Callas, Mafalda Micheluzzi, Dora Minarchi, Vera C. Montanari, Adelaide Montano, Maria Noe, Alda Noni, Amalia Oliva, Magda Olivero, Norma Palmieri, Nicoletta Panni, Gianna Pederzini, Clara Petrella, Amalia Pini, Myriam Pirazzini, Liliana Poli, Verz Presti, Giuliana Raimondi, Lia Ranzini, Elena Rizzieri, Angela Rocco, Lari Scipioni, Giulietta Simionato, Antonietta Stella, Pia Tassinari, Gabriella Tucci, Angelica Tuccari, Corinna Vozza, Luciana Zanolli, Virginia Zeani.

Francesco Albanese, Giovanni Amodeo, Angelo Cartoli, Mario Borriello, Paulo Caroli, Antonio Cassinelli, Carlo Cava, Michele Cazzato, Renato Cesari, Athos Cesarini, Boris Christoff, Plinio Clabassi, Alfredo Colella, Gino Conti, Franco Corelli, Armando Dadò, Gianni Dal Ferro, Paulo Dari, Piero De Palma, Valerio Degli Abbati, Raffaele De Falchi, Mario Del Monaco, Fernando Delle Fornaci, Vito De Taranto, Salvatore Di Tommaso, Giuseppe Di Stefano, Dante Eleuteri, Renato Ercolani, Mario Filippeschi, Giulio Fioravanti, Carlo Franzini, Umberto Frisaldi, Antonio Galiè, Blando Giusti, Tito Gobbi, Enzo Guagni, Alfredo Kraus, Gianni Jaia, Arturo La Porta, Agostino Lazzari, Fernando Lidonni, Sergio Liviabella, Melchiorre Luise, Giampiero Malaspina, Enzo Mascherini, Giulio Neri, Giorgio Onesti, Adolfo Pacini, Piero Passarotti, Filiberto Picozzi,

Antonio Pirino, Carlo Platania, Afro Poli, Giacinto Prandelli, Franco Pugliese, Nicola Rossi-Lemini, Mino Russo, Antonio Sacchetti, Ugo Savarese, Bruno Sbalchiero, Osvaldo Scrigna, Gino Sinimberghi, Enzo Sordello, Tommaso Spataro, Virgilio Stocco, Italo Tajo, Ferruccio Tagliavini, Vito Tatone, Sergio Tedesco, Enzo Titta, Giulio Tomei, Fernando Valentini, Adelio Zagonara and for *Parsifal*: Rita Gorr, Gottlob Frick, Walter Hagen, Tomislav Neralic, Georg Stern, Wolfgang Windgassen.

CONDUCTORS

Napoleone Annovazzi, Vincenzo Bellezza, Franco Capuana, André Cluytens, Oliviero De Fabritiis, Vittorio Gui, Armando La Rosa Parodi, Angelo Questa, Gabriele Santini, Emidio Tieri.

TRIESTE. TEATRO COMUNALE— GIUSEPPE VERDI
Sovrintendente: Giuseppe Antonielli

REPERTORY

Bohème, Boris Godunov, Carmina Burana*, Dialogues des Carmélites*, Fledermaus, Lucia di Lammermoor, Mefistofele, Pagliacci, Tristan und Isolde, Trovatore.

ARTISTS

Annamaria Anelli, Sandra Ballinari, Edda Bradaschia, Rosanna Carteri, Laura Cavalieri, Nora De Rosa, Oralia Dominguez, Leyla Gencer, Liliana Hussu, Dora Minarchi, Nicoletta Panni, Gianna Pederzini, Rita Pierobon, Eugenia Ratti, Esther Réthy, Elda Ribetti, Hilde Roessl-Majdan, Bruna Ronchini, Renata Scotto, Luciana Serafini, Helene Werth, Silvana Zanolli.

Bernd Aldenhoff, Antonio Annaloro, Raffaele Ariè, Franco Artioli, Ettore Bastianini, Raimondo Botteghelli, Nino Carta, Renato Cesari, Marcello Cortis, Enrico Dezan, Gaetano Fanelli, Mario Filippeschi, Carlo Franzini, Carlos Guichandut, Friedrick Guthrie, Alfredo Kraus, Nicolo Macillis, Alessandro Maddalena, Antonio Massaria, Guido Mazzini, Andrea Mongelli, Eno Mucchiutti, Giuseppe Nadalin, Gianni Poggi, Giacinto Prandelli, Leo Pudis, Lorenzo Sabatucci, Ugo Savarese, Glauco Scarlini, Paul Schoeffler, Enzo Sordello, Vito Susca, Ferruccio Tagliavini, Sergio Tedesco Adelio Zagonara.

CONDUCTORS

Vincenzo Bellezza, Oliviero de Fabritiis, Richard Kraus, Armando La Rosa Parodi, Rudolf Moralt, Anton Paulik, Ugo Rapalò.

TURIN. TEATRO REGIO al CARIGNANO and al NUOVO
Sovrintendente: Ferruccio Negrelli

REPERTORY
Amelia al Ballo, Barbiere di Siviglia, Bohème, Buricchino (Trecate)*, Due Foscari, Furie di Arlecchino (Lualdi), Manon, Rigoletto, Rita, Traviata, Turco in Italia.

ARTISTS
Clara Betner, Rosanna Carteri, Maria Luisa Cioni, Gianna d'Angelo, Jolanda Gardino, Dora Gatta, Leyla Gencer, Giusa Gerbino, Adalgisa Giordano, Jolanda Mancini, Mafalda Masini, Mafalda Micheluzzi, Eugenia Ratti, Elena Rizzieri, Giulietta Simionato, Ermina Spledore, Ivana Tosini, Silvana Zanolli.

Alberto Albertini, Carlo Badioli, Ottorino Begali, Armando Benzi, Renato Capecchi, Renato Ercolani, Eugenio Fernandi, Carlo Franzini, Amerigo Gentilini, Gian Giacomo Guelfi, Pier Luigi Latinucci, Agostino Lazzari, Melchiorre Luise, Alessandra Maddalena, Jole Marchese, Angelo Marchiandi, Guido Mazzini, Carlo Meliciani, Alvinio Misciano, Ugo Novelli, Mirto Picchi, Gianni Poggi, Afro Poli, Luigi Pontiggia, Leo Pudis, Lino Puglisi, Nicola Rossi-Lemeni, Ugo Savarese, Mariano Stabile, Sergio Tedesco, Giuseppe Valdengo, Paolo Washington, Giovanni Zabin, Adelio Zagonara, Mario Zorgniotti.

CONDUCTORS
Mario Braggio, Franco Capuana, Carlo Cillario, Oliviero de Fabritiis, Franco Ghione.

VENICE. TEATRO la FENICE
Sovrintendente: Virgilio Mortari

REPERTORY
Campiello, Cenerentola, Don Giovanni, Due Foscari*, Love for Three Oranges, Rusalka*, Tosca, Tristan und Isolde, Trovatore, Vergilii Aeneis (Malipiero)*(world première).

ARTISTS
Mariella Adani, Maria Amadini, Clara Betner, Anna de Cavalieri, Dora Gatta, Leyla Gencer, Magda Laszlò, Ilva Ligabue, Rina Malatrasi, Jolanda Michieli, Dora Minarchi, Orietta Moscucci, Vittoria Palombini, Elena Rizzieri, Anna Maria Rovere, Marisa Salimbeni, Giulietta Simionato, Eva Tomassy, Emelina de Vito.

Luigi Alva, Florindo Andreolli, Carlo Badioli, Ottorino Begali, Sesto Bruscantini, Giangiacomo Guelfi, Giacomo Lauri-Volpi, Alessandro Madda-lena, Giampiero Malaspina, Santo Messina, Nicola Monti, Leonardo Monreale, Alfredo Nobile, Paolo Pedani, Mirto Picchi, Gianni Poggi, Afro Poli, Luigi Pontiggia, Guerrando Rigiri, Nicola Rossi-Lemeni, Ugo Savarese, Uberto Scaglione, Giorgio Tadeo, Augusto Veronese.

CONDUCTORS
Zdenek Chalabala, Carlo Cillario, Ettore Gracis, Vittorio Gui, Armando la Rosa Parodi, Bogo Leskovic, Angelo Questa, Tullio Serafin.

GUEST ARTISTS
The company of the Prague National Theatre in *Rusalka* including: Miroslava Fidlerova, Marta Krasova, Vera Krilova, Jarmila Pechova, Marie Podvalova, Milada Subrtova, Dagmar Zizkova, Eduard Haken, Premysl Koci, Antonin Votava, Ivo Zidek; the Bayreuth 1957 comapny in *Tristan und Isolde* including Birgit Nilsson, Grace Hoffman, Wolfgang Windgassen, Gustav Neidlinger, Arnold van Mill; Conductor Wolfgang Sawallisch; and the Ljublana National Theatre Company for the *Love for Three Oranges*, including Vilma Bukovec, Simeon Car, Drago Cuden, Vladimir Dolnicar, Vanda Gerovic, Bozena Glavak, Sonja Hocevar, Vekoslav Janko, Ladko Korosec, Zdravko Kovac, Janez Lipuscek, Friderik Lupsa, Danilo Merlak, Manja Mlejnik, Marusa Patik, Samo Smerkolj, Slavko Strukelj, Bogdana Stritear, Vanda Ziherl.

MONACO

MONTE CARLO. THÉÂTRE de l'OPÉRA
Director: Maurice Besnard

REPERTORY
Carmen, Elektra, Lohengrin, Lucia di Lammermoor, Otello, Pêcheurs de Perles, Turandot.

ARTISTS
Martha Angelici, Vivette Barthelmy, Christel Goltz, Giuiditta Mazzoleni, Margherita Roberti, Consuelo Rubio, Leonie Rysanek, Hilde Zadek.

Ernest Blanc, Renato Cesari, José Figianelli, Piero Guelfi, Carlos Guichandut, Hans Hopf, Hans Hotter, Flaviano Labò, Richard Martell, Vittorio Pandano, Rolando Panerai, Glauco Scarlini, Alain Vanzo, Ivo Vincò.

CONDUCTORS
Gianfranco Rivoli, Heinrich Hollreiser.

PORTUGAL

LISBON. TEATRO NACIONAL DE S. CARLOS

REPERTORY

Carmina Burana*, Così fan tutte, Dialogues des Carmélites, Elektra, Falstaff, Fliegende Holländer, Gerura*, Hänsel und Gretel, Italiana in Algieri, Manon Lescaut, Pagliacci, Prince Igor, Rigoletto, Ta-Mar (Coelho)*; Traviata, Walküre.

ARTISTS

Anna Maria Canali, Rina Cavallari, Prisca Dietrich, Siw Ericsdotter, Res Fischer, Christel Goltz, Grace Hoffman, Irma Keller, Maria Meneghini Callas, Malfalda Micheluzzi, Orietta Moscucci, Birgit Nilsson, Magda Olivero, Lisa Otto, Nicoletta Panni, Antonietta Pastori, Gianni Pederzini, Clara Petrella, Elda Ribetti, Nora de Rosa, Hella Ruttkowsky, Franca Sacchi, Renata Scotto, Luciana Serafini, Giulietta Simionato, Teresa Stich-Randall, Liane Synek, Eva Tamassy, Herta Töpper, Susanne Will, Ingeborg Weiss, Maria Wolkowsky.

Luigi Alva, Antonio Annaloro, Raffaele Arie, Umberto Borso, Heinz Borst, Rolf Böttcher, Sesto Bruscantini, Renato Cesari, Anton Dermota, Karl Dönch, Renato Ercolani, Deszö Ernster, Gaetano Fanelli, Walter Geisler, Giorgio Giorgetti, Tito Gobbi, Carlos Guichandut, Walter Hagner, Alfredo Kraus, Karl Krollmann, Erich Kunz, Alessandro Maddalena, Giampiero Malaspina, Alfredo Mariotti, Tomislav Neralic, Piero de Palma, Albrecht Peter, Mario Petri, Leo Pudis, Ugo Savarese, Mario Sereni, Paul Schöffler, Vito Susca, Josef Traxel, Otto Wiener.

CONDUCTORS

Ruy Coelho, Oliviero de Fabritiis, Pedro de Freitas Branco, Franco Ghione, Alexander Krannhals, George Sebastian.

SPAIN

BARCELONA. GRAN TEATRO DEL LICEO
Manager: Jose F. Arquer

REPERTORY

Adriana Lecouvreur, Bohème, Cosí fan tutte, Don Pasquale, Faust, Gianni Schicchi, Guerra*, Madama Butterfly, Maria Egiziaca (Respighi)*, Parsifal, Retablo de Maese Pedro*, Rigoletto, Rosenkavalier, Saint of Bleecker Street*, Salome, Suor Angelica, Thais, Tristan und Isolde, Trovatore, Vida Breve.

ARTISTS

Fedora Barbieri, Francisca Callao, Floriana Cavalli, Virginia Copeland, Rina Corsi, Gianna d'Angelo, Marie Louise Debierre, Maria Fabregas, Elvira Galassi, Margarita Gonzalez, Anneliese Kupper, Adriana Lazzarini, Emmy Loose, Ira Malaniuk, Kerstin Meyer, Jeanette Navarre, Birgit Nilsson, Alda Noni, Augusta Oltrabella, Dolores Ottani, Dolores Perez, Lina Richarte, Anna Maria Rovere, Amelia Ruival, Micheline Sanders, Lari Scipioni, Marianne Schech, Enriqueta Tarrés, Renata Tebaldi, Helene Werth, Silvana Zanolli.

Miguel Aguerri, Luis Ma Andrey, Antonio Annaloro, Guillermo Arroniz, Manuel Ausensi, René Bianco, Otello Borgonovo, Hans Braun, Renato Capecchi, Walter Cassel, Julio Catania, Oskar Czerwenka, Marcello de Giovanni, Libero de Luca, José Escola, Eugenio Fernandi, Josef Gostic, Josef Graendl, Alfons Herwig, Melchoirre Luise, Giuseppe Modesti, Ugo Novelli, Juan Oncina, Alios Pernerstorfer, Alfred Poell, Gianni Poggi, Giacinto Prandelli, Juan Rico, Manuel Santullano, Ugo Savarese, Paul Savignol, Laszlo Szemere, André Testai, Wolfgang Windgassen, Ernst Wiemann, Adelio Zagonara, Ivo Zidek.

CONDUCTORS

Carlo Felice Cillario, Gustave Cloez, Laszlo Halasz, Heinrich Hollreiser, José Iturbi, Franz Konwitschny, Rafael Pou, Angelo Questa, Nino Verchi

SWEDEN

STOCKHOLM. ROYAL OPERA
(including Blanche Theatre and Drottningholm)
Director: Set Svanholm

REPERTORY

Ballo in Maschera, Barbiere di Siviglia*, Boris Godunov, Carmen, Cavalleria Rusticana, Entführung aus dem Serail, Fanal (Atterberg), Fidelio, Fledermaus, Fridas Visor, Götterdämmerung, Louise*, Madama Butterfly, Nozze di Figaro, Orfeo, Pagliacci, Parsifal, Rape of Lucretia*, Rheingold, Rigoletto, Salome, Schule der Frauen*, Siegfried, Tannhäuser, Tranfjädrarna (Bäck)*, Tristan und Isolde, Trojans (Berlioz)*, Trovatore, Turn of the Screw, Walküre, Wozzeck, Zauberflöte.

ARTISTS

Margareta Bakker, Margareta Bergström, Brita Christiansen, Kjerstin Dellert, Mattiwilda Dobbs (guest), Barbro Ericson, Judith Garellick, Margareta Hallin, Busk-Margit Jonsson, Ingeborg Kjellgren, Karin Langebo, Kerstin Meyer, Ruth

Moburg, Birgit Nilsson, Carrie Nilsson, Aase Nördmo-Lövberg, Sonja Norin, Florence Pilotti, Eva Prytz, Hjördis Schymberg, Margit Sehlmark, Anna-Greta Söderholm, Elisabeth Söderström.

Bertil Alstergärd, Einar Andersson, Joel Berglund (guest), Lars Billengren, Leon Björker, Jussi Björling (guest), Sigurd Björling, Luigi Carrara, Jurgen Edman, Eric Gustafson, Carl-Axel Hallgren, Hugo Hasslo, Arne Hendriksen, Kolbjörn Höiseth, Sven-Eric Jacobsson, Folke Jonsson, Anders Näslund, Sven Nilsson, Arne Ohlson, Eric Saeden, Olle Sivall, Conny Söderström, Uno Stjernquist, Eric Sundquist, Gunner Suttner, Set Svanholm, Georg Svedenbrant, Ingemar Swahn, Ernö Talas, Arne Tyren, Ragnar Ulfung (guest), Sven-Eric Vikström, Sven Wallskog, Arne Wiren, Ingvar Wixell.

CONDUCTORS

Sixten Ehrling, Kurt Bendix, Bertil Bokstadt, Bengt Lagerkrist, Lars af Malmborg, Bruno Rigacci, Herbert Sandberg, Arne Sunnegärdh, Albert Wolff.

SWITZERLAND

BASEL. STADTTHEATER
Intendant: Hermann Wedekind

REPERTORY

Aïda, Bluebeard's Castle, Così fan tutte, Contes d'Hoffmann, Fliegende Holländer, Giulio Cesare, Lohengrin, Lustigen Weiber von Windsor, Salome, Tilman Riemerschneider (Paszthory)*, Titus Feuerfuchs* (Sutermeister) (world première).

ARTISTS

Monserrat Caballé, Eva Daehne, Ingeborg Felderer, Jutta Lehmann, Ruth Schneider, Herta Schomburg, Ingeborg Wieser, Sabine Zimmer.

Willy Ackermann, Richard Alexander, Michael Arco, Hanns Bastian, Karl Brock, Berthold Büche, Eduard Heindrichs, Kurd E. Heyne, Johannes Kathol, Gottard Kronstein, Dr. Peter Schnyder, Herbert Simon, Wenko Wenkoff, Zbyslaw Wozniak.

CONDUCTORS

Silvio Varviso, Harry Rodmann, Karl Kuerleber, Paul Zelter.

GUEST ARTISTS during the season included:
Inge Borkh, Elsa Cavelti, Grace Hoffman, Colette Lorand, Hilde Zadek, Scipio Colombo, Ernest Häfliger, Derrick Olsen, Heinz Rehfuss, Alexander Welitsch, Wolfgang Windgassen; Hans Münch.

BERNE. STADTHEATER
Director: Stephan Beinl

REPERTORY

Bernauerin (Orff), Così fan tutte, Don Giovanni, Fidelio, Fliegende Holländer, Manon Lescaut, Notre Dame (Schmidt)*, Nozze di Figaro, Rigoletto, Simon Boccanegra, Trovatore, Waffenschinied, Walküre, Zauberflöte.

ARTISTS

Melanie Geissler, Helga Kosta, Chlöe Owen, Luise Paichl, Isabel Strauss, Nata Tüscher, Lucia Wehr, Christine von Widmann, Gerty Wiessner.

Richard Bedel, Tino Bertrand, Theodor Bitzos, Gottfried Fehr, Max Jakisch, Jacob Keller, Albert Kunz, Felix Loeffel, Spiro Makri, Fridolin Mosbacher, Ulo Panizza, Adolf Veuhoff.

CONDUCTORS

Otto Ackermann (guest), Robert F. Denzler (guest), Georg Meyer, Otto Osterwalder, Fritz Janota, Anton Knüsel.

GENEVA. GRAND CASINO
Artistic Director: Charles Held

REPERTORY

Angélique, Bohème, Faust, Fidelio, Heure Espagnole, Jongleur de Notre-Dame, Lohengrin, Lucia di Lammermoor, Nozze di Figaro, Tristan und Isolde, Tosca.

ARTISTS.

Geori Boué, Jacqueline Brumaire, Maud Cunitz, Denise Duval, Monique Florence, Josette Favey, Christel Goltz, Marina Hotine, Else Liebesberg, Janine Ribot, Marianne Schech, Hanny Steffek.

Victor Autran, Georges Bouvier, Kurt Böhme, Hugues Cuenod, Xavier Depraz, Leon Ferly, Josef Greindl, Paul Kuen, Albert Lance, Karl Liebl, Fritz Ollendorff, Alain Vanco, Eberhard Wächter, Wolfgang Windgassen.

CONDUCTORS

Robert F. Denzler, Heinrich Hollreiser, Leopold Ludwig.

ZÜRICH. STADTTHEATER
Intendant: Karl Heinz Krahl

REPERTORY

Barbiere di Siviglia*, Carmen*, Elektra*, Falstaff*, Fidelio, Freischütz*, Macbeth*, Rheingold*, Schwanda the Bagpiper*, Schule der Frauen*, Trovatore*, Turandot*, Walküre*, Zar und Zimmermann.

ARTISTS

Hilde Büchel, Jacqueline Bügler, Mary Davenport, Ingeborg Fanger, Ingeborg Friedrich, Hilde Koch, Elsa Matheis, Eva Maria Rogner, Vera Schlosser.

Robert Bernauer, Heinz Borst, Rolf Böttcher, Hans Dahmen, Erwin Deblitz, Hans-Bert Dick, Willy Ferenz, Charles Gillig, Reinhold Güther, Walter Hesse, Ernst Koschnitzke, Franz Lechleitner, Wolfram Mertz, Karl Pistorius, Heinz Rhöden, Werner Rüegsegger, Ernst-August Steinhoff, Alfred Strasser, Siegfried Tappolet, Nikolaus Toth, Gottlieb Zeithammer.

CONDUCTORS

Hans Rosbaud, Hans Walter Kämpfel, Victor Reinshagen, Eduard Hartogs, Fred Widmer, Hans Rohrer.

GUEST ARTISTS during the season included: Melitta Muszely, Birgit Nilsson, Helga Pilarczyk, Marianna Radev, Marte Asse, Astrid Varnay, Giuseppe di Stefano, Helge Roswaenge, Heinz Imdahl.

UNITED STATES OF AMERICA

CHICAGO. LYRIC OPERA OF CHICAGO
General Manager: Carol Fox

REPERTORY

Adriana Lecouvreur*, Andrea Chénier, Ballo in Maschera, Bohème, Cavalleria Rusticana, Don Carlos*, Gioconda, Lucia di Lammermoor, Manon Lescaut, Mignon, Nozze di Figaro, Otello, Pagliacci, Tosca.

ARTISTS

Anita Cerquetti, Jeanne Diamond, Eileen Farrell, Patricia Frahner, Ardis Krainik, Irene Kramarich, Anna Maria Kuhn, Eva Likova, Anna Moffo, Nlle Rankin, Rosalind Nadell, Giulietta Simionato, Sylvia Stahlman, Eleanor Steber, Renata Tebaldi, Claramae Turner.

Carlo Badioli, Walter Berry, Jussi Björling, Mariano Caruso, Leslie Chabay, Boris Christoff, Mario del Monaco, Giuseppe di Stefano, Andrew Foldi, Tito Gobbi, Lloyd Harris, Bernard Izzo, Cornell MacNeil, Alvinio Misciano, Miles Nekolny, Henri Noel, Aldo Protti, Kenneth Smith, Brian Sullivan, Richard Tucker, Jonas Vaznelis, Andrew Velis, William Wilderman.

CONDUCTORS

Bruno Bartoletti, Gianandrea Gavazzeni, Leo Kopp, Tullio Serafin, Georg Solti.

CINCINATTI SUMMER OPERA (1957)

REPERTORY

Barbiere di Siviglia, Bohème, Carmen, Faust, Lucia di Lammermoor, Madama Butterfly, Nozze di Figaro, Rosenkavalier, Tosca, Traviata, Trovatore.

ARTISTS

Thelma Altman, Frances Bible, Nadine Conner, Maria di Giovanza, Laurel Hurley, Tomika Kanazawa, Irene Kramarich, Eva Likova, Gloria Lind, Antonietta Stella, Eleanor Steber, Claramae Turner, Dorothy Warenskjold.

Virginio Assandri, Cesare Bardelli, Napoleon Bisson, John Brownlee, Giuseppe Campora, Eugene Conley, Lawrence Davidson, Wilfrid Engleman, Barry Morell, James Pease, Rudolph Petrak, Georg Tallone, Roberto Turrini, Frank Valentino, William Wildermann.

CONDUCTORS

Fausto Cleva, Antonio Coppola, Carlo Moresco, Thor Johnson,

NEW YORK. METROPOLITAN OPERA
General Manager: Rudolf Bing

REPERTORY

Aïda, Andrea Chénier, Barbiere di Siviglia, Bohème, Carmen, Don Giovanni*, Eugene Onegin*, Faust, Forza del Destino, Gianni Schicchi, Lucia di Lammermoor, Madama Butterfly*, Nozze di Figaro, Orfeo, Otello, Parsifal, Perichole, Rosenkavalier, Salome, Samson et Dalilah, Tosca, Traviata, Tristan und Isolde, Vanessa* (Barber) (world première), Walküre.

ARTISTS

Licia Albanese, Mildred Allen, Lucine Amara, Belen Amparan, Inge Borkh, Maria Meneghini Callas, Madelaine Chambers, Nadine Conner, Emilia Cundari, Mary Curtis-Verna, Irene Dalis, Gloria Davy, Lisa Della Casa, Victoria de los Angeles, Mattiwilda Dobbs, Rosalind Elias, Hilde Gueden, Margaret Harshaw, Laurel Hurley, Sena Jurinac, Dorothy Kirsten, Heidi Krall, Brenda Lewis, Gloria Lind, Martha Lipton, Virginia MacWatters, Jean Madeira, Zinka Milanov, Mildred Miller, Martha Moedl, Mariquita Moll, Patrice Munsel, Carlotta Ordassy, Roberta Peters, Marcella Pobbe, Lily Pons, Nell Rankin, Regina Resnik, Delia Rigal, Margaret Roggero, Marianne Schech, Eleanor Steber, Antonietta Stella, Risë Stevens, Renata Tebaldi, Helen Vanni, Thelma Votipka.

Lorenzo Alvary, Charles Anthony, Salvatore Baccaloni, Cesare Bardelli, Daniele Barioni, Kurt Baum, Carlo Bergonzi, John Brownlee, Giuseppe Campora, Gabor Carelli, Walter Cassel, George Cehanovsky, Fernando Corena, Jon Crain, Albert Da Costa, Lawrence Davidson, Mario Del Monaco, Alessio De Paolis, Otto Edelmann, Dezoe Ernster, Eugenio Fernandi, Ezio Flagello, Paul Franke, Giulio Gari, Nicolai Gedda, Frank Guarrera, Mack Harrell, Clifford Harvuot, Osie Hawkins, Ralph Herbert, Jerome Hines, Norman Kelley, Charles Kullman, Flaviano Labò, William Lewis, George London, Robert McFerrin, Calvin Marsh, Robert Merrill, Nicola Moscona, Robert Nogy, Gerhard Pechner, Jan Peerce, Norman Scott, Mario Sereni, Louis Sgarro, Cesare Siepi, Martial Singher, Giorgio Tozzi, Richard Tucker, Theodor Uppman, Frank Valentino, Cesare Valletti, Ramon Vinay, Leonard Warren, William Wildermann, Mario Zanasi.

CONDUCTORS

Karl Boehm, Fausto Cleva, Erich Leinsdorf, Dimitri Mitropoulos, Jean Morel, Max Rudolf, Thomas Schippers, Fritz Stiedry.

NEW YORK. CITY CENTRE
General Director: Julius Rudel

REPERTORY

Ballad of Baby Doe (Douglas Moore)*, Bohème, Carmen, Entführung aus dem Serail*, Faust, Fledermaus, Good Soldier Schweik (Kurka) (world première)*, Lost in the Stars (Weill)*, Macbeth*, Madama Butterfly, Medium, Old Maid and the Thief, Regina (Blitzstein)*, Susannah (Carlisle Floyd)*, Tale for a Deaf Ear (Bucci)*, Taming of the Shrew (Vittorio Giannini)*, Traviata, Trouble in Tahiti (Bernstein)*, Turandot, Vida Breve*.

ARTISTS

Adele Addison, Helen Baisley, Olivia Bonelli, Peggy Bonini, Beverly Bower, Carol Brice, Joan Carroll, Elisabeth Carron, Phyllis Curtin, Mignon Dunn, Ellen Faull, Phyllis Frank, Virginia Haskins, Mary Hensley, Irene Jordan, Ruth Kobart, Rita Kolasz, Beatrice Krebs, Gloria Lane, Mary Lesawyer, Brenda Lewis, Eva Likova, Martha Lipton, Gail Manners, Dolores Mari, Jacquelynne Moody, Patricia Neway, Graziella Polacco, Consuelo Rubio, Jean Sanders, Mathilde Sarrand, Beverly Sills, Sonia Stolin, Claramae Turner, Lee Venora, Beverly Wolff, Frances Yeend.

John Alexander, David Atkinson, Herbert Beattie, Arthur Budney, Walter Cassel, Richard Cassilly, William Chapman, Loren Driscoll, Howard Fried, Giuseppe Gismondo, Donald Gramm, Joshua Hecht, Paul Huddleston, Richard Humphrey, Keith Kaldenberg, Norman Kelley, William Lewis, David Lloyd, Chester Ludgin, Ernest McChesney, William Metcalf, Giovanni Millo, Barry Morell, Robert Moulson, Arthur Newman, Hernan Pelayo, Frank Poretta, Louis Quilico, John Reardon, Emile Renan, Robert Rounseville, Norman Treigle, Paul Ukena, Richard Wentworth, David Williams, Lawrence Winters.

CONDUCTORS

Peter Hermann Adler, Franz Allers, Arturo Basile, Theodore Bloomfield, Emerson Buckley, Arnold Gamson, Jose Iturbi, Samuel Krachmalnick, Seymour Lipkin, Julius Rudel, Gino Smart, Evan Whallon.

GUEST CONDUCTOR: Leonard Bernstein.

PHILADELPHIA GRAND OPERA ASSOCIATION
Director: Giuseppe Bamboschek

REPERTORY

Aïda, Cavalleria Rusticana, Elisir d'Amore, Forza del Destino, Norma, Rigoletto, Pagliacci, Tosca, Werther.

ARTISTS

Anita Cerquetti, Licia Albanese, Eva Likova, Sonia Leone, Dolores Mari, Herva Nelli, Gabriella Ruggiero, Nell Rankin.

Edward Doe, Salvatore Baccaloni, Cesare Bardelli, Kurt Baum, Richard Cassilly, Eugene Conley, Walter Fredericks, Raoul Jobin, Philip Maero, Giovanni Millo, Cornell MacNeil, Ben Scacher, Norman Scott, Martial Singher, Cesare Valletti, Frank Valentino, William Wildermann.

CONDUCTORS

Giuseppe Bamboschek, Vernon Hammond.

SAN FRANCISCO. WAR MEMORIAL OPERA HOUSE
General Director: Kurt Herbert Adler

REPERTORY

Aïda, Ariadne auf Naxos*, Ballo in Maschera, Così fan tutte, Dialogues des Carmélites*, Lucia di Lammermoor, Macbeth, Madama Butterfly, Rosenkavalier, Tosca, Traviata, Turandot.

ARTISTS

Licia Albanese, Frances Bible, Leyla Gencer, Helen George, Katherine Hilgenberg, Dorothy Kirsten, Jan McArt, Nan Merriman, Leontyne Price, Leonie Rysanek, Elisabeth Schwarzkopf, Sylvia Stahlman, Rita Streich, Blanch Thebom, Claramae Turner.

Lorenzo Alvary, Virginio Assandri, Heinz Blankenburg, Umberto Borghi, Jon Crain, Cesare Curzi, Otto Edelmann, Harold Enns, Howard Fried, Colin Harvey, Ralph Herbert, Murray Kenig, Richard Lewis, Raymond Manton, Robert Merrill, Nicola Moscona, Carl Palangi, Jan Peerce, Harve Presnell, Gianni Raimondi, Giuseppe Taddei, Eugene Tobin.

CONDUCTORS

Erich Leonsdorf, Francesco Molinari-Pradelli, William Steinberg, Glauco Curiel, Karl Kritz, Rudolph Fellner, Marcel Frank, Otto Guth, Armando Romano.

APPENDIX 1A

For the first time, we are listing this year, most of the important European Summer Operatic Festivals. As the Annual goes to press roughly at the same time as the first of this year's Festivals are beginning, we thought it logical to include the 1957 Festivals in our appendices, as they in fact can be regarded as the beginning of the 1957-8 Opera Season. This summer's (1958) Festivals will therefore be listed in next year's Annual as part of the 1958-9 season.

AIX-EN-PROVENCE.
INTERNATIONAL MUSIC FESTIVAL
9 to 31 July, 1957

REPERTORY

Carmen, Così fan tutte, Nozze di Figaro.

ARTISTS

Mariella Adani, Vivette Barthelemy, Teresa Berganza, Freda Betti, Jean Madeira, Geneviève Roblot, Graziella Sciutti, Irène Sicot, Teresa Stich-Randall, Janette Vivalda.

Luigi Alva, Henri Bedex, Christophe Benoit, Antonio Campo, Marcello Cortis, Nicola Filacuridi, Gerard Friedmann, Robert Geay, Michel Hamel, Daniel Marty, Rolando Panerai, Michel Roux, Michel Sénéchal.

CONDUCTORS

Pierre Dervaux, Hans Rosbaud.

BAYREUTH
RICHARD WAGNER FESTSPIELE
23 July to 25 August 1957

REPERTORY

Götterdämmerung, Meistersinger, Parsifal, Rheingold, Siegfried, Tristan und Isolde, Walküre.

ARTISTS

Elisabeth Grümmer, Grace Hoffman, Ilse Hollweg, Maria von Ilosvay, Sena Jurinac, Gerda Lammers, Paula Lenchner, Jean Madeira, Georgine von Milinkovic, Martha Mödl, Birgit Nilsson, Friedl Pöltinger, Lotte Rysanek, Dorothea Siebert, Elisabeth Schärtel, Astrid Varnay, Jutta Vulpius, Lore Wissmann.

Erich Benke, Toni Blankenheim, Kim Borg, Hans Krotthammer, Alexander Fenyves, Gottlob Frick, Eugen Fuchs, Walter Geisler, Josef Greindl, Hans Habietinek, Alfons Herwig, Hans Hotter, Josef Janko, Egmont Koch, George London, Arnold van Mill, Gustav Neidlinger, Karl Schmitt-Walter, Gerhard Stolze, Ludwig Suthaus, Josef Traxel, Hermann Uhde, Fritz Uhl, Ramon Vinay, Otto Wiener, Hermann Winkler, Wolfgang Windgassen, Heinz-Gunther Zimmermann.

CONDUCTORS

André Cluytens, Hans Knappertsbusch, Wolfgang Sawallisch.

EDINBURGH.
XI INTERNATIONAL FESTIVAL
18 August to 7 September 1957
The Company of La Piccola Scala, Milan

REPERTORY

Elisir d'Amore, Matrimonio Segreto, Sonnambula, Turco in Italia.

ARTISTS

Mariella Angioletti, Rosanna Carteri, Gabrieall

Caturan, Fiorenza Cossoto, Edith Martelli, Maria Meneghini Callas, Eugenia Ratti, Graziella Sciutti, Renata Scotto.

Luigi Alva, Carlo Badioli, Sesto Bruscantini, Franco Calabrese, Fernando Corena, Giuseppe di Stefano, Giulio Fioravanti, Angelo Mercuriali, Nicola Monti, Franco Ricciardi, Nicola Zaccaria.

CONDUCTORS
Gianandrea Gavazzeni, Nino Sanzogno, Antonino Votto.

FLORENCE.
XX MAGGIO MUSICALE FIORENTINO
9 May to 9 July 1957

REPERTORY
Abencérages (Cherubini), Ernani, Figliuol Prodigo (world première) (G. F. Malipiero), Katya Kabanova, Orfeo (Monteverdi), Tristan und Isolde, Venere Prigioniera (world première) (G. F. Malipiero).

ARTISTS
Cesy Broggini, Parehana Sethami, Melanie Bugarinovic, Anita Cerquetti, Irene Companeez, Valeria Heybalova, Grace Hoffman, Jolanda Meneguzzer, Birgit Nilsson, Lucille Udovik, Ettore Bastianini, Amedeo Berdini, Boris Christoff, Fernando Corena, Piero di Palma, Giulio Fioravanti, Mario del Monaco, Augusto Frati, Dino Fermichini, Herbert Handt, Robert Lauhöfer Angelo Loforese, Alvinio Misciano, Gustav Neidlinger, Aurelio Oppicelli, Mario Petri, Louis Roney, Angelo Rossi, Drago Stavc, Nicola Tzveych, Giuseppe Valdengo, Paolo Washington, Wolfgang Windgassen.

CONDUCTORS
Bruno Bartoletti, Kresimin Bavanovic, Carlo Maria Giulini, Dimitri Mitropoulos, Artur Rodzinski, Emidio Tieri.

GLYNDEBOURNE FESTIVAL OPERA
Artistic Director: Carl Ebert
General Manager: Moran Caplat
11 June to 13 August 1957

REPERTORY
Ariadne auf Naxos, Comte Ory, Entführung aus dem Serail, Falstaff, Italiana in Algeri*, Schauspieldirektor (Mozart)*, Zauberflöte.

ARTISTS
Lucine Amara, Sari Barabas, Fernanda Cadoni, Oralia Dominguez, Nancy Evans, Edna Graham,

Margareta Hallin, Heather Harper, Nadia Labay, Wilma Lipp, Pilar Lorengar, Orietta Moscucci, Antonietta Pastori, Rosl Schwaiger, Monica Sinclair, Elisabeth Soderström, Mimi Coertse, Joan Sutherland, Josephine Veasey.

Hervey Alan, James Atkins, Leo Bieber, Heinz Blankenburg, Antonio Boyer, Edward Byles, Marcello Cortis, Hugues Cuenod, Geraint Evans, Gwyn Griffiths, Ernst Haefliger, Thomas Hemsley, Peter Lagger, John Lewis, David Lloyd, Kevin Miller, Paolo Montarsolo, Juan Oncina, Mihaly Szekely.

CONDUCTORS
Vittorio Gui, John Pritchard, Paul Sacher, Bryan Balkwill, Peter Gellhorn.

HOLLAND FESTIVAL
15 June to 15 July 1957

REPERTORY
Don Pasquale, Otello, Rake's Progress.

ARTISTS
Mimi Aarden, Gré Brouwenstijn, Eugenia Ratti, Graziella Sciutti, Jo van de Meent.
Scipio Colombo, Eugene Conley, Guus Hoekman, Otakar Kraus, Chris Scheffer, Gé Smit, Mario Spina, Ramon Vinay, Frans Vroons.

CONDUCTORS
Bruno Bartoletti, Rafael Kubelik, Erich Leinsdorf, Maurits Sillem.

INGESTRE HALL. STAFFORD
10 to 12 May 1957
Manager: Barrie Hall

REPERTORY
Dido and Aeneas, Master Peter's Puppet Show.

ARTISTS
Magda Laszlò, Adèle Leigh, Monica Sinclair.
Bernhard Sonnerstedt, Alexander Young.

CONDUCTOR
John Pritchard.

MUNICH FESTIVAL
Prinzregententheater and Residenztheater
11 August to 10 September 1957

REPERTORY
Aegyptische Helena, Ariadne auf Naxos, Capriccio, Così fan tutte, Elektra, Entführung aus dem Serail, Frau ohne Schatten, Giulio Cesare (Händel), Harmonie der Welt (world première) (Hindemith), Lohengrin, Meistersinger von Nürn-

berg, Nozze di Figaro, Otello, Palestrina, Parsifal, Rosenkavalier, Salome, Wozzeck.

ARTISTS

Irmgard Barth, Lilian Benningsen, Maud Cunitz, Lisa Della Casa, Trude Eipperle, Antonie Fahberg, Liselotte Fölser, Ina Gerhein, Christel Goltz, Elisabeth Grümmer, Erika Köth, Anny van Kruyswyk, Annelies Kupper, Elisabeth Lindermeier, Gisela Litz, Liselotte Losch, Ira Malaniuk, Ruth Michaelis, Birgit Nilsson, Leonie Rysanek, Lotte Schädle, Marianne Schech, Rosl Schwaiger, Gerda Sommerschuh, Hanny Steffek, Hertha Töpper. Bernd Aldenhoff, Kurt Böhme, Walther Carnuth, Marcel Cordes, Otto Edelmann, Keith Engen, Lorenz Fehenberger, Ferdinand Frantz, Gottlob Frick, Richard Holm, Hans Hopf, Karl Hoppe, Hans Hotter, Adolf Keil, Franz Klarwein, Josef Knapp, Paul Kuen, Benno Kusche, Friedrich Lenz, Josef Metternich, Hans Hermann Nissen, Karl Ostertag, Albrecht Peter, Hermann Prey, Max Proebstl, Karl Schmitt-Walter, August Seider, Mihaly Szekely, Howard Vandenburg, Kurt Wehofschitz, Georg Wieter, Rudolf Wünzer.

CONDUCTORS

Karl Böhm, Ferenc Fricsay, Robert Heger, Paul Hindemith, Eugen Jochum, Joseph Keilberth, Hans Knappertsbusch, Fritz Rieger, Meinhard von Zallinger.

NAPLES. ARENA FLEGREA
6 July to 25 August 1957—X Season

REPERTORY

Elisir d'Amore, Gioconda, Otello, Tosca, Turandot.

ARTISTS

Aureliana Beltrami, Adelina Cambi, Anna De Cavalieri, Anna Di Stasio, Gigliola Frazzoni, Leyla Gencer, Adriana Martino, Neda Monte, Rosetta Noli, Miriam Pirazzini, Marcella Pobbe, Lari Scipioni.

Giorgio Algorta, Giovanni Amodeo, Ettore Bastianini, Mario Borriello, Salvatore Catania, Fernando Corena, Piero De Palma, Renato Ercolani, Mario Filippeschi, Antonio Galiè, Gerardo Gaudioso, Giuseppe Gismondo, Giangiacomo Guelfi, Carlos Guichandut, Gianni Poggi, Afro Poli, Leo Pudis, Iginio Riccò, Antonio Sacchetti, Ferruccio Tagliavini, Giuseppe Valdengo.

CONDUCTORS

Vincenzo Bellezza, Oliviero De Fabritiis, Franco Ghione, Angelo Questa, Ugo Rapalò.

ROME. TERME DI CARACALLA
21 June to 1 September 1957

REPERTORY

Aïda, Andrea Chénier, Carmen, Faust, Forza del Destino, Guillaume Tell, Tosca, Traviata.

ARTISTS

Fedora Barbieri, Fernanda Cadoni, Maria Caniglia, Gabriella Caturan, Anita Cerquetti, Magda Olivero, Clara Petrella, Amalia Pini, Marcella Pobbe, Lari Scipioni, Gabriella Tucci.

Francesco Albanese, Mario Carlin, Franco Corelli, Mario del Monaco, Eugenio Fernandi, Mario Filippeschi, Giangiacomo Guelfi, Saturno Meletti, Giulio Neri, Mario Petri, Aldo Protti, Giuseppe Taddei, Roberto Turrini.

CONDUCTORS

Vincenzo Bellezza, Alberto Erede, Oliviero de Fabritiis, Gabriele Santini, Emidio Tieri, Ottavio Ziino.

SALZBURG
27 July to 31 August 1957

REPERTORY

Così fan tutte, Elektra, Entführung aus dem Serail, Falstaff, Fidelio, Nozze di Figaro, Schule der Frauern (world première of new version).

ARTISTS

Inge Borkh, Anna Maria Canali, Lisa Della Casa, Sonja Draksler, Anny Felbermayer, Christel Goltz, Marilyn Horne, Sena Jurinac, Erika Köth, Karol Loraine, Christa Ludwig, Jean Madeira, Kerstin Meyer, Anna Moffo, Lisa Otto, Anneliese Rothenberger, Elisabeth Schwarzkopf, Irmgard Seefried, Rita Streich, Giulietta Simionato, Sieglinde Wagner, Lore Wissmann.

Luigi Alva, Walter Berry, Kurt Böhme, Anton Dermota, Murray Dickie, Otto Edelmann, Dietrich Fischer-Dieskau, Renato Ercolani, Nicolai Gedda, Tito Gobbi, Waldemar Kmentt, Erich Kunz, Hansgeorg Laubenthal, Erich Makjut, Georg Littasy, Max Lorenz, Rolando Panerai, Alois Pernerstorfer, Mario Petri, Paul Schöffler, Tomaso Spataro, Georg Stern, Nicola Zaccaria, Giuseppe Zampieri.

CONDUCTORS

Karl Böhm, Josef Krips, Dimitri Mitropoulos, Georg Szell, Herbert von Karajan.

STOCKHOLM. ROYAL OPERA AND DROTTNINGHOLM THEATRE
2 June to 14 June 1957

REPERTORY

Aïda, Fidelio, Idomeneo, Master Peter's Puppet Show, Orfeo, Portrait (Hilding Rosenberg), Tannhäuser, Tristan und Isolde, Trovatore, Turandot, Wozzeck.

ARTISTS

Margareta Bergström, Kjerstin Dellert, Busk-Margit Jonsson, Kerstin Meyer, Birgit Nilsson, Aase Nördmo-Lövberg, Eva Prytz, Hjördis Schymberg Elisabeth Söderström.

Leon Björker, Jussi Björling, Luigi Carrara, Hugo Hasslo, Folke Jonsson, Anders Näslund, Sven Nilsson, Erik Saeden, Conny Söderström, Set Svanholm, Arne Tyren, Sven-Erik Vikström, Arne Wiren.

CONDUCTORS

Kurt Bendix, Sixten Ehrling, Herbert Sandberg, Albert Wolff.

35th SEASON VERONA. ARENA
18 July to 24 August 1957

REPERTORY

Bohème, Carmen, Norma, Rigoletto.

ARTISTS

Rita Bellini, Giulia Benini, Fedora Barbieri, Margherita Bennetti, Cesy Broggini, Aurora Cattelani, Anita Cerquetti, Renata Ongaro, Giulietta Simionato, Antonietta Stella, Silvana Zanolli.

Attilio Barbesi, Ettore Bastianini, Ottorino Begali, Vasco Campagnano, Mariano Caruso, Franco Corelli, Giuseppe di Stefano, Danilo Franchi, Giorgio Giorgetti, Melchiorre Luise, Silvio Maionica, Giulio Neri, Salvatore Puma, Gianni Raimondi, Ugo Savarese, Ivo Vinco, Mario Zanasi.

CONDUCTORS

Francesco Molinari Pradelli, Nicola Rescigno, Nino Sanzogno.

WIESBADEN. INTERNATIONAL MAY FESTIVAL
5 May to 31 May 1957

REPERTORY

Boris Godunov, Cunning Little Vixen, Don Quichotte, Lucia di Lammermoor, Mathis der Maler, Rigoletto.

ARTISTS

Irmgard Armgard, Irmgard Arnold, Hannelore Backrass, Gianna d'Angelo, Adelheid Müller-Hess, Susanne Muser, Ursula Richter, Liane Synek, Erina Valli.

Rudolf Asmus, Reinhold Bartel, Georg Baumgartner, Wolf von Beneckendorff, Josef Burgwinkel, Werner Enders, Anton John, Manfred Jungwirth, Alfredo Kraus, Gerhard Misske, Rolando Panerai, Gianni Raimondi, Herbert Rössler, Ugo Savarese—and the Company of Belgrade State Opera for *Boris Godunov* and *Don Quichotte*.

CONDUCTORS

Alberto Erede, Paul Hindemith, Ludwig Kaufman, Angelo Questa.

ZÜRICH
2 June to 29 June 1957

REPERTORY

Ballo in Maschera, Fanciulla del West, Moses und Aron (Schönberg—world première)*. Twilight Heron (Ikuma Dan).

ARTISTS

Gianella Borelli, Lucia Danieli, Mary Davenport, Gigliola Frazzoni, Ingeborg Friedrich, Dora Gatta, Irma Keller, Anna Maria Rovere, Michiko Sunahara, Ilse Wallenstein.

Carlo Bergonzi, Umberto Borsò, Mariano Caruso, Plinio Clabassi, Hans-Bert Dick, Willi Ferenz, Rudolf Fiebelkorn, Herbert Fiedler, Charles Gillig, Giangiacomo Guelfi, Antonio Massaria, Helmut Melchert, Vico Polotto, Aldo Protti, Nikolaus Toth.

CONDUCTORS

Franco Capuana, E. Hartogs, Hans Rosbaud.

OPERATIC PREMIÈRES

July 1957 to June 1958

1957

23 July   Sadler's Wells, London.
A TALE OF TWO CITIES. Opera in a prologue and three acts by Arthur Benjamin. Text by Cedric Cliffe after the novel by Charles Dickens. With Heather Harper, Ruth Packer, John Kentish, Heddle Nash, John Cameron, Leyland White. Conductor Leon Lovett; producer Anthony Besch.

2 August   Santa Fé, U.S.A.
THE TOWER. Opera in one act by Marvin David Levy. With Carol Bergey, Peter Binder, William McGrath, Robert Rue. Conductor Robert Baustian; producer Marvin David Levy.

5 August   Tanglewood Festival, Berkshire, U.S.A.
THE TALE FOR A DEAF EAR. Opera in one act by Samuel Weschler. Conductor James Billings; producer Boris Goldovsky.

11 August   Prinzregententheater, Munich.
DIE HARMONIE DER WELT. Opera in five scenes by Paul Hindemith; text by the composer. With Liselotte Fölser, Hertha Töpper, Richard Holm, Kurt Wehofschitz, Josef Metternich, Marcel Cordes. Conductor Paul Hindemith; producer Rudolf Hartmann.

12 September   King George's Hall, London.
ELANDA AND ECLIPSE. Opera in two acts by Guy Halahan. Text by the composer. With Doreen Murray, Johanna Peters, Alan Brafield, John Stoddart, Norman Tattersall. Conductor Eric Stanley; producer John Copley.

1 October   Théâtre Royal de la Monnaie, Brussels.
THYLE DE FLANDRE. Opera in four acts by Jacques Chailley. Text by Jose Bruyr (after Charles de Coster). With Mmes. Lange, Patris, Cortois, Masset, Danlée; MM. Vernay, Ghislain, Dubuc, Wierzbicki, Fischer, Lits, Piergyl, Michel Trempont, Pol Trempont. Conductor René Defossez; producer Roger Lefèvre.

3 October   Teatro Donizetti, Bergamo.
LA NUOVA EURIDICE. Opera in three acts by Roberto Lupi. Text by Maria delle Guercia. With Gianna Maritati, Giuseppina Salvi, Rinaldo Pelizzoni, Guglielmo Ferrara, Giorgio Giorgetti. Conductor Roberto Lupi; producer Friedhelm Gillert.

13 October   Státní Divadlo, Brno.
ZENICHOVE (The Bridegrooms). Opera in three acts by Jan Fischer. Text by S. K. Machacek. With Jindra Pokorná, Libuše Lesmanová, Zdeněk Sousek, František Roesler, Jaroslav Ulrych, František Kunc. Conductor Václav Nosek; producer Oskar Linhart.

13 October   Teatro Donizetti, Bergamo.
REQUIEM PER ELISA. Opera in two acts by Roberto Hazon. Text by the composer. With Adriana Martino, Laura Zannini, Luisana Zerbini, Nello Romato, Gino Orlandini, Franco Ricciardi. Conductor Umberto Cattini.

26 October   Bolshoi Theatre, Moscow.
THE MOTHER. Opera by Chrinnikov. Text by A. Fajko.

16 November   Cincinatti Conservatory of Music.
MAYERLING. Opera in three acts by Henry Rauscher Humphreys. Text by the composer. With Carolyn Goodbar, Miriam Broderick, John Lankson, John Vian. Conductor William Byrd; producer Wilfred Engleman.

22 November   Juilliard School, New York.
THE SWEET BYE AND BYE. Opera in three acts by Jack Beesin. Text by Kenward Elmslie. With Shirlee Emmons, Ruth Kobart, William McGrath. Conductor Frederick Waldman. Producer Frederic Cohen.

26 November   Teatro Comunale, Bologna.
IL CANTO DEL CIGNO. Opera in one act by Luciano Chailly. Text by the composer after Tchekov. With Edda Vicenzi, Franco Ricciardi, Franco Calabrese. Conductor Armando La Rosa Parodi; producer Sandro Bolchi.

30 November   Städtische Bühnen, Opernhaus, Erfurt.
DIE SPIELDOSE. Opera in three acts by Robert Hanell. Text by Georg Kaiser. With Christel Garduhn, Günter Schneewitz, Hellmut Gritzka, Helmut Bante. Conductor Udo Nissen; producer Georg Leopold.

5 December   Státní divaldo, Brno.
JAN HUS. Opera by Karel Horký. Text by Vladimír Kanton. With Vladimír Bauer, Eduard Hrubeš, Antonín Jurečka, František Roesler, Jaroslav Ulrych. Conductor František Jílek; producer Oskar Linhart.

1958

7 January   Teatro La Fenice, Venice.
VERGILII AENIIS. Opera in two parts by Gian Francesco Malipiero. Text by the composer after the Aeneid. With Magda Laszlò, Eva Tomassy, Clara Betner, Maria Amadini, Alfredo Nobile, Giampiero Malaspina, Giorgio Taddeo, Paolo Pedani. Conductor Tullio Serafin; producer Adolf Rott.

15 January   Metropolitan Opera, New York.
VANESSA. Opera in four acts by Samuel Barber. Text by Gian-Carlo Menotti. With Eleanor Steber, Rosalind Elias, Regina Resnik, Nicolai Gedda, Giorgio Tozzi, George Cehanovsky. Conductor Dimitri Mitropoulos; producer Menotti.

19 January   Städtische Bühnen, Openhaus, Erfurt.
KÖNIG DROSSELBART. Opera by Diether Noll. Text by Alexander Stillmark after the story by Grimm. Conductor Diether Noll; producer Günther Imbiell.

6 February   Hall of Fame Playhouse, New York.
THE DRAGON. Opera in three acts by Deems Taylor; text by the composer after the play "Lady Gregory". With Sandra Banette, Violet Serwin, Rita Falbel, Raleston Hill. Conductor John Lovell; producer William Vorenburg.

6 February   Stadttheater, Meissen.
DER BAUER IM FEGEFEUER. Opera in one act by Manfred Grafe. Text by the composer after Hans Sachs. With Marianne Kaufchmann, Margot Glitzka, Werner Stransky, Wolfgang Emmerich, Karl Göhler. Conductor Manfred Grafe, producer Hanns Matz.

8 February   Teatro San Carlo, Naples.
IL VORTICE. Opera in three acts by Renzo Rossellini. Text by the composer. With Clara Petrella, Pia Tassinari, Palmira Vitali-Marini, Anna di Stasio, Ferrando Ferrari, Piero di Palma, Antonio Sacchetti. Conductor Oliviero de Fabritiis; producer Margherita Wallmann.

16 February   Severočeske divadlo, Liberec.
ROZMBERSTI BYBNIKARI (The Fishers of Rožmberk). Opera by Maximilian Hájek. Text by the composer. With Marie Rathouská, Arnost Klíma, Vojtěch Zouhar, Jan Malík. Conductor Jindrich Bubenicek; producer Rudolf Malek.

25 February   Teatro dell'Opera, Rome.
IL TESORO. Opera in four acts by Jacopo Napoli. Text by Vittorio Viviani. With Elena Rizzieri, Giacinto Prandelli, Tito Gobbi, Fernando Lidonni, Adelio Zagonara, Giampiero Malaspina, Carlo Cava. Conductor Oliviero de Fabritiis; producer Vittorio Viviani.

25 February   Städtische Bühnen, Theater Hiltropwall, Dortmund.
YÜ-NÜ. Opera by Erich Riede. Text by Willy Werner Göttig after the story "Die Edelstein-sklaven". Conductor Erich Riede; producer Hörst Günther Schwarz.

1 March   La Scala, Milan.
L'ASSASSINIO NELLA CATTEDRALE. Opera in two acts by Ildebrando Pizzetti. Text by Alberto Castelli after the play by T. S. Eliot. With Leyla Gencer, Gabriella Carturan, Aldo Bertocci, Mario Ortica, Dino Dondi, Rinaldo Pellizzoni, Nicola Rossi-Lemeni, Antonio Cassinelli, Enrico Campi, Silvio Maionica, Marco Stefanoni. Conductor Gianandrea Gavazzeni; producer Margherita Wallmann.

11 March   Cecil Sharp House, London.
LORD BATEMAN. Opera in three acts by Arnold Forster. Text by Jan Sharp. With Heather Goddin, Noel Banke, Peter Hemmings. Conductor Alan Boustead; producer Colin Graham.

19 March   Columbia University, New York.
GALLANTRY. Opera in one act by Douglas Moore. Text by Arnold Sundgaard. With Bonnie Murray, David Atkinson, Joseph Sopher, Cecilia Ward. Conductor Emmerson Buckley; producer Day Tuttle.

19 March   Columbia University, New York.
THE BOOR. Opera in one act by Dominick Argento. Text by John Olon. With Mary Henderson, Hugh Thompson, Grant Williams. Conductor Emmerson Buckley.

22 March   Stadttheater, Köthen.
CARL MICHAEL BELLMAN. Opera in one act by Heinz Röttger. Text by Eva Johnn. With Erika Bärthel. Horst Pehrend Conductor Hans-Joachim Marx; producer Klaus Barnikol.

14 April   Kaufmann Concert Hall, New York.
THE ROBBERS. Opera in one act by Ned Rorem. Text by the composer after Chaucer's "The Pardoner's Tale". With Daniel Caruso, Robert Schmorr, Herold Sien. Conductor Carl Bamberger; producer Ralph Herbert.

14 April   Kaufmann Concert Hall, New York.
THE PET SHOP. Opera in one act by Vittorio Rieti. Text by the composer. With Joan Wall, Sheila Breidach, Edward Eriksen. Conductor Carl Bamberger; producer Ralph Herbert.

15 April   Stadttheater, Basel.
TITUS FEUERFUCHS. Opera by Heinrich Sutermeister. Text by the composer after Nestroy-Posse's "Der Talisman". With Ingeborg Wieser, Herta Schomburg, Salbsire Zimmer, Marcel Cordes. Conductor Silvio Varviso; producer Hermann Wedekind.

16 April   Louisville University, U.S.A.
THE HOLY DEVIL. Opera in two acts by Nicolas Nabokov. Text by Stephen Spender. With Robert Fischer, William Pickett. Conductor Moritz Bomhard.

16 April   Städtische Bühnen, Theater Hiltropwall, Dortmund.
NANA. Opera in two acts by Manfred Gurlitt. Text by Max Brod, after Zola. With Marie Lacorn, R. Fiebelkorn, K. Armaan, Willy Ferenz. Conductor Manfred Gurlittt; producer A. Assmann.

21 April Pyramind Theatre, New York.
CHANTICLEER. Opera in one act by Seymour Barab. Text by M. C. Richards after Chaucer. With Marion Manderen, Linda Newman, James Stuart, Robert Howard. Conductor Robert Colston; producer Patricia Neway.

23 April New York City Center.
THE GOOD SOLDIER SCHWEIK. Opera in two acts by Robert Kurka. Text by Lewis Allan. With Mary LeSawyer, Helen Baisley, Ruth Hubart, Norman Kelley, Joshua Hecht, Emile Renan, Chester Watson. Conductor Julius Rudel; producer Carmen Capalbo.

23 April Teatro San Carlo, Naples.
LA JURA. Opera in two acts by Gavino Gabriel. Text by the composer. With Rina Gigli, Anna Maria Borrelli, Elena Todeschi, Lari Scipioni, Gino Pasquale, Enzo Viaro, Enzo Feliciati. Conductor Alessandro Derevitzky; producer Giulio Bragaglia.

24 April County Theatre, Holton cum Beckering, Lincoln.
THE OPEN WINDOW. Opera in one act by Malcolm Arnold. Text by Sydney Gilliat based on a short story by H. H. Munro. (Previously broadcast in December, 1955).

11 May Deutsche Oper am Rhein, Opernhaus, Düsseldorf.
KARL V (new version). Opera in two parts by Ernst Krenek. Text by the composer. With Valerie Bak, Ingeborg Lasser, Elisabeth Schwarzenberg, Karl Wolfram, Walter Raninger. Conductor Reinhard Peters; producer Heinz Arnold.

15 June Stadsschouwberg, Amsterdam.
FRANÇOIS VILLON. Opera in one act by Sam Dresden. Text by the composer. With Anny Delorie, Maria Van Dongen, Cora Canne Meyer, Greet Keeman, Hans Wilbrink, Chris Scheffen, Jos Barcksen, Susen Jongsma, Gerard Holthaus, Rudolf Kat. Conductor Alfred Eichmann; producer Wolf-Dicher Ludwig.

21 June Städtische Bühnen, Opernhaus, Graz.
DAS KATCHEN VON HEILBRONN. Opera by Waldemar Bloch. With Eleanor Schneider, Robert Charlebois. Conductor Gustav Cerny; producer André Diehl.

22 June Park Lane House, London.
THE ABBOT OF DRIMOCK. Opera in one act by Thea Musgrave. Text by Maurice Lindsay. With Jill Nott-Bower, Constance Mullay, Margaret Fraser, David Hartley, Duncan Robertson, Donald Francke, John Davies. Conductor Myer Fredman.

APPENDIX III

OPERATIC OBITUARY

August 1957 to July 1958

1957

Hermann Lümmer (bs). 4 August
Josef Degler (b). 6 August
Hermine Herma-Klausner (s). 5 August
Emilio Bione (b). 9 August
Giuseppe Cavadore (t). 14 August
Edward J. Dent (Musicologist). 22 August
Ilse Jacobs (s). — August
Sabine Kalter 1 September
Olga Lynn (s). 1 September
Margaret Eichenwald (s). 11 September
Cornelis Bronsgeest (b). 22 September
Dina Notargiacomo (s). 24 September
Ernst Marboe (Administrator). 28 September
Wilhelm Noll (bs). 29 September
Hans Witt (t). — September
Gosta Bjoerling (t). 10 October
Gustav Kösyti (bs). 27 October
Mstisldav Dobujinsky (Designer). 20 November
Tom Williams (b). 28 November
Erich Korngold (comp). 29 November
Beniamino Gigli (t). 30 November
Domenico Viglione Borghese (b). — November
Evan Gorga (t). 6 December
Giovanni Binetti (c). 14 December
Louis Hasselmans (cond). 27 December
Maurice Decléry (b). 27 December
Carmen Toschi-Carpi (s). — December
Eugenio Sandrini (bs). — December

1958

Emmi Leisner (c). 10 January
Vittorio Veneziani (Chorus Master). 12 January
Vittorio Trevisan (bs). 27 January
William Michael (b). 5 February
Waldemar Staegemann (b). 11 February
Emil Graf (t). 26 February
Alice Gentle (mezzo). 28 February
Maria Mueller (s). 13 March
Jeanne Hatto (s). — March
Paul Razavet (t). — March
Tudor Davies (t). 2 April
Charlotte Kuhn-Brunne (s). 11 April
Margaret Sheridan (s). 17 April
Giulio Neri (bs). 21 April
Irmgard Meinig (s). — April
Alfred Muzzarelli (t). 13 May
Heinrich Niggemeier (t). 21 May
Elfriede Trötschel (s). 20 June
Marie Sundelius (s). 21 June
Alf Rauch (t). — June
Erwin Stein (Musicologist.) 19 July

NOTES
ON THE COLOURED ILLUSTRATIONS

ENRICO TAMBERLIK

Tamberlik was one of the most famous tenors of last century. He was born in Rome in 1820 and made his début at Naples in 1840 in Bellini's *I Capuletti ed I Montecchi*. After appearances in Italy, Spain and elsewhere on the continent he made his London début at Covent Garden in 1850 in *Masaniello*.

He returned regularly to Covent Garden until 1864, and was famous in such roles as Arnold *Guglielmo Tell*), Raoul (*Huguenots*), Otello (Rossini) and John of Leyden (*Le Prophète*).

He was the first Covent Garden Manrico, Benvenuto Cellini, and Faust; and he created the role of Alvaro in *Forza del Destino* at its world première in St. Petersburg in 1862.

Tamberlik returned to London to sing at Her Majesty's Theatre in 1877, and died in Paris some twelve years later.

MARIE MIOLAN-CARVALHO

Covent Garden's first Marguerite was also the creator of the part when *Faust* had its première at the Théâtre-Lyrique, Paris in 1859.

Marie Miolan was born in Marseilles in 1827 and studied singing with Duprez at the Paris Conservatoire where she gained first prize in singing. She made her début at a benefit performance for her teacher in 1849 in the first act of *Lucia* and in a scene from *La Juive*. She then was engaged for the Opéra-Comique, and in 1853 she married Leon Carvalho the manager of that theatre. From 1855-66 she was at the Théâtre-Lyrique where her husband became manager. Then from 1868-83 she was heard regularly at the Opéra and Opéra-Comique.

Her London début was at Covent Garden in 1859 in the title role of *Dinorah*. She sang regularly in London for several seasons and besides singing Marguerite in *Faust* was heard as Zerlina in *Fra Diavolo* and *Don Giovanni*, Marguerite de Valois in *Les Huguenots*, Gilda, Rosina, Oscar, Mathilde, Caterina in *L'Etoile du Nord*, Marie in *La Fille du Regiment*; and then, later in her career as the *Figaro* Countess and Donna Elvira.

ANGIOLINA BOSIO

The soprano who sang the title role in *Martha* at its first Covent Garden performance with Mario in 1858 enjoyed a short but brilliant career.

She was born in Turin in 1829 and died in St. Petersburg suddenly in 1859, She studied in Milan under Cataneo, and made her début in that city in 1846 in *I Due Foscari*.

Bosio's Covent Garden début was in 1852 as Adina in *L'Elisir d'Amore*, and was not a particularly successful one. It was only when she assumed the role of Elvira in *Puritani* replacing Grisi, that her true worth was discovered, and she returned to London regularly until the time of her death.

Bosio was London's first Gilda in 1853, Alice (*Comte Ory*) the following year, and Martha. She also sang Violetta, Rosina, Zerlina, Elvira (*Ernani*), the title role in Rossini's '*Mathilde di Shabran*', Catherine in *L'Etoile du Nord*, Leonora, and Zerlina in *Fra Diavolo*.

GIOVANNI MATTEO MARIO, CAVALIERE DI CANDIA

Mario the legendary tenor who is depicted as Lionel in *Martha*, was born in Cagliari in 1810. He came from a noble family, and his father was a general in the Piedmontese army. When he first went to Paris, he was only an amateur, and soon became a great favourite in society. Eventually he was persuaded by Duponchel, Director of the Opéra, to sign a contract to sing at that house, but being unwilling to use his full name professionally, he merely signed the contract with his Christian name, Mario, by which he was known ever since.

He made his début in the title role of Meyerbeer's *Robert le Diable* in 1838, and after two seasons at the Opéra, transferred to the Théâtre des Italiens.

Mario first sang in London in 1839, and returned every season for more than a quarter of a century. He was associated with the great galaxy of "stars" that included Grisi, whom he married, Tamburini and Lablache. In 1846 he was one of the moving spirits in the group of singers who deserted Lumley and set up the Royal Italian Opera at Covent Garden, where he became the leading tenor, remaining there until 1868 and returning for his farewell performances in 1871.

He participated in many first performances in London, including *Lucrezia Borgia*, *Don Pasquale*, *Rigoletto*, *Le Prophéte* and *Roméo et Juliette*.

AÏNO ACKTÉ

Finland has not produced very many famous singers; but outstanding among those that she has was Aïno Ackté. She was born in Helinski in 1876. Her father Lorenz Nikolai Ackté was both a singer and a conductor and her mother, Emmy Stromer leading soprano at the Helsingfors Opera. After studying with her mother she went to Paris where she continued vocal studies with Duvernoy.

In 1897 she made her début at the Paris Opéra, where she remained until 1903. It was during this period that she sang such roles as Ophélie, Micaëla, Juliette and Marguerite. She then began to assume heavier roles, and at the Metropolitan in the 1904-5 season sang Eva, the 'Siegfried' Brünnhilde and Elisabeth in *Tannhäuser*.

It was as a Wagnerian too that she was first heard in London when she took part in the 1907 winter season of German opera singing, Senta, Elsa, Eva and Elisabeth. Perhaps her most famous role was Salome which she sang in the first London performance of Strauss's opera in 1910 under Beecham.

In 1938 Ackté became director of the Finnish Opera at Helsingfors; and she died in 1944.

FELIA LITVINNE

This Russian soprano, born Françoise-Jeanne (Fanny) Schütz in St. Petersburg in 1861, received her vocal training in Paris under Mme. Barth-Banderali and the great baritone Maurel who was responsible for her engagement and début at the Théâtre Lyrique in 1885 in the title role of *Hérodiade* with a cast that included Jean and Edouard de Reszke—the latter singer married Litvinne's sister.

After appearances in America and elsewhere she made her Covent Garden début in the 1899 season as Isolde opposite Jean de Reszke. She sang intermittently in London until 1910, being heard as Aida, Donna Anna, Brünnhilde and Gioconda. Alceste, which was considered possibly her greatest role, she sang in Paris.

When Litvinne retired from the stage in 1917 she devoted the rest of her life to teaching. She died in 1936.

ANNA ZERR

This German soprano who is depicted as Queen of Night, was born at Baden-Baden in 1822. She studied with Bordogni, and made her début at Carlsruhe in 1839. From there she went to Vienna in 1846.

In 1851 she came to London, and while there sang at a concert for the benefit of Hungarian refugees; for this action she was deprived of her title of Austrian Kammersängerin, and not permitted to sing again in Vienna.

Her Covent Garden début, also in 1851, was as Queen of Night. She returned the following season and was heard in Spohr's *Faust*, and Jullien's *Pietro il Grande*. She retired from the stage on her marriage in 1857, and died in 1881.

MARIETTA PICCOLOMINI

Piccolomini was one of the most famous interpreters of Violetta in *Traviata's* early days. She sang the role at its first London production at Her Majesty's Theatre in 1856.

She was born in Siena in 1834 (some authorities give 1836) and came from a famous Tuscan family which had boasted two popes, numerous cardinals, bishops, and literary figures. She studied in Florence with Mazzarelli and Pietro Romani, and made her début in that city in 1852 as Lucrezia Borgia.

She sang in London between 1856 and 1860 at both Her Majesty's and Drury Lane. Her roles included —Arline in the Italian version of *The Bohemian Girl*, Zerlina, Adina, Susanna and Luisa Miller.

In 1860 she made her farewell appearances and shortly afterwards married the Marchese Gaetani della Fargia. However, she returned to London in 1863 to sing in four special performances at Drury Lane organised for the benefit of Lumley, the former manager of Her Majesty's. Piccolomini died in Florence in 1899.

PAULINE VIARDOT

Garcia's younger daughter, and sister of the immortal Malibran, Pauline Viardot was considered by many to be one of the greatest artists of the century.

She was born in Paris in 1821 and, although it was her mother who was her formal teacher, she could not but have obtained first hand knowledge of her father's vocal methods, for she accompanied his pupils at the piano.

Viardot made her début in Brussels in 1837; two years later she came to London and was heard as Desdemona in Rossini's *Otello* at Her Majesty's. Then followed a period at the Théâtre des Italiens in Paris with Grisi, Persiani, Rubini, Tamburini and Lablache. At this period she was known as Pauline Garcia, for her marriage to Viardot did not take place until 1841. Her voice was a mezzo-soprano with a compass of three octaves which enabled her to sing soprano roles.

Her real London successes were in the years 1848-58 when she appeared at Covent Garden, and where her great triumphs were not always to the liking of Grisi. She sang with great success as Donna Anna, Valentine (*Huguenots*), Amina, Fidès in *Le Prophète* which she had created at its Paris première, Rachel in *La Juive*, Adina, Saffo, Rosina and Azucena in the first London *Trovatore*.

She was the Orfeo in the famous Paris revival of Gluck's opera in 1859, and the following year was heard as Alceste. After 1863 Viardot gave up singing in opera, though she was heard in concerts for another seven or eight years. She was friendly with Brahms, Schumann and other great figures in music and also with Turgenev. She taught at the Paris Conservatoire and her pupils included Desirée Artôt, and Marianne Brandt. She died in Paris in 1910.

MARIETTA ALBONI

One of the most famous contralto singers of last century Alboni was born at Citta di Castello in 1826. She studied with Bertolotti at Bologna, and made her début in that city in 1842 in Pacini's *Saffo*. She then sang with success all over Italy, in Germany and Austria, and in 1847 was engaged for the new Royal Italian Opera, Covent Garden at a salary of £500 which was immediately raised to £2,000 following her success on the opening night as Arsace in Rossini's *Semiramide*. She was also heard as Jane Seymour in *Anna Bolena*, Rosina, Cherubino, Isabella (*L'Italiana*), in the baritone (!) role of Carlos in *Ernani*, and in *Donna del Lago*, *Gazza Ladra*, *Maria di Rohan* and *Lucrezia Borgia*. In 1848 she sang Cenerentola, Urbaine in *Les Huguenots* and in *Tancredi*, in addition to repeating roles from the previous year.

These were her only two Covent Garden seasons, for she deserted that house and joined the rival company at Her Majesty's. She sang with Patti at Rossini's funeral, and was heard as late as 1871 in London when she sang in Rossini's *Petite Messe Solennelle*. She died at Ville d'Avray in 1894.

NOTES ON CONTRIBUTORS

ERNEST BRADBURY. Critic of the *Yorkshire Post*, contributor to a number of musical journals, and a newcomer to our pages.

ROBERT BREUER. American musicologist. Regular contributor to *Musical America*, *Opera News* etc. A newcomer to our pages.

GABRIEL DUSURGET. Founder and Artistic Director of the Aix-en-Provence Festival. Has probably discovered more 'new' singers than anyone else in the post-war operatic scene.

RAYMOND ERICSON. American critic and Managing Editor of *Musical America*, who once again collaborates with

FRANK MILBURN, Jr. to produce the American report and other features for the ANNUAL.

VIKTOR FUCHS. Teacher of voice, lecturer and critic. Well-known in Europe in pre-Hitler days, now resident in America. Returned last year to Europe to lecture at the Academy in Vienna.

EDWARD GREENFIELD. One of the younger generation of British critics. He writes for the *Manchester Guardian*, and has recently been heard in various record programmes on the B.B.C. Another newcomer to our pages.

ROY HENDERSON. British baritone and member of the Glyndebourne Company from 1934-9 where he sang Count Almaviva, Masetto, Guglielmo and Papageno with great success. Now teaches in London.

JOHN W. KLEIN. British writer and musicologist, whose writings, especially on operatic subjects appear regularly in the British Musical press.

HORST KOEGLER. One of the leading post-war German critics. A regular contributor to German and American periodicals, and also to the ANNUAL.

LOTTE LEHMANN. One of the greatest sopranos of this century. She appeared regularly at Salzburg and Vienna until the advent of Hitler, and was also a regular visitor to London. She now lives in America where she teaches. She returned to London last autumn for the first time for many years.

ERICH LEINSDORF. Austrian born conductor, now a naturalised American, and conductor of the Metropolitan Opera. Was Toscanini's assistant at pre-war Salzburg.

ROBERT PONSONBY. Artistic Director of the Edinburgh Festival since 1956. Educated at Eton and Oxford and has always had a consuming interest in opera.

CHARLES REID. Regular contributor to the ANNUAL. English critic and writer. Music critic of the *News Chronicle* and *Punch*.

MARGHERITA WALLMANN. Formerly a ballet dancer and now the foremost woman producer of opera in the world. Greatly in demand at all the leading opera houses. Last season she produced *Aïda* and *The Carmelites* at Covent Garden.

JOSEPH WECHSBERG. Another regular contributor to the ANNUAL. Viennese critic and humourist, erstwhile member of the famous claque at the Vienna Staatsoper. Regular correspondent to *The New Yorker*.

CHARLES WEBBER (the late). Chief conductor of the Carl Rosa Opera for many years. One of the few British repetiteurs at pre-1914 Bayreuth.

HAROLD ROSENTHAL. Editor of OPERA ANNUAL since 1954 and of *Opera* since 1953, broadcaster and critic. His *Two Centuries of Opera at Covent Garden* was published earlier this year.